"Amazing, a year long devotional guide of hearing God say: 'Trust me, do not be afraid.' Fear creates the inability to trust, which keeps us from experiencing the intimate daily walk God desires. Sue Falcone's *The Lighthouse of Hope* is a practical and powerful tool that will help draw you into the Savior's presence, trusting Him day by day by day."

Pastor Don Miller
Senior Pastor
Westover Church
Greensboro, North Carolina

"A Touching and honest account of inspiring daily devotionals on how God helped one brave soul face and overcome her mountain of fears. This book will give readers courage to face their fears and to realize no matter what life brings, God is in complete and total control of everything."

Barbara Rheingrover-Stohlmann
International Painter/Sculptor and Author of
My Love Affair in Stone
Canton, Georgia

The
LIGHTHOUSE
of
HOPE

The
LIGHTHOUSE
of
HOPE

A Day by Day Journey to Fear Free Living

SUE
FALCONE

WINEPRESS (WP) PUBLISHING

WinePress Publishing (PO Box 428, Enumclaw, WA 98022) functions only as book publisher. As such, the ultimate design, content, editorial accuracy, and views expressed or implied in this work are those of the author.

Unless otherwise noted, all Scriptures are taken from the *Holy Bible, New International Version*®, *NIV*®. Copyright © 1973, 1978, 1984 by the International Bible Society. Used by permission of Zondervan. All rights reserved.

Scripture references marked NASB are taken from the *New American Standard Bible,* © 1960, 1963, 1968, 1971, 1972, 1973, 1975, 1977 by The Lockman Foundation. Used by permission.

Scripture references marked AMP are taken from *The Amplified Bible, Old Testament,* © 1965 and 1987 by The Zondervan Corporation, and from *The Amplified New Testament,* © 1954, 1958, 1987 by The Lockman Foundation. Used by permission.

Scripture references marked NKJV are taken from the *New King James Version,* © 1979, 1980, 1982 by Thomas Nelson, Inc., Publishers. Used by permission.

Scripture references marked KJV are taken from the *King James Version* of the Bible.

Scripture references marked NLT are taken from the Holy Bible, *New Living Translation,* copyright © 1996, 2004 by Tyndale Charitable Trust. Used by permission of Tyndale House Publishers, Wheaton, Illinois 60189. All rights reserved.

Scripture references marked THE MESSAGE are taken from *The Message Bible* © 1993 by Eugene N. Peterson, NavPress, PO Box 35001, Colorado Springs, CO 80935, 4th printing in USA 1994. Published in association with the literary agency—Alive Comm. PO Box 49068, Colorado Springs, CO 80949. Used by permission.

ISBN 13: 978-1-57921-949-9
ISBN 10: 1-57921-949-7
Library of Congress Catalog Card Number: 2007943938

To the One True God,
who gives us all we need
to resist and overcome fear.

And for showing us His heart
and plan of how to do so.

ACKNOWLEDGEMENTS

My appreciation goes to Dr. David Jeremiah for offering me the challenge of finding in God's Word, The Holy Bible, an instance for every day of the year, including Leap Year, where God said or implied the words "Fear Not."

I also thank God for showing me this was my story to share through these situations. In the journey, I have had to face all my fears, see how to overcome them, and then encourage and help each of you to see you can do the same.

A special thank you to my family: my awesome husband, Carmen, who had to live with me while I worked through these fears, and to my blended family of 4 children and 6 grandchildren who has seen the change in me as a result of facing my fears.

Also my heartfelt appreciation to my aunt, Eletha McCollum, who gives me hope, love, and encouragement still today. And also to my pastor, Don Miller, Westover Church, who encouraged and endorsed my book, to Andy and Joan Horner, Founders of Premier Designs, Inc. for their support and endorsement, and to Barbara Rheingrover-Stohlmann, for her support and endorsement. And to my Prayer Partners, the Hope Builders, our "Purpose Gang" small group, my Inspired Writers Group, Abby Sutton of Westover Church, and to WinePress Publishing Group for their encouragement to pursue the dream God gave me many years ago—to Inspire, Teach, and Write for His glory.

INTRODUCTION

For God has not given us a spirit of fear, but of power and of love and of a sound mind.

—2 Tim. 1:7 NKJV

On March 3, 2003, I undertook the challenge from my radio pastor, Dr. David Jeremiah, to find 366 instances in the Bible where God said for us to "fear not" in one way or another.

I am not saying we should never fear because some fears are good for us, and they protect us. The fear Dr. Jeremiah pointed out to me was the "spirit of fear" that we can allow to dominate and take over our lives and paralyze us from becoming whom God wants us to be and doing what He wants us to do.

Dr. Jeremiah shared a great definition of fear that defined what I was writing about in this book. Someone has said that fear is "a small trickle of doubt that runs through our minds and eventually wears such a great channel that all our thoughts drain into it." From an early age I saw how that trickle of doubt became a great river of fear in my life.

Now I love the beach and lighthouses. My husband and I have climbed most of them on the East Coast, so it is no wonder God showed me to name this book, *The Lighthouse of Hope.* I even received an idea for a song to go along with this awesome adventure with the Lord.

But as songwriting is not my gift, I sought help to make that idea a reality. I am grateful to Abby Sutton, Director of Service Programming at Westover Church, located in Greensboro, NC for undertaking this project; and the fantastic joy God gave us as we worked together to create a God honoring addition to this book.

This book became a day by day journey to FEAR Free Living. It is an inspired 366 day devotional that has the power and truth to encourage all who open its pages. It can also be used as a teaching tool to impact change in your life as you learn how to face and overcome the fears of your life—God's way.

You can begin your journey today, and my prayer for you is that you see: "*You* are the **one** Jesus loves."

And that He is the answer to facing and overcoming your fears. You will see how God weaves our paths, not by chance, but by perfect order. And how, (when we allow Him to invade our inner being), God completes in us an intentional, purposed-filled life to be lived without fear—a life to be filled with hope, joy, peace, and contentment.

Loving and Living fearlessly in Him Alone,

Sue Falcone

Day 1

DO NOT FEAR, GOD IS HERE

> After these things the word of the Lord came to Abram in a vision, saying, "Do not be afraid, Abram. I am your shield, your exceedingly great reward."
>
> —Gen. 15:1 NKJV

Even great Abram, (soon to be known as Abraham), expressed fear. So God came to Abram in a vision to assure him not to be afraid. God also told Abram that He would bless, reward, and take care of him.

We really don't know what Abram feared at this time in his life, but whatever it was, it definitely was real. We know he had just defeated kings, and he was about to do something that would change and influence our world when God came to him and told him not to fear.

God has come to me many times in my life. Not quite as dramatic as a vision, but still assuring me everything was going to be all right in my life. God showed me I was not to fear, but to let Him be in total control of my life.

HOPE FOR YOU

Do you know God intimately enough to take this "fear not" promise and put it into practice in your life now? No matter what you are facing, big or small, God wants to be your assurance that you have nothing to fear. He will bless and reward you. Trust Him. God is your Protector.

Day 2

DO NOT BE AFRAID TO GO

So He said, "I am God, the God of your father, do not fear to go down to Egypt, for I will make of you a great nation there."

—Gen. 46:3 NKJV

A re you afraid of what God is asking you to be or do? Experiencing fear is normal, but living and remaining in that fear means we don't trust God to take care of us. God at this time told Jacob His plan and purpose for him. He also assured Jacob not to be afraid to go and do.

I spent many wasted hours working on my own to fix it all. I also took well meaning advice from others who did not know and trust God for their answers either.

There are so many times I did not listen or seek God. I lived in total fear, even resulting in panic attacks. Be honest, has that ever happened to you? But I do know when I got to those places; by focusing on God I could escape.

HOPE FOR YOU

What do you need to let God "in on" in your life? He is only a cry away. God will show you just as He showed Israel (Jacob), His plan and purpose for you. Are you willing to *ask*? God is ready to listen and act, so do not delay, His plan and peace are waiting for you.

GOD IS HERE

"Fear not, for I am with you, I will bring your descendants from the east, and gather you from the west."

—Isa. 43:5 NKJV

Just as Isaiah was speaking of Israel's return from Babylon, God has a wonderful promise concerning fear. He constantly reminds us that He is with us at all times. Whatever you are facing, do you know God is with you? Are you afraid because He doesn't appear to be with you? You can be sure He is.

God has never failed me, and He is ready to show you the way. God is the only one, through His Son, Jesus Christ, who can give you peace over your fears. Read God's powerful words daily, and you will receive peace from your fears. Think, say, trust, and believe, and see how God helps you overcome and defeat your fears.

Hope for You

God knows and loves you. There is nothing about you that surprises God or causes Him to be mad at you. Trust Him with every fear and see how He will work out every detail.

Day 4

STEP OUT OF YOUR FEAR

And Moses said to the people, "Do not be afraid. Stand still, and see the salvation of the Lord, which He will accomplish for you today. For the Egyptians whom you see today, you shall see again no more forever."

—Exod. 14:13, 15 NKJV

This is one of the first times Moses had to face the moaning and groaning of the Israelite people on their journey to the Promised Land. He asked them to stop and see what the Lord was going to do to deliver them from the hands of the Egyptians and not to be afraid.

I once had a terrible fear of snakes. I would literally faint just looking at one small garden variety. One day the Lord advised me, through a complete stranger I had just met, that I needed to face my deadly fear—snakes.

I knew God demanded action from me. I was not to stand still any longer. I was not sure how to obey, so I prayed and was directed to my computer. I trembled as I approached web sites to learn more about my fear—snakes. I was delivered from my fear as God showed me He has a plan and purpose for snakes just as He has a plan and purpose for me.

HOPE FOR YOU

Is there a fear that has defeated you? It may not be as dramatic as mine, but step out in faith with God and ask Him to deliver you. Believe, trust, and obey; God will do the rest.

Day 5

GOD TESTS

Moses said to the people, "Do not fear, for God has come to test you, and that His fear may be before you, so that you may not sin."

—Exod. 20:20 NKJV

O ur true God is not trying to scare us into obedience. At this time, the people of Israel feared for their lives because of what was going on around them, and they asked Moses to be their mediator because they were afraid to ask God to help them.

Have you ever been so afraid of life and your circumstances that you were afraid to approach God? I have. Why was that? The Bible clearly tells us God loves us so much, and there is no reason to fear Him even though life is not as we expected it to be.

God's love was not easy for me to receive because I did not feel worthy or accepted by Him. I felt I had to earn God's love and when I failed, I feared what would happen to me. What a hopeless way to live. But God showed me that because of Jesus, I am worthy, fully accepted, and forgiven of all my sins. Then I saw and received His love for me. All fear left, and now I live in God's grace and want to help others do the same.

HOPE FOR YOU

I pray you choose Jesus and let Him into your total being. Then you will be able to make the changes to overcome your fears. God wants to show you His love, acceptance, forgiveness, and how to really know His grace and live no longer in fear.

Day 6

YOU ARE NOT ALONE

"No man shall be able to stand before you all the days of your life, for as I was with Moses, so I will be with you. I will not leave you nor forsake you. Be strong and of good courage, for to this people you shall divide an inheritance the land which I swore to their fathers to give them."
—Josh. 1:5–6 NKJV

This is a promise to us just as it was to Joshua when he was chosen after Moses' death to lead the Israelites into the Promised Land. God, just as He did then, wants each of us who are His to know He is with us. We are not alone.

Fear always comes when we leave God out of our lives. Throughout my life I can look back at the times when I lived in the most fear. My pattern shows I was running from God, thinking I could handle my life. How about you? Does this fit some of your patterns too?

God will not necessarily change your circumstance or situations, but you will have Him with you to handle it in His power and strength rather than your own. It is such a simpler and easier way to live.

HOPE FOR YOU

I pray right now that you will know you are not alone in your fear. God is with you, and He wants to help you be strong. He wants to face everything with you. Won't you let Him?

Day 7

GOD NEVER LEAVES

"The Lord Himself goes before you and will be with you; He
will never leave you nor forsake you. Do not be afraid, do
not be discouraged."

—Deut. 31:8

Moses said to Joshua in front of all Israel that the Lord was with
them. How often do we remember that God is here with us?
He even goes before us and is with us and does not leave us. Why are
we afraid or discouraged about anything?

It is a daily choice to live in His plan of obedience. Fear is not of
God, but He knows we must face it as a test of true faith in Him. He
has prepared the way so that we can allow Him to control, lead, and
guide us right on through.

With that attitude of faith, we can overcome all fear and discouragement. Walk in His strength and power and see the difference in how
you sleep at night.

HOPE FOR YOU

What is it you are so fearful about? Is anything discouraging you? Just
remember God is here with you. He wants to go before you. He is not
leaving you. When you trust and obey His promises are yours.

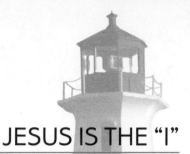

Day 8

JESUS IS THE "I"

Now when evening came, His disciples went down to the sea, got into the boat, and went over the sea toward Capernaum. And it was already dark, and Jesus had not come to them. Then the sea arose because a great wind was blowing. So when they had rowed about three or four miles, they saw Jesus walking on the sea and drawing near the boat, and they were afraid. But He said to them, "It is I, do not be afraid. Then they willingly received Him into the boat, and immediately the boat was at the land where they were going."

—John 6:16–21 NKJV

As experienced fishermen, the disciples knew a lot about the sea. How could they possibly be afraid? It is recorded that when they saw Jesus walking to them on the water they thought He was a ghost. Wouldn't you have been afraid?

Jesus gives us a true look at His character. He is the great I Am and in control of everything. I have been just as fearful as the disciples were because I took my spiritual eyes off of who He is and wants to be in my life. He is Lord of all and that includes my fears and your fears, whatever they may be.

HOPE FOR YOU

What fear are you facing? Isn't it time to come to Jesus, who is the great "I Am," and let Him handle it totally? He is willing and waiting for you to do so.

Day 9

GOD WILL TAKE CARE
OF ALL YOUR FEAR

Then an angel of the Lord appeared to him, standing at the right side of the altar of incense. When Zacharias saw him, he was startled and was gripped with fear. But the angel said to him: "Do not be afraid, Zacharias: your prayer has been heard. Your wife Elizabeth will bear you a son, and you are to give him the name John."

—Luke 1:11–13

H ave you ever been afraid of God and what He wanted to do with your life? I have not seen an angel in person, but Luke recorded how Zacharias, (John the Baptist's father), was told by an angel about the coming birth of his son, and he was afraid. So afraid and unbelieving was Zacharias that, during the time of waiting for John to be born, the Lord silenced his speech. Zacharias should have known that he had nothing to fear—that God would take care of it all.

It took me a long time to finally say yes to God about writing and spending time with Him. Through my journey, this book was written to please and glorify God. And also to let you know as a believer that He wants to take care of everything you face in your life, including your fears.

HOPE FOR YOU

Have you been asking for something from God so long that you are afraid when it comes to receive it? God wants to free you from that fear. Won't you let Him?

Day 10

GOOD NEWS, DO NOT BE AFRAID

But the angel said to them, "Do not be afraid, I bring you good news of great joy that will be for all the people."
—Luke 2:10

I don't know about you, but I imagine if I was out doing my job as the shepherds were and angels and the glory of the Lord surrounded me, I would be just a little bit afraid.

Does God do the dramatic in our lives today? He does more than we take the time to realize. He really wants to be our friend and show us how to live a fearless life. It is said that the true definition of fear is "false evidence appearing real."

I lived in that lie for many years. I let the fears of my own making or made by others control me as if they were real and the only truth.

But God's plan is for us to trust and depend on Him only so we will not live in fear. Why would Jesus give His life for us, if not to give us eternal life forever, and to help us live in His complete peace now?

HOPE FOR YOU

What fear is robbing you of the joy, peace, and contentment God has waiting for you right now? Once you admit your fear, *ask* God believing He can take it away. I assure you God is the only one who can, and He will give you the sweet release and freedom from fear.

Day 11

GOD HEARS AND RESPONDS

Then He continued, "Do not be afraid, Daniel. Since the first day that you set your mind to gain understanding and to humble yourself before your God, your words were heard, and I have come in response to them."

—Dan. 10:12

Daniel was definitely afraid when he was having this vision. He had even lost his speech. But the messenger assured him that his prayers had been heard, and restored his speech.

Daniel realized the only way he could live without being afraid was to develop a daily close relationship with God. This included spending time with God, reading His Word, and in prayer to Him.

This is great encouragement because I have found this is so true today. God speaks to me through His Word and hears my prayers and gives me strength to face my fearful situations. I no longer have to let my fears overtake me. When they come, I know where to go, and how to seek the strength and power to overcome both physical and spiritual fear.

HOPE FOR YOU

What is God saying to you right now about the fear in your life? He wants to be your life, won't you let Him? Your life will never be the same.

Day 12

THE SPIRIT OF FEAR DOES NOT COME FROM GOD

For God has not given us a spirit of fear, but of power, and of love and of a sound mind.

—2 Tim. 1:7 NKJV

No matter your age or experience, God is saying we are not to fear what others say or think. Timothy was young, and when preaching God's message, he faced much opposition. He was encouraged by God and Paul not to let anyone intimidate and cause him to fear.

Have you ever felt fearful and intimidated by others and by circumstances? I have, over and over again. But I have found by trusting in God and staying close to Him, I do not have to live in fear of anything. And when I do, I have to stop and realize my fear is not from God.

I don't know about you, but a sound mind was not something I asked and sought God for every day. But I am learning the need to do so because my mind is where my fears begin, and should end before fear can overtake me.

HOPE FOR YOU

Understand that God did not give us the spirit of fear. But when it comes, we are to run to Him and He will take it from us. God's power and love for us overcomes all fear. What fear do you need to lay down before Him? He is ready to take it from you.

Day 13

TRUST IN THE LORD AND BE SAFE

The fear of man brings a snare, but whoever trusts in the Lord shall be safe.

—Prov. 29:25 NKJV

S olomon was gifted to be able to share the wise things of the Lord that help us face life today. He knew he had failed to listen and obey as God intended, but God could still use him for the good of all.

There are so many people who live in fear of others and spend a lifetime seeking their approval. I was one of them. God had to show me through some pretty dramatic circumstances (divorce, death, loss of income, and obesity) so I could see clearly I am not to seek the approval of men. I only have to please God, and He will handle the rest.

HOPE FOR YOU

Have you made the choice to please God instead of men? By choosing to trust and receive Jesus Christ as your personal Lord and Savior you have God's promise He will help you through anything. You are safe; you don't need the approval of others.

Day 14

DO NOT WORRY ABOUT YOUR LIFE

"Therefore I tell you, do not worry about your life, what you will eat or drink, or about your body, what you will wear. Is not life more important than food, and the body more important than clothes?"

—Matt. 6:25

Jesus tells us not to worry about anything. He is assuring us that God is in control and will take care of all our needs, because He knows what is best for us. An ancient Chinese proverb says that "planning for tomorrow is time well spent, worrying about tomorrow is time wasted." Are you a planner or a worrier?

Most worriers are so consumed with fear of everything around them that they find it hard to trust God with anything. They think that they have to work it all out in their own way, and when all else fails consult God.

I can remember living this way for a large part of my life. Looking back I did not seek God's plan for my life but instead chose to follow my own ways. I am so grateful God gave me a new beginning and has never left me alone to go my own ways.

HOPE FOR YOU

What are you so worried, fearful, and upset about? Did you know there is another option? It is trusting God first and seeking His plan instead of making up your own.

Day 15

YOU DO NOT HAVE TO FEAR DEATH ANY LONGER

Free those who all their lives were held in slavery by their
fear of death.

—Heb. 2:15

I t is said that death is the number one fear of most people. The Bible
clearly explains Jesus came to die so that we who trust and believe in
Him would no longer be bound by the fear of death because we know
we will live forever with Him. Do you truly believe that? Why then do
we fear death?

Is it because we do not want to leave this world and our loved ones,
or is it just fear of the unknown? Or are you one of those who really
are not sure you will have eternal life and you fear the outcome? I
once chose not to even think or have an opinion about death. But by
avoiding it, I knew I feared it.

Later, the Bible and God's promises became clear to me. The birth,
death, and resurrection of our Lord Jesus Christ took care of the fear
of death. When we truly believe Jesus is alive and personally our Savior
and Lord, all fear of death has to flee.

HOPE FOR YOU

My husband and I sat down and discussed this. We have lost many
people in our lifetime. We do not fear dying at all. We know we will be
with the Lord, not by what we have been or done, but because of what
our Lord and Savior Jesus Christ did for us. Do you have this peace and
joy in your life about death? If not, don't you think *now* is the time to
handle this most important event of your life?

Day 16

DO NOT BE AFRAID OF ANY MAN

"You shall not show partiality in judgment, you shall hear the small as well as the great, you shall not be afraid in any man's presence, for the judgment is God's."

—Deut. 1:17 NKJV

This was how Moses trained the judges who were to govern the people. Do you see some similar guidelines that are present in our government? Just as Moses instructed his people, we need to learn that we are not to be afraid to counsel or give advice based on fear of what others think or say.

We need to speak the truth of the Lord in love, and He will give us the strength to do just that. I know there is so much discussion now concerning what we can or should say to those in our government and those all around us.

Many times I was afraid to speak up for the Lord for fear of what others might say or do to me. I did not feel confident about sharing what the Lord had done for me and wanted to do in our world and in our government. But God can show us the right way to do so, and He will handle all the details.

HOPE FOR YOU

Are you at peace with the people in our government? Do you know the options of what to do about it? Do you fear certain people in your life, but won't ask or say what needs to be said? God wants to show you that you no longer have to fear others, and He will give you the right way to handle those who would oppose you.

Day 17

GOD WILL DELIVER YOU FROM ANYTHING

And the Lord said to Joshua, "Do not fear them, for I have delivered them into your hand; not a man of them shall stand before you."

—Josh. 10:8 NKJV

J ust like Joshua who went into battle for the land God had promised him and his people, we need to know that God is on our side in our daily battles of life. We have nothing to fear.

The stakes in our lives may not be as large as were Joshua's, but they are just as important to God. I have come to realize that God wants me to trust Him and not fear in the small areas of life in the same way He wants me to trust in the larger ones. Isn't it true that fear in the small things often leads to fear in the larger areas as well?

I came from a home based on fear and rejection, so I can understand how the circumstances of life can lead us into a pattern of fearing others. I am so thankful God showed me a way out of that choice of life.

HOPE FOR YOU

Are you letting the Lord fight your battles, or are you facing them all alone? God promises to give us courage when we allow Him to be in control.

Day 18

LIVE IN THE NOW AND DO NOT WORRY

"Therefore do not worry about tomorrow, for tomorrow will worry about itself. Each day has enough trouble of its own."

—Matt. 6:34

A re you living in the past, the future, or in this moment as it is right now? So many are so concerned about what *might* happen that they cannot live as God has planned for them right now. Jesus said we are not to worry about life at all.

Taking a day at a time is fearful to some. They are not contented and are not trusting God for all of life. I too have lived this way, and I can assure you it is a life not closely connected to God. It is a selfish life of more about me than all about Him.

Can you change and not let this world and others rob you of what God has for you? Can you truly live free from worry and stress? Yes, I am here to assure you that you can.

How? By accepting and trusting Jesus as the only way and allowing Him to change you. Also by spending time in His Word so that you are more closely linked to God than to this world. Will you still fail? Yes, but God will forgive you and will once again put you on the right path with no worries, fear, or guilt of failure.

HOPE FOR YOU

Have you left God out of your daily life? Is He the first one you think of when you arise? God wants to be the one to guide you through each day, won't you let Him?

Day 19

IS GOD FIRST WHEN FEAR GRIPS YOU?

Then Samuel said to the people, "Do not fear. You have done all this wickedness, yet do not turn aside from following the Lord with all your heart."

—1 Sam. 12:20 NKJV

What is the first thing you do when fear grips you? Is your first reaction and thought to pray to God? Faith in our wonderful Creator, Friend, and Judge will overcome anything that confronts you in this world!

It means you need a clean heart to be able to call upon your Father and know that He is waiting to help you. Samuel told his people that even though they had done some awful things, they still should not fear to turn back once again to serving and following the Lord.

God heard the Israelites' plea. Will He hear yours? I once thought I was not worthy or good enough to pray to God. I did not know the right words or the way to say them to Him. I let others intimidate me so that I would avoid this part of my life at all costs.

But I learned that prayer is our link and connection to God. He listens no matter how you say it, and He can see your heart's desire. Do I always get the answers I seek? No, but I have come to understand that God knows much better than I do, and I can accept His Word on that promise to me.

HOPE FOR YOU

Do you believe God is waiting to hear from you no matter where you have been or what you have done? Pray and be free from your fear right now. God is waiting to listen and answer.

Day 20

DO NOT BE AFRAID OF FALSE TEACHERS

> If what a prophet proclaims in the name of the Lord does not take place or come true, that is a message the Lord has not spoken. That prophet has spoken presumptuously. Do not be afraid of him.
>
> —Deut. 18:22

Moses was telling his people once again that they needed to make sure whom they were listening to, and that the words were truly of God. Also they were not to be afraid of false teachers.

I see many people constantly changing opinions and lifestyles based on the words of others rather than on the blueprint of life—the Bible. I got caught up in that thinking at different points of my life as well. There are so many "self-help" doctrines available that I wonder what the heart of God must be feeling.

The God of our Bible assures us, "He is the same yesterday, today, and forever" (Heb. 13:8), and we are not to fear Him or anything else because He will take care of us. Have we lost that message and replaced it with something else?

Hope for You

Do you believe, trust, and live the truth the Lord has given us in His Word, the Bible? The Bible is the test of all truth. You can be assured it is the whole truth, and not to be feared or replaced. It is not just another self-help book, but the truth of God that we need to live victorious lives for Him.

Day 21

WHY FEAR THE EVIL DAYS?

Why should I fear when evil days come, when wicked deceivers surround me?

—Ps. 49:5

The writers wanted us to know that even when the fearful times surround us we can choose not to go there. Depression is said to be the most common emotional ailment in our country. Americans take more medication for the treatment of depression than for any other known ailment. But I am here to share with you, there is hope.

I understand depression because, based on my past and my family situations and all the evil I see around me, I could easily live there. I have lots of friends and loved ones who are totally consumed by depression every day.

But I chose to let God become first over anything else. By focusing on Him and His Word, as He shows me to do; God gives me back hope as I praise Him alone as my Savior and my God.

HOPE FOR YOU

If you are living in a fog of medication and nothing seems to be working for you, I urge you to take the time to lift up your eyes, think of your Lord and Savior, and get into His Word. I know God has a plan of how to face the depression of your life. He wants to give you back His hope for your future—no matter what the past has been.

Day 22

GOD IS WITH US, EVEN IN DEATH

Even though I walk through the valley of the shadow of death, I will fear no evil, for you are with me, your rod and your staff, they comfort me.

—Ps. 23:4

David knew the fear of death; first, as a mere shepherd, and then as a mighty king. He faced death at every stage of his life.

We too face many fears that can cause us to become as dead already. We can choose to live in helplessness and hopelessness, or we can allow God to give us the strength and courage to walk through the valleys and onto the mountaintops that await us when we reach our literal, physical death.

Does that mean we never are to have the valleys? No, we will have valleys. But God knows where we are at every moment. Nothing surprises Him. Most of us don't want to think about the valleys.

My life has been more about valleys than about mountaintops. God has shown up at every instance so that now I have no fear. I am able to enjoy the mountaintops when I see all the valleys I have come through to be there.

HOPE FOR YOU

When you acknowledge God, you will be able to face all the abuse, illness, pain, and suffering that you are in now. You will know you are not alone and that He is right there ready to walk with you through all you are facing.

Day 23

DO NOT BE AFRAID TO FAIL OR SUCCEED

Then the Lord said to Joshua, "Do not be afraid, do not be discouraged."

—Josh. 8:1a

A re you afraid to fail? Or perhaps you are even afraid of success. God shows us that through both failure and success we can learn some valuable lessons. Even the strong leader, Joshua, needed encouragement and strength from God to continue to do what he had to do.

When you fail or are anxious about anything, what is your first reaction? Is it to go to God and let Him show you His love and grace? Only then can He help you deal with the problem so you can move on and not become discouraged.

I have spent many wasted hours letting myself get caught up in my fears and letting discouragement overtake me. Now I know that it is not a way of life God has for me or for you either.

Hope for You

God has the answer just waiting for you. Begin again. He is ready to see you through. Don't give up and quit, for if you do, you will never see the entire plan God has for your life.

Day 24

GO FORWARD WITH GOD

When you go out to battle against your enemies, and see
horses and chariots and people more numerous than you,
do not be afraid of them, for the Lord your God is with you,
who brought you up from the land of Egypt.

—Deut. 20:1 NKJV

M oses assured the people they were going to be all right and not
to be afraid of those they were going to face. He reminded
them what the Lord had done and was going to do now.

I have feared many times in the struggles of my life. My main two
fears are food and finances. They are my "drugs of choice." I have lived
through bankruptcy and weighed more than 300 pounds.

Once I finally faced my fears and came to God with them, He showed
me His plan to move me forward and into new beginnings with a
change of heart and attitude. Can I go back and lose sight of how far
the Lord has brought me through these fears? I assure you I can, but I
make a daily choice to put God first, and let Him handle anything that
comes; His way, and not mine.

HOPE FOR YOU

What is it right now you need to turn over completely to God? Do not
be afraid to do so. He is here to show you the way. Let Him show you
how far you have come and the new beginning He has for you.

Day 25

FAITH IN THE GOD OF THE BIBLE OVERCOMES FEAR

> The disciples went and woke Him, saying, Lord save us! We're going to drown! He replied, "You of little faith, why are you so afraid?" Then He got up and rebuked the winds and the waves, and it was completely calm.
>
> —Matt. 8:25–26

Jesus knew His disciples very well. He taught them to have faith in Him, but when the winds and waves came they gave into their fear instead of faith in the one who could save them. But Jesus forgave them and calmed the situation.

Like the disciples, I have faced many a moment when my fear seemed far more a reality than my faith and love of the Lord. I have had a fear of water all my life. I loved the sun, ocean, and beach more than anything else, but going in the water terrified me. I have learned that even though I am not a great swimmer, God is there and He is the reason I do not have to fear drowning. He will take care of me there just as He does in the many storms of life that come.

How did I get to that point of calm assurance? I have learned that trials, situations, and storms of many kinds will come, but Jesus is the only way through and out of them.

HOPE FOR YOU

Are you drowning today? Does it look as if there is no way out and you are living in so much fear and pain that no one can understand and help? Take it to Jesus. Only He can unlock and calm your storm and help you see clearly where He is leading you.

Day 26

WHY FEAR, THE LORD IS MY STRENGTH

In God (I will praise His word), In God I have put my trust;
I will not fear. What can flesh do to me?

—Ps. 56:4 NKJV

David knew that God was to be praised and trusted far above the mortal men in his world. At the time of this writing, he was running and having to trust in God alone for his very life.

Do you fear gloomy, dark, rainy days? Does the lack of light and sunshine take away your hope and joy? I didn't realize how much I was affected by weather until I started a business in my home instead of going out regularly to an office to work.

I found that when those gray days would come, I just wanted to waste time and not do what God had for me that day. I would even put off working on this book when the weather was bad.

I have found that no matter the weather, the Lord God is my Lighthouse of Hope, and nothing can rob me of His joy, peace, and contentment. He leads and guides me even on gloomy days.

HOPE FOR YOU

What have you allowed to affect your effectiveness for Christ? Are you ready to begin again and let the light of the Lord flood your soul and change your outlook on this day? God is ready to show you how.

Day 27

DO NOT LET FEAR SHAKE YOU, STAND FIRM

Now the house of David was told, "Aram has allied itself with Ephraim"; so the hearts of Ahaz and his people were shaken, as the trees of the forest are shaken by the wind. Say to him, "Be careful, keep calm, and don't be afraid. Do not lose heart because of these two smoldering stubs of firewood—because of the fierce anger of Rezin and Aram and the son of Remaliah."

—Isa. 7:2, 4

I saiah the prophet saw people shaken with fear and not living as God planned for them. Looking around we see wars and rumors of wars, evil, and people living messy lives without God, and we too can become shaken.

But God does not want any one of us to live a shaken life. I have many times allowed things and people to shake my very existence. I wanted to be a help and an encourager to others, but I didn't even have peace in my own life. But God never left me. He brought me through to a place where fear does not rule, and I am not shaken by life.

HOPE FOR YOU

What is your level of faith? Are you living a shaken life of fear or a hopeful life firm in the faith of our Lord Jesus? Allow God to be in control, and nothing will be able to shake you for long.

Day 28

THE LORD IS WITH ME, WHAT CAN MAN DO TO ME?

The Lord is with me, I will not be afraid. What can man do to me? The Lord is with me, He is my helper, I will look in triumph on my enemies.

—Ps. 118:6–7

The writer shows us that when we place our confidence in the Lord, and not our fears, there is nothing man can do to us.

During my life I didn't look or act very different than a lot of you. I could pretend and play the games and make it look like I was living a good "Christian" life.

But in 1997 life changed. I ended up being very afraid. I was facing retirement, I was overweight, and I had no direction or true purpose in my life. I thought I had it all figured out, but life caught up with my true self.

However, God didn't give up on me. He had waited fifty-one long years to hear me finally say, "God, I no longer know what to do, I need You, and I am ready to trust and obey and do as You want." My family has seen me change from the inside out, and I am still changing day by day.

HOPE FOR YOU

What kind of life are you living? Is it one of pretense, pride, and self motivation? Or is it one of full trust and faith in Jesus Christ? No matter how long you have put it off, now is the time to let God be in full control and see the plan He has for you.

Day 29

DO NOT BE FRIGHTENED, THE END IS NOT YET

And you will hear of wars and rumors of wars, see that you are not frightened or troubled, for this must take place, but the end is not yet.

—Matt. 24:6 AMP

J esus is showing us that no matter what is going on around us, we are not to be alarmed, upset, or live in fear. This is hard to do when all we hear and read would tell us otherwise.

As we have so much instant communication and information available to us, how do we hear and not be fearful? How do we know what is really the truth? We need to spend as much time with God as we do with all the outside information we receive. Each of us has the same amount of time and choices about how we spend our time. We need to discern what really controls our lives.

I have let a lot of untruthful information around me come in so that at some point I began to believe it rather than what God told me. But now I know that I need to filter what comes in and goes through my mind so that God can be in total control.

HOPE FOR YOU

Are you letting God control and plan your day? Do you wake up excited about what He has for you right now? Is He first on your mind? God is waiting to show you His promises and information.

Day 30

DO NOT BE AFRAID, I AM THE FIRST AND THE LAST

And when I saw Him, I fell at His feet as dead. But He laid His right hand on me, saying to me, "Do not be afraid, I am the First and the Last."

—Rev. 1:17–18 NKJV

I s Jesus' word good enough for us? There is nothing that Jesus doesn't know and hasn't experienced. He holds the key to everything in His hands. This scripture is in the back of His Word for us, and we win.

A lot of people would have you believe that this passage, as recorded by John, the beloved disciple, is not to be taken literally. When I was first led into a study of Revelation, I approached it just as I do the rest of God's Word, as truth that He would show me personally if I would be willing to let Him.

I take the Book of Revelation as encouragement to not fear, no matter what may come. In the end, I will live forever with Him, and that is the good news. I have found that in order to overcome any fear you now hold onto, you must know the way to live forever. Then you will be able to see God's perspective and be able to overcome your fear.

HOPE FOR YOU

Jesus is waiting now to show you true joy, peace, and contentment without fear. Isn't it time you gave everything to Him and let Him show you the path and direction He has for you? He is the only way.

Day 31

DO NOT BE AFRAID, GOD FINDS FAVOR WITH YOU

Then the angel said to her, "Do not be afraid, Mary, for you have found favor with God."

—Luke 1:30 NKJV

D o you have God's favor? Can you now focus on the blessings you have versus what you don't have? Are you content no matter the situation? Or are you living in fear, despair, and hopelessness?

God's favor does not necessarily bring you what you want. Do you think that Mary, when she was told what was going to happen, was excited about having to go through pain, ridicule, rejection, and child-birth, and then see her Son murdered so horrifically? Not quite my idea of God's favor. But she trusted and believed God first and above herself. He carried her through all that came into her life. It was not so that she could be glorified, but so that He could be. She knew the difference.

I would not have chosen the life God brought me into many years ago. I was not born into a loving, caring family who wanted me. Instead I was born to parents who were not married and gave me away to be raised without a father and with little else. But God knew the plan that I didn't know. He has given me much favor, and continues to do so.

HOPE FOR YOU

God wants to show you favor now. There is nothing too big or too surprising to God. He is in control of it all and wants to work it out for His glory, and for your good. Will you let Him? This is the most important choice you will ever make now and for your eternity.

Day 32

DO NOT BE AFRAID OR TERRIFIED TO GO FORWARD

Then I said to you, "Do not be terrified or afraid of them. The Lord your God, who goes before you, He will fight for you, according to all He did for you in Egypt before your eyes, and in the wilderness where you saw how the Lord your God carried you, as a man carries his son, in all the way that you went until you came to this place."

—Deut. 1:29–31 NKJV

Moses was addressing the Israelites regarding their past history. He reminded them why it had taken so long to finally get to the Promised Land. It was because of their fear, unbelief, and rebellion against the Lord.

I can see very similar patterns between myself and the Israelites. I have been a fearful, easily intimidated person, who did not depend and rely on God's promises. I rebelled against what He had for me, and I ended up almost missing the promised life God had for me all along.

God in His grace and mercy never wants us to continue to miss out on Him, no matter how far we may have strayed. He is the God of redemption, forgiveness, and love.

HOPE FOR YOU

How far have you gone away from the true God of the Bible and the promises He has for you? You can return and He will forgive, forget, and bless you.

Day 33

PERFECT LOVE DRIVES OUT ALL FEAR

There is no fear in love, but perfect loves casts out fear, because fear involves torment. But he who fears has not been made perfect in love.

—1 John 4:18 NKJV

There is but one perfect lover of your soul and that is God. When focusing on His love for us there can be no fear because His love drives all that out. John is not suggesting sinless, perfect love on our part, but total confidence in the Lord, so that through His love for each of us personally, we can love Him and others. This growing and mature love will then banish fear from our lives.

Most of my life I found it hard to love. I did not feel I was conceived in love, nor did I grow up with love shown to me. I was afraid of loving because I did not want to be hurt as I had been in the past.

But God has shown me His love is all I need. He revealed to me that I was conceived in His love, regardless of who actually gave birth to me. Once I accepted that gift, I then could truly share my love with others and myself as well.

HOPE FOR YOU

Do you see God's love in your life? If not, it is time to open up your heart and receive it. His love will set you free from the fears you face. It will be one of the best gifts you will ever receive.

Day 34

YOU ARE NO LONGER A SLAVE TO FEAR, YOU ARE A CHILD OF GOD

> For you did not receive a spirit that makes you a slave again to fear, but you received the Spirit of sonship. And by Him we cry, "Abba, Father."
>
> —Rom. 8:15

For a long time I dealt with who I really was, based not on the world or my standards, but on the Word of God. Paul shows us clearly that we are no longer slaves of this world, but we are sons and daughters of the one true King.

I realize when I received and trusted Jesus Christ as my personal Lord and Savior, I got so much more than I had heard about before. It is certainly more than I deserve.

I have accepted who I am in my new nature. It is an identity based on the Spirit of the Lord Jesus. Knowing this has shown me why I do not have to allow fear to control me. I can rely on Him. Now I can take God at His literal Word and receive and claim the promises He has for me personally.

HOPE FOR YOU

Do you know your true identity in Christ? Do you know you are "a saint, a work of art, accepted, forgiven, righteous, and holy?" Before you can change and overcome fear God's way, it is important to know who you are in Him. It's all about Him, and not about you.

Day 35

SUBMIT TO GOD AND TO MARRIAGE

It was thus that Sarah obeyed Abraham [following his guidance and acknowledging his headship over her by] calling him lord (master, leader authority). And you are now her true daughters if you do right and let nothing terrify you [not giving way to hysterical fears or letting anxieties unnerve you].

—1 Pet. 3:6 AMP

Peter felt the need to address the issues of marriage because many of us choose not to discuss our Christian views with our potential husband or wife. We marry unsaved people or those who are not faithful to God. Then how do we handle the situation in which we find ourselves?

We should do all we can to make sure we have God's plan and blessing before we marry. Then we are to submit to each other in love. This certainly does not mean we have the right to disobey God's commandments or cause physical harm to one another in the process. I did not seek God's approval, and I paid dearly, as did my daughter and many others.

Marriage is a gift from God and is to be enjoyed and not endured in fear. God shows us how to have a wonderful life together when it is based totally on Him as the head of the marriage. I am so blessed to have had another chance at marriage, and this time I listened to God.

HOPE FOR YOU

No matter the situation, God is always there for you. Trust Him, live, and become one in Christ. It can always be worked out His way.

Day 36

A WONDERFUL PROMISE TO US, HIS CHURCH

> In righteousness you shall be established; You shall be far from oppression, for you shall not fear; And from terror, for it shall not come near you.
>
> —Isa. 54:14 NKJV

What a wonderful promise of God which Isaiah shares with his people. He foretold the promises of Christ and gave us a picture of what life forever will be with Him.

I admit I did not always live in the promises of God. I let the fears and insecurities overwhelm me. I lost all sight of my righteousness in Christ and let the world and my feelings control me instead of God. But God is a gracious and loving God, and He forgave all my unbelief and showed me how to begin and live in His promises for me.

Doesn't it put the fears you have in perspective when you understand the love and promises God has for you? The amazing grace of it all is that it is a free gift to you. You are protected by a loving God who cares about every part of your life.

HOPE FOR YOU

What is stopping you from living as God intends? You are His family, and He is in control. There is no need to let your fears overcome His promises to you. You can have His joy, peace, and contentment.

Day 37

ARE YOUR IDOLS CAUSING YOU GREAT FEAR AND DESPAIR?

> They are upright, like a palm tree, and they cannot speak, they must be carried, because they cannot go by themselves. Do not be afraid of them, for they cannot do evil, nor can they do any good.
>
> —Jer. 10:5 NKJV

Jeremiah saw his people being taken in by the culture of the land where they were living. He urged them not to get caught up in the worship of idols nor be afraid of those who did. He wanted them to know that God was their Protector, and to return to His ways.

Do we have idols in our world today? It is said an idol is defined as: anything that is sacred to a person, in that it defines self-worth, becomes the controlling center of life, and takes priority over all other loyalties.

I can see lots of these idols in our world, and I have allowed many of these to become a part of my life. The two that I let trap and cause me fear and guilt the most were food and money. It took many years to see that they are not real persons and have no truth in the way they can control me. God showed me how to overcome their control His way, and use them the way He intended in my life.

I found God is worth so much more of our loyalty than any idol we may have. No one else can give us His true joy, peace, and contentment.

HOPE FOR YOU

What is it you need to quit fearing and following? God is the one who has the plan for you—not anything or anyone else. Find His truth now.

Day 38

DO NOT BE AFRAID OF THEM, REMEMBER WHAT GOD HAS DONE

You shall not be afraid of them, but you shall remember well
what the Lord your God did to Pharaoh and to all Egypt.
—Deut. 7:18 NKJV

How many times have we forgotten what the Lord has done for us? How many times do we get tangled up again in the depths of our fears? Moses was urging the Israelites to keep going. He reminded them what the Lord had already done for them, and not to be afraid.

We must remember fear is not a person. It cannot consume us when we are walking with God. God wants us to live in faith and love, not in fear. I have let fear be the other person in my life for many years. I became fearful at the least sign of any interruption that I did not expect or want.

But God showed me He is the truth, and I do not have to let the ordinary happenings of life rob me of the joy, peace, and contentment that only He can give to me.

A lot of people feel that the words of the Bible are not real or relevant for us today. They are depending on other sources to free them from their fears, doubts, anxieties, and worry. How can we ever think that God would protect and preserve His Word if it were not for us right now?

HOPE FOR YOU

Are you depending on God's Word or something else to free you from the pain of fear? Reach out to the Bible on your shelf, and see what God has for you.

Day 39

DO NOT BE AFRAID, ONLY BELIEVE

As soon as Jesus heard the word that was spoken, He said to the ruler of the synagogue, "Do not be afraid; only believe."

—Mark 5:36 NKJV

What a wonderful promise Jesus gave to this ruler after being summoned to heal his daughter. Everyone told the ruler there was no hope, but he had seen what Jesus was doing and so he came and believed.

Isn't it wonderful that all Jesus asked of the ruler then, and of us today, is to believe? Is it so hard to believe that Jesus can handle every fear we have, even the fear of death? Why then are we not running to Him at all times?

I asked many questions before I finally found the answers I had sought for so long. In my humanistic mind I found it hard to understand the truth of faith in the one living God. I thought I had to be somebody or do something before God would grant me freedom from my fears. When all He wanted was for me to believe. It sounded too simple. But God has shown me that He is a simple God, and I am to be just "Simply Sue," and He will give me the desires of my heart.

HOPE FOR YOU

Do you truly believe the Bible and what Jesus has and wants to do for you? Have you given Him your all, and have you let Him give you an exchanged life? This is the only hope for overcoming your fears, and all He asks is for you to believe.

GREATER IS HE WHO IS IN YOU

> You are of God, little children, and have overcome them, because He who is in you is greater than he who is in the world.
>
> —1 John 4:4 NKJV

D o you find it easier to live a fearful life, and become overwhelmed by the situations and problems you encounter? John is saying that we don't have to live that way, nor did God intend for us to do so.

John shows us the assurance we have as believers to call upon God and know that He is greater than anything of this world. Isn't that good news and freedom for us?

It is for me now, but I remember when that was not the case. I had heard God's promises and believed them, but I thought I had to do something to be good enough to receive them. Is that your view of God too? I hope you can see the free gift Jesus is offering each of us—freedom to bring everything to Him.

HOPE FOR YOU

Is God in you? Are you living in the faith and love of our Savior and Lord, or are you still "working" to measure up? Know that the God in you is stronger than anything you will ever have to face, and He is here to free you so that you can live without fear.

Day 41

THE LORD, YOUR GOD HIMSELF, FIGHTS FOR YOU

> You must not fear them, for the Lord your God Himself fights for you.
>
> —Deut. 3:22 NKJV

When you are with others, do you talk about your own fears, life, what you have or know, or what you don't have and don't know? Or do you talk about what the Lord is doing in your life and how He can help them too?

Moses commanded Joshua not to be afraid because the Lord Himself was going to provide supernatural power and give them the victory. My battles may not be the same as Joshua's were, but they are just as real. Whether I am facing fear or resisting the temptation to fear, God has promised to fight alongside me and for me as I obey Him.

HOPE FOR YOU

Is it you or God fighting your battles? I have learned God has the power and I am a weak person. I need Him to be able to face anything, so I am willing to ask and let Him do the work. Let God show you His power and what He has for you to be and do.

Day 42

THERE IS NO PEACE IN FEAR

Peace I leave with you, my peace I give you. I do not give to you as the world gives. Do not let your hearts be troubled and do not be afraid.

—John 14:27

J esus knew He had to let His disciples in on the plans He had for them. He was not going to be with them in the flesh much longer, and He wanted them to know He was leaving His Holy Spirit alive in each one of them, and not to be afraid.

Are you at peace in your life? Or are you afraid, stressed out, and can't seem to understand how others handle life so calmly? I have come to realize, as Rick Warren wrote in "The Purpose Driven Life", that my life is not about me but about God in me. As deeply as I allow Him to work through His Holy Spirit living in me, is the depth to which I can live in His peace and not be afraid—no matter what the situation may be.

HOPE FOR YOU

So, what is your choice? Is it to be afraid, stressed, and live as the world lives? Or will it be to call upon the Lord God and find His joy, peace, and contentment? It is up to you.

Day 43

GOD CAN DELIVER QUICKLY, HAVE YOU ASKED BELIEVING?

The Lord said to Joshua, "Do not be afraid because of them for tomorrow about this time I will deliver all of them slain before Israel. You shall hamstring their horses and burn their chariots with fire."

—Josh. 11:6 NKJV

Have you seen God move quickly into action in your life? Joshua was facing a major battle and he needed help right then. The Lord told him not to fear, and gave him a timeframe of what would happen. Then He secured His words by showing Joshua what to do after the defeat.

Have you asked God, believing He can go into action right now? I have not always thought God could or would answer me quickly. I took my own way, and then when I made a mess of it I would once again return to Him.

I finally got tired of that spiritual and physical merry-go-round, and learned to seek His action and answers first, not last. I know sometimes we have to wait for good reasons, but God can act quickly when it is important for Him to do so. I also know that God wants all the credit for winning the battles of our lives, and He demands our obedience for what is to follow as well.

HOPE FOR YOU

What quick action do you need from God? Are you facing major battles within a certain timeframe? Have you asked Him for His help? Are you willing to do what He is asking of you once it is over?

Day 44

GOD SHOWS YOU NOT TO BE AFRAID

And the angel of the Lord said to Elijah, "Go down with him, do not be afraid of him." So he arose and went down with him to the king.

—2 Kgs. 1:15 NKJV

Elijah was a unique prophet God sent to Israel. He faced things that we probably will not have to encounter. God's message is still the same for us as it was for Elijah. No matter what is happening, God is here and He can be trusted.

Trust Him from the depths of your heart and don't waste time working it all out on your own. I have had to learn many tough lessons in applying this to my life. Those tough lessons have given me the freedom to keep going.

Trust Him with your finances, your health, the health of others, your relationships, your emotions, and everything this day may bring. You do not have to live in fear of anything or anyone. God is taking care of it all.

HOPE FOR YOU

What have you been working on without asking God for help? Trust God right now, and let Him show you His plan and His love for you. Remember, "God is big enough to perform any miracle as needed. His answers are bigger than our prayers, and His promises are greater than our problems" (Author unknown).

Day 45

GOD WILL GUIDE YOU SAFELY

He guided them safely, so they were unafraid, but the sea engulfed their enemies.

—Ps. 78:53

The writer Asaph retells the history of the Jewish nation so that each generation would not forget God and repeat the errors of their forefathers. It is great encouragement to us still today.

Do you trust God completely to guide you to safety and to be unafraid? It has taken me a long time to trust God completely with everything. It takes honesty and humility to face Him, and then acceptance of His forgiveness to receive all the gifts He has for us.

His forgiveness is what He offers each of us who believe. How many of us receive God's gift as our own? Whatever is here or coming or has already past, God is faithful. He will guide you through, and by knowing it is Him, you can help others know not to be afraid as well.

HOPE FOR YOU

Are you ready to give up your own ways and honestly and humbly face God with all of it? Are you willing to receive His forgiveness and then forgive yourself? This is a major step to becoming all He created you to be and do.

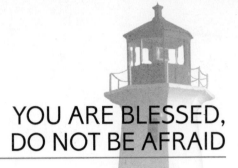

Day 46

YOU ARE BLESSED, DO NOT BE AFRAID

Who is going to harm you if you are eager to do good? But even if you should suffer for what is right, you are blessed. Do not fear what they fear, do not be frightened.

—1 Pet. 3:13–14

Doesn't God's way to live make more sense than the way we have been living—afraid and fearful? Peter shares that we should fear no one, and that even if we have to suffer for what is right in order to learn the lessons God has for us, we are still blessed.

For many years I did not take God at His word, I did not let Him control all parts of my life. Looking back, I see that I faced many people and situations my way instead of His. I can't go back and change what happened, but I can move forward in forgiveness and encourage others to do the same. Life is a gift to me, and God has redeemed all my wasted years into ones of His joy, peace, and contentment.

HOPE FOR YOU

What does God want to redeem for you? Are you willing to let go of the past, receive His forgiveness, and go forward His way? He has His joy, peace, and contentment waiting for you.

Day 47

GOD NEEDS EVERYONE
IN THE BATTLE

> The officers shall speak further to the people, and say, "What man is there who is fearful and fainthearted? Let him go and return to his house, lest the heart of his brethren faint like his heart."
>
> —Deut. 20:8 NKJV

To serve in Israel's volunteer army, the Israelites had to have strong faith in the Lord. The leaders knew if one lacked this, or was distracted, he might be an influence on others to do the same. They required each warrior to search himself and if he was fearful he had to be willing to take himself out of the battle until he could regain the heart and strength of the Lord.

I have been one who thought I could stay in the battle in my own strength, when in fact I should have taken myself out of it and sought God. I kept going for many years until I was finally forced to spend time with the Lord to renew my faith and strength in Him alone. I had to quit depending on myself. Only then can I be of help to others as I truly want to be.

HOPE FOR YOU

Are you really helping others win? Are you in the battle of life without the faith of the Lord to give you strength and courage to win? If you are, it is time to take yourself out of the battle and spend time with the Lord. Let Him show you the true way to overcome fear and a weak spirit, and become ready and equipped to handle life His way.

Day 48

GOD'S PROMISES ARE TRUE

Do not fear, you will not suffer shame. Do not fear disgrace,
you will not be humiliated.

—Isa. 54:4

God was assuring the Israelites through the prophet Isaiah, that even though they had sinned and had chosen not to obey Him, He still loved them and He would take care of them.

God is also assuring us now, once He has forgiven us, He forgets our sin so there is nothing to separate us from all He has for us. Isn't that a wonderful promise of life now and forever?

I once thought I had lived so badly, and committed so many sins that there was no way God could ever totally forgive me. Also I couldn't even imagine He would forget each and every one of those as well. I didn't think I deserved another chance because I could not begin to forgive myself. I was so wrong. Once I came in true repentance, I found He was willing and waiting for me.

HOPE FOR YOU

Are you at peace with God? He is waiting to give you life more abundantly than you can ever imagine. Don't wait another minute to come totally to Him.

Day 49

DO NOT BE AFRAID TO SUFFER, AND EVEN TO DIE

> Do not be afraid of what you are about to suffer. I tell you, the devil will put some of you in prison to test you, and you will suffer persecution for ten days. Be faithful, even to the point of death and I will give you the crown of life.
> —Rev. 2:10

John was a witness to the wonderful things Jesus revealed to him. He was instructed to write them down so that all of us through the ages would be able to hear and know that we have nothing to fear. We are to know that what happened in the past or what we face right now or what is to come is only a test. It does not last very long.

I thought for many years that the last book of the Bible was one of those mystical and inaccessible areas only to be pursued by those highly esteemed theologians, of which I knew I was not called to be! I found many have feared to read the book of Revelation, because it is our future, and it is in a form most of us are not familiar with in everyday living. But I encourage you to dig in deep and read the whole book for yourself and see God's revealed plan to all of us.

Hope for You

Our challenge in life is to be faithful to Jesus as He is to us. I am full of hope. I know God is in control, Jesus Christ is victorious, and all who trust Him will be saved. Do you have that assurance?

Day 50

PRAY DAILY, BE PREPARED FOR THE CRISIS WITHOUT FEAR

Isaiah said to them, "Tell your master, 'This is what the Lord says: Do not be afraid of what you have heard—those words with which the underlings of the king of Assyria have blasphemed me.'"

—2 Kgs. 19:6

King Hezekiah had just received a message from his enemy to surrender. The situation looked hopeless and very fearful. Hezekiah went to the temple to pray. His officials went to Isaiah for guidance.

When you are in a seemingly hopeless situation, what is your first response? Is it as King Hezekiah's was, to go and pray and seek guidance from the local prophet?

Or do you sit in fear, working to figure it all out and listening to all the advice around you from non-Christians? That's what I did many times in my life. But I finally realized that way never gave me the answers for very long, and certainly no peace. I know now I must pray daily for guidance from the Lord. I am not to wait until my situation gets to the hopeless stage before I pray and seek godly wisdom.

HOPE FOR YOU

Have you prayed about your situation? Are you seeking godly council for guidance? What is keeping you from doing this? Remember "our problems are God's opportunities" (Author unknown).

Day 51

CAN YOU LAUGH AT FEAR?

He laughs at fear, afraid of nothing, he does not shy away from the sword.

—Job 39:22

C an you laugh at your fears? God asked Job several questions, not expecting him to answer. He just wanted Job to see His power and submit to His authority. I am sure with all that Job was going through it was hard to laugh and see God's plan in it. But that is exactly what God wants us to do.

Laughter is a great medicine for everything, and it sure puts many of my problems in proper perspective. I thank God for His gift of laughter so that I can overcome whatever I may have to face.

When we let our fears consume us, and not the power and sovereignty of God, it is hard to laugh. Once we focus on Him and not the fear, laughter becomes the instant cure.

HOPE FOR YOU

How long has it been since you really laughed? Are you in good health? Are life and all your fears blocking you from the gift God has given you? Children laugh all the time, why not join them?

Day 52

FEAR NOT, BE GLAD AND REJOICE

> Fear not, O land, be glad and rejoice, for the Lord has done marvelous things!
>
> —Joel 2:21 NKJV

Have you ever rejoiced and been glad *in* your fears? Joel was warning the people of Judah about the coming judgment of the Lord. They had sinned and turned away from God, and Joel was telling them what God had for those who believe and return to Him.

God loves you and wants you not to fear. He wants you to be glad in Him alone. I fought this for such a long time, until I came to the point where I cried out and left my burden with Him. The Lord has blessed me so much—even with the breath of life. Without anything else from Him, I am glad and rejoice in Him. He has done marvelous things for me.

HOPE FOR YOU

Are you glad and rejoicing? Or does fear have you trapped in its never ending stronghold? God is willing to love and forgive you and give you a purpose in life and surround you with caring people. Be glad in the journey and walk with Him.

Day 53

FREE TO SERVE ANYWHERE, WHERE WOULD YOU CHOOSE?

> Gedaliah the son of Ahikam, the son of Shaphanm took an oath before them and their men saying, "Do not be afraid to serve the Chaldeans. Dwell in the land and serve the king of Babylon, and it shall be well with you."
>
> —Jer. 40:9 NKJV

God saved a part of the tribe of Judah to prosper. Jeremiah went to Gedaliah, the newly appointed governor, to dwell with him. He could have gone where it was safe and where he felt wanted and accepted. But he chose to return to the Judean exiles (even though they did not like him) so that they would not think him a traitor who had sold out to the Babylonians.

When given such difficult circumstances, are we willing to choose the hard path, or do we want the pleasurable and comfortable way? I always wanted an easy pace, but I never seemed to be able to pursue it. I always ended up choosing the hard way. But I finally realized God has always led me to Him through the hard choices I made. He wanted me to become totally dependent on Him. By doing so I learned to dwell with those who are not believers and not be afraid of them.

HOPE FOR YOU

What decisions and choices are you facing? Are you seeking the comfortable way or God's way for yourself and your family? Is it hard to trust Him? Are you afraid? God has the right choice for you.

Day 54

DO NOT BE AFRAID OF ANYONE WHO WANTS TO KILL YOU

I tell you, my friends, do not be afraid of those who kill the body and after that can do no more.

—Luke 12:4

Jesus is reminding the people not to fear any person, even in harmful situations. Jesus wanted them to know they should be bold witnesses for Him and not let anyone threaten them from doing so.

The same is true for us today. I am sure in reading this verse you might have thought, as I once did, that it is a great promise for those who were called to full time Christian ministry. But how does it apply to those of us who work regular jobs, have families and friends, and attend and sometimes serve in church?

I have found that God has so much more for us than being comfortable and seeking the things of this world. He has exchanged our lives with His, and He wants us to go, care and share Him, and not be afraid to do so. We have placed so much emphasis on being "people pleasers" it is hard to realize the only one we should seek to please is God.

HOPE FOR YOU

Are you living to please God or man? Are you afraid of those who could kill you for choosing God first? God is the answer, and you no longer have to be afraid of men.

Day 55

FEAR NOT, THE KING HAS COME

> Jesus found a young donkey and sat upon it, as it is written, "Do not be afraid, O Daughter of Zion, see, your king is coming, seated on a donkey's colt."
>
> —John 12:14–15

This shows the fulfillment of how Jesus would enter Jerusalem before His death as stated in Zechariah 9:9. The words "do not be afraid" were added because of the confusion that would go on after the death of Jesus. That fear and confusion still goes on today, even though we know the whole truth and the total picture.

God never intended us to fear or be confused concerning who we are in Christ or what He came to do through His death and Resurrection. It took me a long time to accept my true identity in Jesus Christ, because I was so insecure in myself, stemming from my past. But I have learned knowing who I am in Christ is more important than any other identity I could have on earth.

HOPE FOR YOU

Do you believe all the words of God to us are truth? He is ready for you to shake off any fear of death and allow Him to live in you and to serve in His will. Are you ready to do so?

Day 56

DO NOT GRIEVE OR BE DEPRESSED, THE JOY OF THE LORD IS YOUR STRENGTH

> Then [Ezra] told them, "Go your way, eat the fat, drink the sweet drink, and send portions to him for whom nothing is prepared, for this day is holy to our Lord. And be not grieved and depressed, for the joy of the Lord is your strength and stronghold."
>
> —Neh. 8:10 AMP

The Israelites had just heard the truth of the law from their leaders and realized they had sinned against God and had received many punishments because of it.

They were convicted in their hearts of their sin and were grieved and depressed because of it. This can happen when we let the knowledge of our sin overcome us. Their leaders encouraged them to begin anew to celebrate and to take care of those who needed to see the blessings the Lord had for them.

This encouraged me in remembering I am forgiven and that I do not have to live in fear, grief, or depression. I must remember that the joy of the Lord is my strength to overcome it all. What an awesome promise, and one that I have learned is mine.

HOPE FOR YOU

Do you have the joy of the Lord? Do you see your life as beyond hope? Are you ready to celebrate or hibernate? God wants to take away all fear and guilt, and give you a life of joy. Come to Him, and He will make you new.

Day 57

THE LORD IS HERE, DO NOT FEAR

> In that day it shall be said to Jerusalem, "Fear not, O Zion.
> Let not your hands sink down or be slow and listless."
> —Zeph. 3:16 AMP

Zephaniah was a prophet sent to urge Judah to come out of their complacency and return to God. Even though this was written many centuries ago, it is not old news, is it? Do we realize America is a blessed nation? Are we losing the blessings our forefathers so bravely fought to preserve and defend? Most Americans agree to the existence of God but have no awareness of His plan through Jesus Christ, His Son, for them.

I can assure you I have been guilty of fear, complacency, and not being totally devoted to God. How about you? We can return at any time to God. He will forgive and forget, and He still wants to use us in the plan He has for us. Our God is still in control, and He is the reason why we do not have to fear.

HOPE FOR YOU

Are you listening and obeying God? He has not changed. He is ready to show you once and for all that fear is not in His plan for you or for our nation.

Day 58

DO NOT BE ANXIOUS ABOUT ANYTHING

Rejoice in the Lord always, I will say it again, Rejoice! Let your gentleness be evident to all. The Lord is near. Do not be anxious about anything, but in everything, by prayer and petition, with thanksgiving, present your requests to God.

—Phil. 4:4–6

Does this sound impossible—to never be anxious about anything? Paul assured us it was not. I am sure you are thinking God must not know about your life and what you are going through. I can't even imagine what your life looks like right now, but God knows.

I do know where I was when these words finally reached my heart to show me God loves me. It was in a time of my life where I thought I had messed up too much, I could never change, and that it was too late for me to begin again! But I learned through trust and total dependence on Him, I don't have to choose to fear, doubt, or be anxious, no matter what the circumstances or the timing appears to be.

Paul's advice was to turn our fears and worries into prayers. A real interesting lesson I had to learn was that God does hear and He does answer. His solution is always much better than all the worry and fear I let myself go through.

Hope for You

Do you pray to the Lord? Do you ever write down your prayers and then see how God answers them? The only way to live without fear and anxiety is to have the peace of God alive in your daily life.

Day 59

WHAT OR WHO ARE YOU AFRAID OF?

> I'm the One comforting you. What are you afraid of—or who? Some man or woman who'll soon be dead? Some poor wretch destined for dust?
>
> —Isa. 51:12 THE MESSAGE

Isaiah's constant theme was to tell the Israelites they should not fear anyone or anything, but they were to trust the one true God their Creator. Just stop and think about it. Are we more faithful to God now than when we began as a believer? Or are we letting ourselves give in and becoming more fearful every day?

Dr. Caroline Leaf, author of "Who Switched Off My Brain," tells us it is a proven fact that "fear is the root of stress." And that according to the American Institute of Stress, "between 75 and 90 percent of visits to primary care physicians result from stress-related disorders."

So with that information, shouldn't we consider what God is showing us through His Word? I am so thankful that I did not become a part of that stress statistic, and that God willingly gives me His comfort and peace in any situation.

HOPE FOR YOU

Are you a part of the stressed-out crowd, letting stress overcome you more and more? I urge you now to consider what God has done for you. It is so much more than you can ever imagine.

Day 60

NO MATTER WHAT COMES, WE WILL NOT FEAR

Therefore we will not fear, though the earth give way, and the mountains fall into the heart of the sea.

—Ps. 46:2

The writers did not experience the same kinds of fears we do now, but they realized that no matter what comes, we are not to fear because God is here. He is in control, and He is our eternal future and hope.

Are you living in fear of what is being reported and happening around you? At one time I dwelt on what I heard. I could easily become fearful over the slightest bad news. I also handled situations in my life the same way. I looked fine on the outside, but I could put up a great front. Inside I was always at turmoil and afraid.

I have found it depends on how you view life as to how fearfully you will live. When you view it from God's perspective it is a totally different world than what we see from our viewpoint. I choose to live from God's viewpoint rather than from mine. Only He can bring me joy, peace, and contentment no matter what is going on around me.

HOPE FOR YOU

It is a choice as to how you view and live your life. Whose viewpoint will you choose—God's view and ways or your own?

Day 61

DO NOT BE AFRAID OF PEOPLE

> Only do not rebel against the Lord. And do not be afraid
> of the people of the land, because we will swallow them up.
> Their protection is gone, but the Lord is with us. Do not be
> afraid of them.
>
> —Num. 14:9

In the same way the Israelites were grumbling and complaining about the people they were going to face, I too wandered around in my own desert for many years before I could finally realize that God wanted me to *ask* Him before I charge off on my own.

We know one of the greatest fears we have is of speaking before other people. I was no exception to that fact. Growing up in Oklahoma, I can imagine there are not many teachers, classmates, or even relatives that remember much about me. I did not say much to anyone because I was afraid they would make fun of me. I had already experienced enough of that, so I did not want to draw any more negative attention from anyone.

What does that tell you about my personal relationship with God? I did not know and was not willing to find out that I could trust Him with every area of my life. I missed out on many blessings God had for me in my beginning years, but I am blessed to know now that He has redeemed that lost time and turned it into a wonderful love relationship with Him.

HOPE FOR YOU

Are you wandering around in your desert just as the Israelites did for 40 years? Do you have a personal relationship with Jesus Christ? He is your way out of your desert, and now is the time to make that choice.

Day 62

GOD KNOWS THE PLAN HE HAS FOR YOU

"For I know the plans I have for you," declares the Lord, "plans to prosper you and not to harm you, plans to give you hope and a future. Then you will call upon me and come and pray to me, and I will listen to you. You will seek me and find me when you seek me with all your heart."

—Jer. 29:11–13

This familiar message is not new to most of us, but we normally do not focus on the entire meaning. Jeremiah wrote this as a letter to the Jews in exile in Babylon. He assured them God is faithful and had a plan for creating them. Then Jeremiah gave them some instructions on how to overcome and defeat fear.

I know, through these words, God is my Creator, and He has a plan for me. God has given me the ways I can know and live the life He planned for me.

It is clear that when I pray and seek God with all my heart and obey and do as He wills, life is much easier and fear has no room to survive. But when I choose not to seek God, and do not allow Him to control each and every day; fear and doubt can grip me as tightly as a vice.

HOPE FOR YOU

What is it that keeps you gripped in fear and apart from God? Right now see God loves you and He has a plan for you. Now is the time to call, come, and pray to the one true God. I can assure you, He will listen and answer you.

Day 63

YOU WILL NOT DROWN

The disciples went and woke Him, saying, "Master, Master, we're going to drown!" He got up and rebuked the wind and the raging waters, the storm subsided, and all was calm. "Where is your faith?" He asked His disciples. In fear and amazement they asked one another, "who is this? He commands even the winds and the water, and they obey Him."
—Luke 8:24–25

Are you like the disciples, fearful of drowning in the storms of your life? Jesus is the one who can calm the storms, and He did just that for His disciples then and now. In Him there is hope, and by faith the disciples went on to impact the world with the message of Jesus Christ.

I have found in the last few years that it is hard for me to handle the physical rainy gray days that come into my life. When it is raining and storming outside I can be like those disciples—fearful and drowning in self-pity. It is so much easier to see God at work when the sun is shining and things are running smoothly, isn't it?

I have learned that God is in control of it all. There is nothing He cannot handle in my life, your life, or the past, present, and future history of our world.

HOPE FOR YOU

There is nothing you are facing that God cannot take care of and work out. Have you asked Him to do so?

Day 64

GOD HEARS, NO MATTER WHERE YOU ARE

God heard the boy crying, and the angel of God called to Hagar from Heaven and said to her, "What is the matter Hagar? Do not be afraid, God has heard the boy crying as he lies there. Lift the boy up and take him by the hand, for I will make him into a great nation."

—Gen. 21:17–18

D oes God hear you and your family cry? Ishmael became the ruler of a large tribe now known as the Arab nations. One of his daughters married Esau. It is recorded that he and his tribes were hostile to Israel, just as they are today!

God took care of Ishmael and his mother Hagar even when they continued to run and not face their problems. God wanted them to trust Him for forgiveness and mercy. Has God heard your cry and taken care of you even though He no longer had first place in your life?

Many times I have run from my problems just as Hagar did. Do you know escape is only a temporary solution? I finally realized God's plan is for us to face our problems with His help. God wants first place in everything of our lives instead of ignoring and running away from Him.

HOPE FOR YOU

Are you walking with God and experiencing His joy, peace, and contentment, or are you on the run from God and your problems and fears?

Day 65

DO NOT BE AFRAID TO SPEAK FOR THE LORD

One night the Lord spoke to Paul in a vision: "Do not be afraid, keep on speaking, do not be silent."

—Acts 18:9

God had a message for Paul and for us as well. We are to keep speaking to everyone about Him, no matter who it is. We are not to be quiet because of our fear.

Often when we see so much that is wrong going on around us, we don't keep focused on what God is doing in our lives. We can get to feeling alone and believe that no one really wants to follow Christ as we do.

I have been lonely and afraid much of my life, even when I had many people around me. That was the time I needed to remember that I was never alone, and that God was still in control, and had a unique and special plan for me. We must continue on to see the joy, peace, and contentment He has for us through it all. We must not be afraid to share that encouragement with others.

HOPE FOR YOU

Are you afraid and discouraged? Was something said or did you hear or see something that made you afraid? God tells all of us not to fear but to focus on Him. He is ready to take care of anything you are facing and He is here for you. Oftentimes He wants you to put your focus on Him and others first, no matter what your fear may be.

Day 66

DO NOT BE AFRAID OF ANYONE OR THEIR WORDS

And you, son of man, do not be afraid of them or their words. Do not be afraid, though briers and thorns are all around you and you live among scorpions. Do not be afraid of what they say or terrified by them, though they are a rebellious house.

—Ezek. 2:6

E zekiel served as a prophet to the Jewish exiles that had been taken as captives to Babylonia. They had become an ungrateful and abusive people. He was called to stay in Babylonia and present the message that God was with them, even though they were far from the Lord both spiritually and physically.

I have faced many difficult people in my life. I did not do so well because for the most part I tried to face them on my own. The message today is that wherever we are, we are not to be afraid because God knows all about it, and He is there to care for and protect us. He also wants to develop our character to be able to handle those difficult people and situations we will face, and do it His way.

HOPE FOR YOU

The Lord knew Ezekiel would need His strength not to give in to what these people would say and react to what He had to tell them. How about you? Do you face difficult people and abusive situations? Do you know God is there for you and wants to give you His strength to be able to care for them and share His love with them?

Day 67

DWELL AND SERVE WITHOUT FEAR

And Gedaliah took an oath before them and their men, and said to them, "Do not be afraid of the servants of the Chaldeans. Dwell in the land and serve the king of Babylon, and it shall be well with you."

—2 Kgs. 25:24 NKJV

It is not always easy to stay and face your fears, is it? Gedaliah, the newly appointed governor, assured the Israelites not to fear and to stay where they were. They were to dwell in Babylon and serve the king.

In looking back at my life, I have not always followed this message. I chose to run without even asking God, and I made choices that could have defeated me for the rest of my life. But once I faced my life and could see my patterns, God showed me how to stay, dwell, and serve where He had placed me, and to be content in doing so.

HOPE FOR YOU

Are you ready to stay and face your fears? Has God placed you where it is not comfortable to be? Listen and obey, He will take care of you.

Day 68

THE LORD IS WITH YOU, READY TO BLESS YOU

That night the Lord appeared to him and said, "I am the God of your father Abraham. Do not be afraid, for I am with you, I will bless you and will increase the number of your descendents for the sake of my servant Abraham."
—Gen. 26:24

Isaac, Abraham's son, was afraid. But he was reminded by God physically that God was with him just as He had been with his father, Abraham. That gave him the strength and courage to go on.

Today I am going on, even though the weather here is a mess and not everything in my life is what I would choose it to be. I have not had a physical visitation from God, but I know by His Word that I am at peace and living in His joy and contentment because God is right here with me. In times like these, I just continue to thank God for not leaving me, even though He has every right to do so. I thank Him for loving me in spite of me.

HOPE FOR YOU

Reach out and know that God loves and cares for you, no matter what, and that He has not left you. Reach out and ask and thank and praise Him. He will give you the strength to get up and go on.

Day 69

IN THE MIDST OF PAIN, DO NOT BE AFRAID

And as she was having great difficulty in childbirth, The midwife said to her, "Don't be afraid, for you have another son."

—Gen. 35:17

As Rachel was dying in childbirth, she was told not to be afraid because she had produced a son who was to be a leader of the Jewish people. Death is a certainty for all of us, but we do not need to fear it. God has a plan of when and how it will happen, and He takes care of all the things leading up to it.

It is not so much the manner and matter of death but the important issues—how you lived and what will live on after you are gone. I have never wanted to think about dying. I guess I thought it really didn't matter anyway. But God showed me how to live in a way that makes death no big deal.

The choices you make today determine where and how you will live forever. Do you ever think about the God you serve and how He wants you to choose to live? Or are you focused only on yourself and not even seeing the choices you have?

HOPE FOR YOU

Focus today on how you are serving God and others, not just on what is happening to you. What will be the end results in your eternal future and the eternal future of others? These are the important issues.

Day 70

DO NOT BE AFRAID OF THOSE WHO INTEND TO HARM YOU

> But Joseph said to them, "Don't be afraid, am I in the place of God? You intended to harm me, but God intended it for good to accomplish what is now being done, the saving of many lives."
>
> —Gen. 50:19–20

A re you afraid of anyone whom you have hurt at sometime? How about those who have hurt you? Are you afraid to face them, see them, or even think of them? Joseph was advising his brothers, who had definitely done harm to him, not to be afraid of him. He saw his opportunity to turn a wrong into a right, and to forgive them, just as he had been forgiven.

I have lived in fear of those who have hurt me. I hurt them in return by refusing to forgive them and pretending not to care. But the Lord showed me that I had to face those hurts if I was going to live in the plan He had for me.

To do this I had to contact my Mom and ask her to forgive me for not being the kind of daughter she needed. First of all, my Mom was the one that caused the harm, so by all human reasoning I thought she should have been seeking *my* forgiveness. But I obeyed God and faced her. From then on until her death our relationship was so different. She had changed and by my forgiving and getting to know her, I became a changed person too. She is now in Heaven, and one day I will see her again.

HOPE FOR YOU

Is there someone or something you need to face God's way? I urge you not to wait. There is no better time than now to be set free of that fear.

GO, TAKE POSSESSION, AND DO NOT BE AFRAID

See, the Lord your God has given you the land. Go up and take possession of it as the Lord, the God of your Fathers, told you. Do not be afraid, do not be discouraged.

—Deut. 1:21

M oses told the Israelites God's plan for them, but did they listen? No, they did not. And as a result, they spent forty years wandering in the desert to reach their destination; when in fact it would have only taken two weeks to complete!

Why did that happen? It was because they did not trust God and believe in His plan for them. Most of the original people who set out on the journey with Moses from Egypt, and even Moses himself, did not get to see what God had for them all along.

I am not so different from the Israelites. I spent more than forty years in my desert journey. But God never left or gave up on me. He knew one day I would seek Him totally to overcome my fears of the Promised Land He had waiting for me. This book is a result of crossing into the land.

HOPE FOR YOU

Are you too afraid to go take what God has for you? Is God showing you what He wants you to be and do? Are you refusing and using all the same excuses just as the Israelites did? How long will you wander? Will you even fail to go and then wish you had? Cross over into what the Lord has for you; He can be trusted.

Day 72

DO NOT PANIC OR FEAR, THE BATTLE IS THE LORD'S

He shall say, Hear, O Israel, today you are going into battle against your enemies. Do not be fainthearted or afraid, do not be terrified or give way to panic before them. For the Lord your God is the one who goes with you to fight for you against your enemies to give you victory.

—Deut. 20:3–4

Just like the Israelites, we face all kinds of enemies that want us to feel outnumbered, helpless, and hopeless. Yours may be at school, work, or even at home. They are everywhere, aren't they?

What battle are you facing today? Is it a job you need, is it to be healthier and lose weight? Is it to be healed, be a better parent and person, or to get along with others better? Or could it be a church issue?

God reminded the Israelites that He was always with them and that He had already saved them from everything they had faced in the past. We have that same assurance. We now can feel secure because God has already overcome anything we may face and will help us through it. He has helped me many times, and now He wants to do the same for you.

HOPE FOR YOU

Now is the right time for you to cry out and ask God to show you the truth. You do not have to live in fear, panic, and hopelessness. You can live in the security of who you are in Christ Jesus. It is an easier and simpler way to live each day.

BE STRONG, NOT AFRAID, GOD IS WITH YOU

Be strong and courageous. Do not be afraid or terrified because of them, for the Lord your God goes with you, He will never leave you nor forsake you.

—Deut. 31:6

Just as Moses was telling the people, and particularly Joshua, the new leader, we are to be strong, knowing God is with us. Do you realize God goes with you and that He will never leave you or forsake you? Because of this, we are not to be afraid.

It has been hard for me to see God at work in my life. Looking back, He never once left me even though I left Him at times. He has never failed to work out all things for my good even though at times I couldn't see it. He has never failed to meet my needs even though I have messed up many things in my life. What a praise I can see it all now.

HOPE FOR YOU

Can you see God at work in your life? Do you believe God wants you to face your fears, whatever they are? He wants you to come and give them to Him so that He can take care of them all. Commit now and obey God and trust Him. He will bless you with a life filled with hope, joy, peace, and contentment, not fear.

Day 74

DO NOT FEAR, I WILL HELP YOU, SAYS THE LORD

For I am the Lord, your God, who takes hold of your right hand and says to you, Do not fear, I will help you.

—Isa. 41:13

Isaiah showed us that we, just as the Israelites, need not fear because we know God is with each of us. He wants a relationship with each of us, and He gives us His strength, help, and victory over sin. So what more do we need?

I have not always made it a practice to let God help me. I have thought I had to do something first, then if I encountered a problem, God was there for me. In truth, the opposite is true. I am learning to begin each day with Him in control and then let Him show me the plan for the day.

HOPE FOR YOU

Choose to place your total trust in the one true God. Then allow Him to be in charge and see what a difference it will make in each new day.

GOD WILL HELP YOU, DO NOT BE AFRAID

This is what the Lord says—he who made you, who formed you in the womb, and who will help you, Do not be afraid, O Jacob, my servant, Jeshuran, (Israel) whom I have chosen.

—Isa. 44:2

I saiah assured the people that God had chosen and made them, and He would take care of them. Isaiah showed us that we, just as the Israelites, need not fear because we know God is with each of us. He wants a relationship with each of us, and He gives us His strength, help, and victory over sin. So what more do we need?

I have found I am not a good "Holy Asker." I often was punished for asking, both in my young and adult life; so I thought I must be an awful person and did not deserve to approach God with anything. I am glad I got my priorities in line with God's and learned that He wants me to seek and ask Him for everything! I don't have to earn my way to God, I just have to willingly ask and receive.

HOPE FOR YOU

Keep your mind focused on God and let nothing rob you of His joy, peace, and contentment. "When fear knocks, your love and faith in God kicks in, and fear will find no one at home in your life" (Author unknown).

Day 76

GOD WILL FIGHT YOUR ENEMIES, DO NOT BE AFRAID

Joshua said to them, "Do not be afraid, do not be discouraged. Be strong and courageous. This is what the Lord will do to all the enemies you are going to fight."

—Josh. 10:25

How could Joshua lead his men and tell them not to be afraid? He could do this because he had experienced God at work in his life and in the battles he had won.

Has God helped you in the past? Doesn't that give you the hope and assurance that He will continue to do so? Even though I made a lot of wrong choices and was not an obedient servant of God, He has always taken care of me. I must never forget that, because then I can face fear—His way.

HOPE FOR YOU

What are you facing right now that has you entrapped and fearful? Is it financial issues, spiritual matters, emotional needs, physical needs, church situations, or relationships? God loves you and is waiting for you to give all your heart, body, and soul to Him, so that you will never need to fear anything again.

Day 77

WOULD YOU BE AFRAID TO DEFEND YOUR COUNTRY AND FAMILY?

Jael went out to meet Sisera and said to him, "Come my lord, come right in, don't be afraid." So he entered her tent and she put a covering over him.

—Judg. 4:18

Jael was the wife of Heber, (who was loyal to Sisera and King Jabin and whom Deborah was working to defeat). Jael, however, was not loyal to King Jabin. She invited Sisera into her tent to hide so that she could help Deborah defeat King Jabin by killing him. She even told Sisera not to be afraid.

I have often wondered if I was ever called to defend my family and my country, would I be afraid? Could I ever see myself like Jael, inviting the enemy in, knowing what I had to do?

God's Word clearly tells us that when God is in charge He will show you, even in the worst circumstances, how to overcome fear. He even used a resourceful woman to accomplish His purpose.

HOPE FOR YOU

Now is the time to come and face God in truth and life. He will restore you and help you become the person He wants you to be. What is your choice? Perhaps God's plan for you is not as dramatic as that of Jael's, but are you willing to find out?

Day 78

YOU CAN KNOW GOD AND LIVE, AND NOT BE AFRAID

But the Lord said to him, "Peace! Do not be afraid. You are not going to die."

—Judg. 6:23

Gideon, whom God had called to be the leader of Israel, had just seen God's angel and was afraid. Why was Gideon so afraid of seeing an angel? The Jews believed that no one could see God and live. As an angel was the closest thing to seeing God that Gideon had faced, he felt that he was going to die. God had to assure him that was not true.

I have feared death because I just didn't take the time to seek God so that I could understand it. I did not know that death had been overcome for me, personally. God has given all of us victory over death, but with a few simple conditions on our part. We must admit we are a sinner, that Jesus Christ paid the price for our sins and forgives us, and that we now turn from our previous lifestyle and let Him be in control of everything as our Lord and Savior.

HOPE FOR YOU

When asked, "Are you going to Heaven, and why?" How do you answer? The Bible tells us plain and simple that each of us can know when we die we will go to Heaven. Jesus Christ is the way, the truth, and the life, and by our trust and belief in Him alone, we will be saved. Along with that belief, we receive forgiveness of all our sins, the Holy Spirit, and we can allow Jesus to live His life through us. It is all about God and not us.

Day 79

ARE YOU A PERSON OF NOBLE CHARACTER?

And now, my daughter, don't be afraid, I will do for you all you ask. All my fellow townsmen know you are a woman of noble character.

—Ruth 3:11

When Ruth obeyed her mother-in-law with regard to Boaz, he told her not to be afraid. Boaz knew Ruth was a woman of character, and he did not take advantage of her. He was an honorable man. He would do the right thing for her. He also rewarded her by feeding her and her mother-in-law, Naomi.

Are you as selective and obedient as Ruth was to make sure you are a person of noble character? Are you one who chooses honorable friends and mates God's way? Do you listen to those God sends into your life for counsel and wisdom in your choices? By doing this, there is no fear.

If you have done as I have, and not consulted God in the choices of friends—and whom I married—or whom I listened to—there is still hope for you. God showed me there is a better way to live, when I choose Him first. He restored my character to that of His nobility.

HOPE FOR YOU

Are you in an abusive relationship? Have you lost the joy, peace, and contentment of the Lord, or did you ever have it? Have you given up on being a person of noble character, or do you even care? You can *ask* God and have everything become clean and whole in the Lord and become the person of noble character as God intended all along.

Day 80

ARE YOU PAYING ATTENTION?

As she was dying, the woman attending her said, "Don't despair, you have given birth to a son." But she did not respond or pay any attention.

—1 Sam. 4:20

This is the true account of one lady losing hope when faced with the tragic death of her husband, Phinehas, in battle and by the death of her father-in-law, Eli, (who died after hearing of the death of his son and the loss of the Ark).

It did not matter to her that she had given birth to a son (which in that day was a great honor), and even though she would have to face a lot, she chose to give up. She even named the boy Ichabod, which means "the glory of the Lord has departed" from Israel.

I can remember when I was faced with many things at one time; I wanted to give up on myself, God, and everyone else as well. But thank God, He kept me close and gave me strength even when I didn't want it, so that I could go on and fulfill the plan He had for me.

HOPE FOR YOU

Does your life seem hopeless? Are you ready to give up and die? God is right here and is waiting for you to come and ask Him to show you how to live and be the person He created you to be.

Day 81

DON'T BE AFRAID,
BE SAFE IN THE LORD

Stay with me, don't be afraid, the man who is seeking your
life is seeking mine also. You will be safe with me.

—1 Sam. 22:23

David assured Abiathar, after hearing that Saul had killed the
priests of the Lord, that he would be safe. David knew God was
going to protect him, and he was willing to encourage others not to
be afraid as well. Do you have peace, knowing that even though the
enemy is after you, God is on your side and will protect you and others
too?

Can you encourage others who suffer as you do? There is hope. What
better way to overcome fear than to know God and set your mind on
Him first. Then you can encourage others to do the same. I have seen
this at work in my life, and I am safe with God in charge.

Once David overcame all the terror of the evil in his land and became
King over Israel, do you know what he did? He kept his promise to
God and also to his friend Abiathar. He made him the new high priest,
and Abiathar remained in that position during the time David was
king.

HOPE FOR YOU

How have you rewarded those who have helped you and who have
encouraged you not to fear? David knew that God would take care of
him, and then he, in turn, could take care of others.

Day 82

DON'T BE AFRAID, KNOW GOD'S PLAN

"Don't be afraid," he said. "My father Saul will not lay a hand on you. You will be king over Israel, and I will be second to you. Even my father Saul knows this."

—1 Sam. 23:17

This may have been the last time Jonathan, son of Saul, and David were together. They were great friends, and they encouraged each other's faith in God. They trusted and valued their friendship.

God sends friends into our lives to show us not to be afraid and that others do care for us. Caring about, praying for, and thinking of God and others first is the best way to overcome fear.

In your life do you have true and trusted friends? Have you been so hurt in the past that you are afraid to trust anyone again? I wanted to shut myself off in this way many times. God always drew me back to the places where I could serve others and encourage them as I had been encouraged.

There are many people living alone who are in need of true friends. Just as God did not want to be alone and created us to trust, live, love, and serve Him, He also knew we needed others in our lives.

HOPE FOR YOU

What is keeping you from serving and caring for those God has placed in your life as friends? Others need you as much as you need them.

Day 83

NO NEED TO FEAR, JESUS IS BIGGER THAN ALL YOUR FEARS

"Don't be afraid," the prophet answered. "Those who are
with us are more than those who are with them."

—2 Kgs. 6:16

The prophet Elisha told his servant not to be afraid even though it looked as if they were completely surrounded by enemies. Elisha knew that the Lord was there first and that all they had to do was open their spiritual eyes to see Him at work.

Do you believe God is with you always even though you physically can't see Him? What do you think of when fear comes and wants to stay and control you, your life, and your time? I know we can get so caught up in our fear, troubles, and everything around us that the last thing we ever think about is our unseen faith in God.

Do you have people in your life who seem not to fear, doubt, and have fewer problems than you do? Is that true, or are they facing them God's way?

HOPE FOR YOU

Do you have true faith in God? Do you see God working in your life even in the state you are in right now? Do you share your faith with others? What an awesome God who is able and willing to do that for us.

Day 84

I AM WITH YOU, DO NOT BE AFRAID

"Do not be afraid of the king of Babylon, whom you now fear. Do not be afraid of him, declares the Lord, for I am with you and will save you and deliver you from his hands."

—Jer. 42:11

The people of Judah were very fearful of the evil king they were under, and they needed Jeremiah to help them know what to do. Jeremiah assured them (after much prayer) that the Lord God was with them. They were not to be afraid. He assured them they should stay where they were and not flee to Egypt. God had a plan for them. Unfortunately the people chose not to listen to Jeremiah.

Isn't it wonderful to know that God sees us in our fears, and He is with us and ready to deliver us from all of it? We have a choice. I have missed many of the blessings the Lord had for me because of my poor choices.

I urge you to follow the Lord, and ask for His plan before you leap out on your own. I am sure these people of Judah, in looking back, would have followed the Lord instead of other men.

HOPE FOR YOU

What are you facing that you need to make sure is God's plan before you make the final choice? Spend time with Him to know for sure.

Day 85

DO NOT BE AFRAID, THE BATTLE IS THE LORD'S NOT YOURS

You will not have to fight this battle. Take up your positions; stand firm and see the deliverance the Lord will give you. O Judah, and Jerusalem. Do not be afraid; do not be discouraged. Go out to face them tomorrow, and the Lord will be with you.

—2 Chron. 20:17

God spoke through Jahaziel as the enemy was close to the people of Judah. He wanted them to know He was there with them and not to be afraid.

How many times do we first try to fight our own battles, then, when we are in a mess and see no way out, we *ask* God for help? I have been doing this most of my life.

I have learned that choosing to fight my own battles gave me none of the daily peace, joy, and contentment the Lord had for me. In fact, it robbed me of peace and the personal relationship God wanted with me.

HOPE FOR YOU

Do you know you no longer have to fight your daily battles? Do you know that God wants you to seek Him and learn to stand firm in His ways?

Where have you put God in your life? Put Him in charge of all your battles, and live and follow Him into them. They are not yours. They can be His.

Day 86

DO NOT WORRY ABOUT THE LEADERS WHO QUESTION YOU

When you are brought before synagogues, rulers and authorities, do not worry about how you will defend yourselves or what you will say.

—Luke 12:11

Jesus assured His disciples and us today that when we stand up for Him in situations in which we do not know what to say or do, we will have the Holy Spirit with us and in us to furnish the right words and actions to take.

Even though I am just a simple girl from a broken home and family, I have found myself in some very interesting places. I once met a famous singer whose name you would all recognize. As I stood in line to meet him, I could have been worrying about what I was going to say to him. But instead I made a choice to ask God to show me the words to say to this man that he needed to hear. I was not afraid.

When I got to meet him, he was so kind and receptive. I remember quoting him Jeremiah 29:11–13 and told him that his music and life had blessed me and many others. He then let me know he was glad I had reminded him that the Lord was responsible for everything in his life. He gave God all the credit. My husband later told me he was proud I took the time to do this, and that the Lord was pleased too.

HOPE FOR YOU

Are you ready to share the Lord's Word at anytime? I am not in the habit of quoting scripture to strangers all the time, but I can assure you God will help you when you ask and are willing to follow as He leads.

Day 87

DO NOT FEAR, GOD WILL COME AND SAVE YOU

Say to those with fearful hearts, "be strong, do not fear; Your God will come, He will come with vengeance; with divine retribution He will come to save you."

—Isa. 35:4

This is Isaiah's beautiful portrayal of the final kingdom where God will establish His justice and will wipe out all evil. This is what we can look forward to every day because we know it will come and we will live in it forever if we have trusted, believed, and welcomed Jesus into our life as Savior and Lord.

Salvation is the only qualification for being able to live in God's world forever. Have you made that choice? Until He does come, God wants to give us hope, peace, and joy right now over whatever fears we have. It is said that faith is the opposite of fear, but we have to make sure we know who our faith is in to avoid the trap of fear.

I have learned to live unafraid means I have to stay focused and renewed in God's Word. I have to let Him saturate my mind. I cannot allow myself to doubt that God is real and personal to me and is working in my life—no matter what the situation looks like at the time.

HOPE FOR YOU

Do you know where you will spend forever? You can know and be sure right now. By knowing that, God will show you daily how to be strong and not fear.

Day 88

DO NOT BE AFRAID, LET THE LORD STRENGTHEN YOU

"Do not be afraid, O man highly esteemed," he said. "Peace! Be strong now; be strong." When He spoke to me, I was strengthened and said, "Speak, my lord, since you have given me strength."

—Dan. 10:19

D aniel was frightened by a messenger coming to him in a vision until God assured him he did not need to fear. Just as God ministered to Daniel those many centuries ago, He is here right now and is ready and able to minister to us.

God is in control of all that is going on around us. He knows what the future will bring. He also knows our personal needs and what we are facing right now.

After spending many years searching for true peace, I have found the Lord is the only source of it. God strengthened Daniel, and He will do the same for me and for you.

HOPE FOR YOU

Will you trust and take God at His Word? I am so glad that God chose to use Daniel's life to show us this is the only way to live.

Day 89

THE LORD WHO REDEEMED YOU SAYS, FEAR NOT

But now, this is what the Lord says—"He who created you, O Jacob, He who formed you, O Israel: Fear not, for I have redeemed you, I have summoned you by name, you are mine."

—Isa. 43:1

God created Israel and made the land special to Him. He also created us and made us special to Him. He summons us by name, gives us His name, and redeems and protects us. He then says this is the reason we should not fear. If we are focused and living a grateful, thankful, and productive life for Christ, how can we allow fear to dominate and entrap us?

I used to think that God must be very tired of me saying to Him that I was sorry about choosing to live in my fears rather than faith in Him. Then I learned I had a choice to get out of that trapped cycle, and God was willing to do whatever was needed and for however long until I gave my fears completely to Him.

HOPE FOR YOU

Has Jesus Christ redeemed you? Does He call you by name and summon you to obey and do His will? Belonging to Him is the only way to overcome all your fears.

Day 90

DO NOT BE AFRAID, I, GOD, WILL HELP YOU

"Do not be afraid, O worm Jacob, O little Israel, for I myself will help you," declares the Lord, your Redeemer, the Holy One of Israel.

—Isa. 41:14

Have you ever been called a worm? This name refers to the contempt of Israel by ungodly nations. It is also the word used of our Lord Jesus on the cross. God is telling us not to be afraid no matter how others think of us. He knows.

Isn't it great to know that God is not limited by time? Just as He calls Himself "Redeemer of the Israelites," He is also our Redeemer. The Israelites are His chosen people even though they disobeyed. Now as believers we are also chosen to be a part of His family and then share Him with everyone in the world.

One day we will all be together, but until then we are not to fear those who choose not to believe in God. He is with us, He wants a relationship with each of us, and offers us His strength and help to overcome sin and death. What more do we need?

HOPE FOR YOU

Is God your Redeemer? Are you glad to be called a worm for Him? I am so blessed to have His help, strength, and the victory He gave me over sin and death.

Day 91

DO NOT LET YOURSELF BE BURDENED, CHRIST HAS SET US FREE

It is for freedom that Christ has set us free. Stand firm, then, and do not let yourselves be burdened again by a yoke of slavery.

—Gal. 5:1

P aul addressed both the church of his time and us now. We are not to let ourselves be caught in the trap of being a slave to our own and other's selfish desires for us.

Jesus paid the price for us and now we are to live in the freedom of His love and grace. Fear has no place in that lifestyle. When we are burdened with living as others expect, or having our own standards that we cannot possibly meet, we give way to becoming overwhelmed and to living in fear and the dread of life itself.

I have lived a life of working at being a people pleaser and a perfectionist. I lived independent of the plan and purpose God had for me. I can assure you the burden and fear of it all took a toll on my life in all areas. This kind of lifestyle is not God's will, and it is such a hard journey to go through.

HOPE FOR YOU

Are you overburdened in life? Have you taken on the world in your own strength instead of what Jesus died to give to you? Are you following your own self and others instead of the Lord? You can be free to see what an exciting journey God has for you.

Day 92

GOD IS JUST, DO NOT FEAR

Do not fear, O Jacob my servant, for I am with you, declares the Lord. Though I completely destroy all the nations among which I scatter you, I will not completely destroy you. I will discipline you but only with justice, I will not let you go entirely unpunished.

—Jer. 46:28

Just as the Lord promised Israel and their descendents He would be with them and not to fear, that same promise is for each one of us right now. No matter what you have done and been before, our Lord God is promising all who trust and believe in Him that He will show us how not to fear or be dismayed or troubled. He is in control, and He will lead us through.

Did I say we would not have to be accountable for the lives we have led and are leading now? No, our Lord is just and He takes us through paths of discipline. He prunes us. There are tough times for us, but we must remember He is God and He only corrects and purifies us so that we will learn to totally depend and trust in Him alone and not on others or the world around us.

HOPE FOR YOU

Where does your relationship with God stand? Is He so personal and real in your daily life that you know when He disciplines, corrects, and prunes you it is so that you will come back to Him in total trust and obedience? You can know that now.

Day 93

CALL OUT, DO NOT FEAR

You came near when I called you, and you said, "Do not fear."

—Lam. 3:57

These are powerful words from the prophet, Jeremiah. At this time in his life, he shared how he was left to die in an empty cistern, how God rescued him, and how God wants to rescue each of us as well as our nation. The condition for rescue is that we must cry out and want God alone to rescue us.

Do you really believe God will take away your fear when you call on Him? Does He have that power and first place in your life so that when fear comes He is the first one you cry out to?

In these times it seems as if there are so many more ways of reporting bad news and suggesting fears in our lives that it is hard not to be fearful, isn't it? But no matter what comes I have found that God is the only one who can calm my fears.

HOPE FOR YOU

Whether it is the terror of weather or evil people wanting to harm us, or the corrupt practices and systems that want to steal what God has given us, there is still no reason to fear. God is in control, and I, for one, have chosen to let Him be my life. How about you? Remember this, "He who created us without our help, will not save us without our consent" (St. Augustine).

Day 94

THE LORD WILL JUDGE, BUT WE ARE NOT TO FEAR HIM

"So I will come near to you for judgment, I will be quick to testify against sorcerers, adulterers and perjurers, against those who defraud laborers of their wages, who oppress the widows and the fatherless, and deprive aliens of justice, but do not fear me," says the Lord Almighty.

—Mal. 3:5

God, through Malachi the prophet, is showing us that even though we sin and are far away from Him, He is still in control and will judge, but He will also be ready to forgive us.

Isn't it awesome to know that we don't have to fear things and people in our lives, and we also don't have to fear God? How blessed it is to be able to believe and serve Him.

God wants a relationship with us, and He is waiting for each of us to come personally to Him and *ask* forgiveness for all we have done, and then let Him be first and in control from now on.

HOPE FOR YOU

It is a choice, and we need to make sure we don't think, as the people in Malachi's time did, that they had not disobeyed and had no reason to *ask* forgiveness. God is patient, but He will not wait forever. I finally realized I didn't want to risk waiting any longer to choose Him to be first and in control of my life. How about you?

Day 95

DON'T BE AFRAID, HE IS NOT HERE

He said, "Don't be afraid. I know you're looking for Jesus the Nazarene, the One they nailed on the cross. He's been raised up, He's here no longer. You can see for yourself that the place is empty. Now—on your way. Tell His disciples and Peter that He is going on ahead of you to Galilee. You'll see Him there, exactly as He said."

—Mark 16:6 THE MESSAGE

Even though Jesus had told everyone the plan, the women who were there to take care of His body were still afraid and were surprised when they went to the tomb and found He was not there. Jesus knew they would be afraid, so He left an angel to tell them not to be afraid and to go tell His disciples they would see Him again.

Are we still afraid today? Do we fear and doubt that He can take care of us, and that He loves us and has provided the way so that we do not have to fear? Do we really believe the truth of the Bible and that He is alive and we will see and live with Him forever?

At times, even recently, I can lose sight of that plan and live life in my own selfish way. I do not take the time to keep His words alive in my heart and mind. I am my own worst enemy. But Jesus keeps His promise. He never leaves me, and He waits for me to come back and relive the simple plan He has for me all along.

HOPE FOR YOU

Have you lost sight of Jesus' plan for you? Are you afraid and wandering away from Him? Come back now; He is waiting for you.

Day 96

BE STRONG, DO NOT BE AFRAID

As you have been an object of cursing among the nations, O Judah and Israel, so will I save you, and you will be a blessing. Do not be afraid, but let your hands be strong.
—Zech. 8:13

God and His prophets had been urging the people to finish building the temple for over 15 years! God encouraged them with hope and promises of a great future. He had made the plan plain and clear, and He knew now the people had to quit listening only and *get to work.*

Is it time for you to do the same? God shares with us that we are to be a blessing and let our hands get on with the work He has given us to do. How can we be a blessing first to God and to others when we are letting our fears stop us?

There may be plenty of logical reasons you feel afraid and want to delay and even quit and give up. We can get discouraged because we don't see results soon enough, or it looks too hard and we feel it is not worth the effort. But God's Word is true, and we must continue on the journey He has for us.

HOPE FOR YOU

What is it you have put off getting started doing, and why? For me it was this book, which is a labor of love for Him. Now is the time to let God become the reason and passion for you to go to work and complete the plan He has for you.

Day 97

DO YOU HAVE DECISIONS TO MAKE? DO NOT BE AFRAID

But after he had considered this, an angel of the Lord appeared to him in a dream and said, "Joseph son of David, do not be afraid to take Mary home as your wife, because what is conceived in her is from the Holy Spirit."

—Matt. 1:20

M ost of us have read these words many times, but have you ever faced major decisions in your life and been afraid? Joseph had a big problem, didn't he? His soon-to-be wife was pregnant, and the baby was not his. The law and culture of that time gave him two options: one was to divorce her quietly and leave her out in the cold; the second was to have her stoned to death for her sin. But God had another option.

When we face situations and are afraid, what do we do first? Joseph had not even considered marrying Mary as another way of handling the situation. God had to send an angel to tell him not to be afraid to do so because of who this child would become to all of us.

HOPE FOR YOU

Have you ever made a decision without consulting God, and it was the wrong option? I have done it many times. What are you facing that you are afraid of and are not sure what to do? Aren't you glad that Joseph listened to the angel and obeyed God? How different it would have been if he had not. It doesn't matter what the situation is, God still wants you to come to Him first so that His option for you will be clear.

Day 98

MORE AFRAID OF PEOPLE THAN GOD?

> Do not be afraid of those who kill the body but cannot kill the soul. Rather, be afraid of the one who can destroy both soul and body in hell.
>
> —Matt. 10:28

We normally are more focused on our physical life than on our spiritual life. What a way we have become accustomed to living! Matthew shared the words of Jesus telling us we are not to fear anyone or anything that can kill our physical body, but we should be concerned about what really counts. If you are *not* truly in the Lord and the Lord is *not* truly in you, you should be afraid.

It is not the physical body and what we have done with it and the things we have achieved that will last forever. It is our choices about whether we truly have chosen Jesus as the *only* way and if we are living for Him. Isn't it the truth that we knowingly choose hell by not accepting Christ?

According to George Barna and the surveys of the Barna Group, 90 percent of all people in America believe there is a God, but only 50 percent believe that Jesus is the only way to Him. Then the next figure shocked me. Only 30 percent of all Americans believe there is literally a place called Hell.

HOPE FOR YOU

Are you at risk? What do you really believe? It is time for you to find out the truth and make sure that fear does not cause you to be caught up with the unbelievers in hell. Hell is real, and God doesn't want anyone to spend eternity there.

Day 99

JESUS IS ALIVE, DO NOT BE AFRAID

The angel said to the women, "do not be afraid, for I know you are looking for Jesus, who was crucified! He is not here, He has risen, just as He said."

—Matt. 28:5–6

This is the key verse in the Scriptures that gives us the reason why we do not have to be afraid. Over 2,000 years ago, just as the angel told the woman (probably Mary) that Jesus, whom she came to take care of, was not there; today we can rejoice and be joyful because His borrowed tomb is empty, and He is alive. The reality of the resurrection of our Lord Jesus Christ brings joy not fear.

I have found you can't live in both joy and fear at the same time. I can become very focused on myself and my world and not remember exactly what Easter is all about. I get caught up in the daily things, even going through physical happenings and pain, and fail to thank God for this blessed event. We should celebrate Easter every day, not just once a year!

HOPE FOR YOU

Whenever fear comes to entrap and ensnare you, remember the empty tomb. Jesus is real. He died and rose again so that believers in Him need not be afraid. We can now share this truth with others. You do not have to fear. You can choose joy and life from Jesus Christ and not fear.

Day 100

YOU HAVE THE KINGDOM, WHY FEAR AND WORRY?

Do not be afraid, little flock, for your Father has been pleased
to give you the kingdom.

—Luke 12:32

J esus commands us not to worry about anything. It is good to work
and plan according to what He wants us to do, but it is wrong to
focus on what might or could go wrong.

It is freedom to know we have been given our eternal kingdom by believing in God through His Son Jesus. How we live here will determine
how we will spend the time in the kingdom He has given us.

Why do we spend this life thinking only of ourselves and living in
fear when God has our eternal plan set, and He is willing to show us
how to live out that plan?

I am learning it is so much greater to live a life focused on Him and
not on what this world can give me. Do I lose sight of this? Sure, but
when I do, I just remember who Jesus is, what He did for me, and then
I ask and receive His forgiveness to begin again.

HOPE FOR YOU

So what if you lose every material possession here? Does that rob you
of the joy, peace, and contentment of knowing your eternal existence
is secure? Do you believe God will meet your needs, or are you afraid
your *greed* will suffer?

Day 101

DON'T BE AFRAID, JUST BELIEVE

Hearing this, Jesus said to Jairus, "Don't be afraid, just believe, and she will be healed."

—Luke 8:50

What is your first reaction when illness comes to you, your family, and friends? Does illness bring you closer to God or chase you further away? Jesus told a father not to be afraid but to believe in Him and who He was, and his daughter would be healed.

This was not only a physical healing but also a spiritual one. This man, Jairus, was the ruler of the Jewish synagogue. When Jesus healed his daughter He told Jairus not to tell anyone because He wanted them to know and love Him personally, and not just for what He could do for them.

I have been blessed to have great health, but recently I experienced a car accident. At first I wanted to process and handle it as I have normally done. But God has shown me a better way while I am recovering from the accident.

Did I choose Him first when it happened? No, I am sorry to say I failed that test. But once I did, I have found Jesus means what He says concerning not to fear at all about anything, including our health issues. He will take care of us.

HOPE FOR YOU

Do you need physical healing? Do you believe Jesus can heal you? Or is it spiritual healing that you really need? Just as Jesus knows your needs physically, He also wants you to be totally *His* spiritually as well.

Day 102

DON'T BE AFRAID, GOD HAS A PLAN FOR YOUR LIFE

For he and all his companions were astonished at the catch of fish they had taken, and so were James and John, the sons of Zebedee, Simon's partners. Then Jesus said to Simon, "Don't be afraid, from now on you will catch men."
—Luke 5:9–10

Jesus was assuring Simon, who we now know as Peter, not to be afraid that his life was changing from a fisherman to a true disciple of Christ. His profession was changing from fishing for food to eat and a way of life, to fishing to give men spiritual food and obeying God.

I can relate to Peter in this situation. I have been in that same spot quite a few times in my life. I can assure you I didn't always listen to what God was showing and telling me. But I now see the joy, peace, and contentment He had for me all along once I agreed with His plan for me.

What was the fear that Peter and many of us have as well? Do we trust that God will take care of us? Or is it that we are not willing to obey and give up what we now see to step out in true faith into something we can't see and feel successful at doing?

HOPE FOR YOU

Do you have an unfulfilled dream and passion? Have you ever asked God if that was really His plan for you? Is there something that is just not complete in your life? You can still have it. It is your choice to trust and follow Jesus, and let Him take care of the rest. Don't wait as long as I did to finally say yes. You may not get another opportunity to do so.

Day 103

DON'T BE AFRAID, YOU ARE WORTH IT

Indeed, the very hairs on your head are all numbered. Don't be afraid, you are worth more than many sparrows.

—Luke 12:7

God cares and loves those who are truly His. Great importance is placed now upon our worth, how we perform, what we accomplish, how much money we have, and how we look. Jesus came to assure us that we no longer have to fear; He cares.

Isn't it great to know that God's values are different than ours? He cares for us because we belong to Him. Because of that right, we can come to God face to face and have no fear of anything.

I am so blessed to know I am His and all that is ahead of me He will and can handle. What a freedom to be able to live without fear.

But what does it cost us to have this freedom? Is there a price to be paid? Two thousand years ago, Jesus Christ paid the price for all who will believe in Him. Yes, there was a great cost to God for us to be free. He gave up His one and only Son for us. For this freedom in Christ, God wants all of us to be totally His.

HOPE FOR YOU

Our world teaches us there must be more to this, doesn't it? God does not want to trap us into obedience and living His way. Remember, you are worth more to God than anything else. What is He worth to you?

Day 104

YOU CAN'T LIE TO GOD OR YOURSELF ABOUT YOUR FEARS

Sarah was afraid, so she lied and said, "I did not laugh." But He said, "Yes, you did laugh."

—Gen. 18:15

Fear is the most common motive and reason for lying. Sarah lied because she was afraid of being discovered by God. But Sarah soon learned there is no way to hide anything from God.

I have a lot of experience in this area. I grew up living a lie, and saw lies practiced all around my home. Once you are on that path, it is very hard to tell the difference between a lie and the truth. Also, in our culture, honesty and integrity are not valued and rewarded. I ended living out the lies for a large part of my life.

I even lived a lie in the spiritual realm as well. I met the Lord at an early age. I did not tell my family about it. Due to my young age, the pastor came to visit my mom to get her permission to baptize me. When my Mom found out, she refused to give permission out of her own fear of water and because of the ridicule of others. I was heartbroken. I remember the Pastor saying that he understood, and he assured me that he would take care of it. From then on, I was a full member of the church, and I didn't have to feel any different because I wasn't baptized. But it did bother me, and many years later, after living that lie, I admitted to my church family what had transpired and I was baptized.

HOPE FOR YOU

Is there some lie you are living and you are afraid to admit it to yourself and to God? Come now to Him and become clean again, you can trust God.

Day 105

DO NOT BE FRIGHTENED, THE END IS NOT YET

When you hear of wars and rumors of war, do not be frightened, those things must take place, but that is not yet the end.

—Mark 13:7 NASB

Jesus was assuring the people not to be afraid of the end of life as we now know it. After Jesus left this earth, He promised to return, and we have been watching for His return ever since.

He gave us certain things to wait for, but we are not to fear as we wait. Many people fear the news they hear and relate it to the return of Jesus. They become very afraid. Jesus assured us that because of our belief and trust in Him we have nothing to fear.

I can remember times in my life when I would get caught up with everyone else and began to speculate about His return. I would become frightened as I did so. What was I afraid of? Was I not living the life and doing as He had commanded? Was I ashamed of my belief in Him? Or did I just fear death so much that thinking about His return brought me to a dread I did not want to face? These fears were the very things He warned us about.

HOPE FOR YOU

Are you afraid of the return of our Lord Jesus? Do you fear death and all that is associated with it? The truth is there is nothing to fear. Jesus is life, and I now gladly look forward to each day as the very day He could return. Do you?

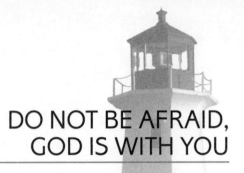

Day 106

DO NOT BE AFRAID, GOD IS WITH YOU

> Do not tremble, do not be afraid. Did I not proclaim this and foretell it long ago?
>
> —Isa. 44:8

Isaiah is showing us that we should have no fear if we have not let other idols become our gods instead of God alone. What is our world focused on today? Have we let money, fame, power, and food take the place of our one true God? No wonder we are fearful. Isaiah's message of hope is still as true as it was centuries ago when given to the Israelites. God knows all.

When we trust and receive Jesus, He doesn't just come into our lives. He comes to change and *be* our life. Once that becomes real to us, we can truly see why there is no fear. He is always in our inner being through the Holy Spirit. The Holy Spirit is in control, and fear has no place with Him.

It took me a long time to finally make my exchanged life a reality day to day. But once I did, He took over from that point on. I am so glad I made that choice.

HOPE FOR YOU

What about you? Where does God fit into your life? Is He your life, or is He just in the part you want Him to have? There is a difference.

Day 107

GOD GIVES US THE STRENGTH AND POWER TO NOT BE AFRAID

I will make your forehead like the hardest stone, harder than flint. Do not be afraid of them or terrified by them, though they are a rebellious house.

—Ezek. 3:9

God was telling Ezekiel that the Israelites, whom he had been sent to serve, would not listen to him. Their hearts were hardened and they were obstinate. God assured Ezekiel to be strong and not be afraid of them or of their reaction to what he had to say.

Are there times when you feel close to God and strong, and nothing seems to come your way to make you afraid, even if you know what you are saying or doing is not heard by others or seems not to matter to them? What about the other times? Which is the majority of your life?

I often wonder if some of the things I have asked God for will ever be revealed in my lifetime for me to see and experience. Then I realize it does not matter because it is for His glory, not mine; He wants me to keep praying and believing, and He alone knows the outcome.

HOPE FOR YOU

Are you close to God and know it, or are you struggling and living your life your own way, letting it overwhelm you? You can be free to live the way Ezekiel chose to live—in total obedience to God.

Day 108

WHY DID YOU DOUBT?

Immediately Jesus stretched out His hand and took hold of him, and said to him, "You of little faith, why did you doubt?"

—Matt. 14:31 NASB

Jesus was in the process of rescuing Peter from the water. Peter had faith to get out of the boat and walk to Him, but he took his eyes off Jesus and started to drown. Then Jesus asked Peter why he had let his fear and doubt almost drown him.

Have you ever been rescued by Jesus when you lost sight of faith in Him? Did you ask yourself why you let that happen? I have many times. I am learning that before I leap out I need to make sure that I continue to trust Him through the whole process. If not, I can be weaker than Peter, and I will lose my way and become a prisoner of my fears once more.

HOPE FOR YOU

Are you drowning? Have you lost the hope that only Jesus can provide for you? No situation is too big and no life is too small for Jesus to rescue. Reach out and ask and He will save you from all harm.

Day 109

GOD GIVES US PEACE FROM BEING AFRAID WHEN WE OBEY

I will give you peace in the land; you shall lie down and none shall fill you with dread or make you afraid; and I will clear ferocious (wild) beasts out of the land, and no sword shall go through your land.

—Lev. 26:6 AMP

M oses shared with the Israelites the way in which God will bless when He is obeyed. It is the same today. God has for us a life filled with peace, not dread or fear. All He wants from us is to live obedient lives and give Him the glory while serving others.

I have not always chosen to obey and follow Jesus all the way. I have let fears and things and others stand in the way. I know that when we do not choose Him, or when we turn away from Him, that is when fear, doubt, anxiety, and despair have the opportunity to take over in our lives, as they did in mine. But God is always there when we come back to Him, and He is willing to forgive and forget.

HOPE FOR YOU

Are you living in obedience and in the will of the Lord? You can, and then peace and joy will override all the fear that has come before you. What is your choice?

Day 110

ARE YOU AFRAID AND CONTROLLED BY MONEY?

> Keep your lives free from the love of money and be content with what you have, because God has said, "Never will I leave you, never will I forsake you." So we say with confidence, "The Lord is my helper, I will not be afraid, what can man do to me?"
>
> —Heb. 13:5–6

God clearly states He is here for us and will not leave us and will take care of our needs. The leaders of our country must have understood this lesson because in 1864 "In God We Trust" was added to our coinage. They wanted to make sure we would all remember where to place our trust as they did. Then by 1957 "In God We Trust" was recognized as our National Motto and added to our paper currency as well.

Money has always been my "drug of choice." I have struggled with it because I have viewed and handled it unwisely, and used it as my security instead of God.

It took me a long time to confront this fear and sin in my life. I had to realize that money is not a person, and I do not have to let it take control over me. I also had to see that God had always taken care of me.

Only then was I able to listen to God in this area and learn that I am to give more, save more, and spend less. He also showed our family a plan of how to live "debt-free" and be financially free for the first time in our lives.

HOPE FOR YOU

Does money control your life? Do you trust it instead of God? This does not have to be your journey any longer. God has a plan; follow Him and be free.

Day 111

DO NOT WORRY ABOUT YOUR LIFE, SAYS THE LORD

Then Jesus said to His disciples: "Therefore I tell you, do not worry about your life, what you will eat, or about your body, what you will wear."

—Luke 12:22

Jesus knew that all of us would need to hear this message over and over again. He wanted us to know that He would take care of all of our needs and we don't need to let worry enter into our minds.

We all know worry is a waste of time. It accomplishes nothing. It is now a proven fact that worry is a major problem with our health. Worry also goes into all areas of our lives. Why, then, do we keep worrying?

I have found that staying in the Word every day gives me a foundation to live worry free by making sure I make the right choices about what I hear, see, and whom I allow to influence my choices. These are the keys to God changing me.

Worry is a choice, so choose God first and see the difference. God is ready and able to keep us worry free.

HOPE FOR YOU

Are you fretting or worried or fearful of anything? Do you trust, ask, and depend on God first in your life? If not, begin to trust Him, and you will be amazed at the joy, peace, and contentment you have been missing.

Day 112

WHOM SHALL I FEAR?

The Lord is my light and my salvation whom—shall I fear?
—Ps. 27:1a

D avid knew the deep dark pit of fear very well. He had faced it many times. He knew the light of the Lord and the security of salvation as his own. There was nothing, nor anyone to fear.

Is the Lord your light, your salvation, and stronghold? I have to admit I have not always chosen the Lord first as my light and strength. But I do know that when I don't, I encounter my most fearful times.

When I take my eyes off who He is and focus on me and my situation, I fear all kinds of things and people. Do you see the same pattern in your life? When I remember that fear is not a person, and the Lord is the light, it takes me out of my darkness and fear. Fear can imprison us within ourselves. God alone can free us and keep us free from fear.

HOPE FOR YOU

Are you in a prison of fear? Have you forgotten how to get out? God does not want us to live in our prison of fear! The good news is, even if you are living in fear and in your own prison, God is ready to set you free.

Day 113

DO NOT FEAR THEM, EVERYTHING WILL BE REVEALED

Therefore do not fear them, for there is nothing concealed
that will not be revealed, or hidden that will not be known.
—Matt. 10:26 NASB

How many people are you afraid to let know you are a follower of Jesus Christ? Do you know what you believe, so that you can stand and know it will all be made known to everyone at some future time? Jesus assured all of us that we can know and not fear when others do not believe what you know is the truth.

Today we have let the world define our beliefs so much that we live less powerful lives than God intended for us as believers. Then the same fears that come to non-believers can come into our lives as well.

I have lived this way for a lot of my life. I wanted to please people and receive the rewards of this world more than I wanted to please God and receive His rewards. It took drastic situations for God to show me His grace and mercy and to give me another chance in life.

HOPE FOR YOU

What is your choice? Is it God and His truth and way to live, or is it as the world lives? God has a plan and wants to show you how to overcome your fears right now.

Day 114

DO NOT FRET, IT LEADS TO EVIL

Refrain from anger and turn from wrath; Do not fret—it only leads to evil.

—Ps. 37:8

As David recorded this, he knew all about anger and worry. He had let it enter into his life, and it had become a way of life. He knew, however, that was not God's way. As he confessed his sin and allowed God to change him, he shares how we can do the same thing.

Worry and anger in America is killing us. We have the highest rate of divorce in the world, the highest *legal* drug use, the highest disease rate, and it all stems from fear. We also have the second highest debt rate per household, and yet we are the country with the most freedoms and the most availability to the gospel of God's peace with little persecution.

We have been taught and encouraged in recent years that life is all about us. When we dwell on ourselves and our problems, we will become angry and anxious. But if we choose to dwell on God first, His goodness, grace, and mercy are the gifts we can receive. We will find peace.

HOPE FOR YOU

Are you angry and worried now? Do you know that you don't have to be? God wants to bring you out of that world and into His joy, love, peace, and contentment for you. Allow Him to do so.

Day 115

DO NOT FEAR, FOR I AM YOUR GOD

> So do not fear, for I am with you, do not be dismayed, for I am your God.
>
> —Isa. 41:10

Isaiah is telling Israel that God is there for them now that they have obeyed. He gives them the comfort, hope, and encouragement of the Lord.

God is faithful to us and there is no reason to live in fear of any kind. He can handle anything as long as we have chosen Jesus as our personal Savior and Lord to control our lives. I did this, but I still let fear creep in and soon I was no longer faithful to God. God did not leave me there. He stayed close knowing I would come back to Him.

It is clear that God has a plan for each of us, and we should live in that joy and excitement daily. We are to have no fear of anything when we focus on what He is doing, has done, and will do for each of us in our lives.

HOPE FOR YOU

Have you realized all the ways God has helped and blessed you? Do you know He is the only one who can calm those fears in your life, no matter what they are?

Day 116

DO NOT BE AFRAID, I WILL BLESS YOU

> Now I have determined to do good again to Jerusalem and Judah. Do not be afraid.
>
> —Zech. 8:15

God delights in blessing us and assuring us not to be afraid. At this time, the Jews had been encouraged after their return from captivity to rebuild the temple. God wanted to bless them, and He kept encouraging them to continue and have hope for the future He had for them.

I have been slow at doing what the Lord wanted me to do for many reasons. I am learning that He keeps His promises, and I am not afraid now to do whatever He has for me. God promises to give us great rewards for enduring and not giving up. He also expects us to do our part.

HOPE FOR YOU

Is there anything the Lord has asked you to do that you are slow at doing? I encourage you to begin again and not delay. The Israelites were glad they did, and you will be too.

Day 117

DO NOT BE AFRAID OR DISCOURAGED, SUCCESS IS YOURS

Then you will have success if you are careful to observe the decrees and laws that the Lord gave Moses for Israel. Be strong and courageous. Do not be afraid or discouraged.

—1 Chron. 22:13

During this time, as recorded here by Ezra, David the king was told by the Lord that he would not be the one to build the temple. His son, Solomon, was the one who would get the honor. David was not upset. He was determined to offer all his help to his son.

Building the temple was a large undertaking. David advised his son and the people of Israel not to be afraid or discouraged.

Many times I have faced large tasks and I did not always remember to do as the Lord has shown me. I would accept the challenge and then charge off in my own strength to complete the project without thought of what the Lord wanted me to accomplish for Him. Then, when I got into problems, I would come back to the Lord. Now I know the difference. It has to be Him in charge, not me.

HOPE FOR YOU

How about you? Are you going to God first with those large or small tasks? Or do you wait till you get into problems to turn to Him? God is willing to show you how to change to His way.

DO NOT BE AFRAID, COME SEE ME, SAYS JESUS

> Then Jesus said to them, "Do not be afraid. Go and tell my brothers to go to Galilee, there they will see me."
>
> —Matt. 28:10

This scene occurs after Jesus had been crucified and rose from the grave. His disciples had scattered and were afraid to be seen. Jesus was alive, as He had promised. The women were the first ones to see the risen Savior. Now Jesus was telling them not to be afraid but to go and tell His disciples to meet Him in Galilee. He had already forgiven them for deserting Him.

Have you deserted Jesus, and are you afraid to establish that relationship again? Do you feel that He won't want you back? Or that you don't deserve being able to come back?

I have run from God many times and then found He was always willing to forgive me for running. He is always ready to welcome me back. I have found once you are His, there is nothing He won't do to bring you back to Himself.

HOPE FOR YOU

How is your relationship with Jesus? Are you running your own life, or are you allowing Him to be in control? He is ready to welcome you back.

Day 119

GOD IS TELLING YOU, DO NOT BE AFRAID

> Therefore, this is what the Lord, the Lord Almighty, says: "O my people who live in Zion, do not be afraid of the Assyrians, who beat you with a rod and lift up a club against you, as Egypt did."
>
> —Isa. 10:24

I saiah was assuring the ones who had been faithful, not to be afraid. These people had been through a lot and didn't always obey God. But God was ready to once more forgive them and bring them hope.

I can relate to these people. God has done so much and has blessed me and I haven't always obeyed Him as I should have been doing. But God is ready to forgive, and with His forgiveness He also forgets as well. We need to keep focused on that truth and not let our fear entrap us.

HOPE FOR YOU

Are you faithful to God? Do you need Him daily in your life? Now is the time to return and be a faithful part of God's family.

Day 120

DO NOT DOUBT, YOUR FAITH CAN MOVE MOUNTAINS

And Jesus answered them, "Truly I say to you, if you have faith (a firm relying trust) and do not doubt, you will not only do what has been done to the fig tree, but even if you say to this mountain, be taken up and cast into the sea, it will be done."

—Matt. 21:21 AMP

Jesus was showing His disciples something they could see—a fig tree withered right before their eyes when Jesus spoke to it. Through their faith in Him, they too could do mighty things, even moving mountains if the need came up!

Have you ever moved mountains in your life through belief, trust, and faith in God? I have had many mountains in my life, and looking back, I know it was only through my total trust in Jesus that they were taken away from me.

They may not have been an actual Mt. Everest, but to me they were as big and real as that, and they caused me great fear and pain. I know now they are no longer there.

HOPE FOR YOU

Do you have mountains that need to be moved in your life? Jesus is ready to show you the way to move them. Are you ready to trust Him totally and not doubt or fear?

Day 121

GOD PROTECTS YOU, SO YOU NEED NOT FEAR

You will be protected from the lash of the tongue, and need not fear when destruction comes.

—Job 5:21

As Job was going through all his pain and suffering, he did not know it was a test from God. His friend Eliphaz shares with him a message of how pain and suffering can be a part of our spiritual growth, and we do not need to be afraid to go through it.

This is great to remember as we face difficult situations in our lives. We do not have to fear when we remember that our faith in God is what our lives are all about. We cannot begin to see God's plan until we realize that very fact.

I know that many times I have listened to the wrong friends, and they have led me into wrong teaching and belief of who God really is and who He wants to be in my life. I found, when I started seeking Him; He revealed all I needed to know. He has given me His strength and power to overcome any situation.

HOPE FOR YOU

Today are you in some bad situations? Do you know God is real and allows tests in our lives? He wants to help you through them and to pass them His way. Trust Him and come to Him right now, and He will answer and show you His way.

Day 122

GOD WILL PROVIDE A WAY, EVEN IF YOU ARE AFRAID

If you are afraid to attack, go down to the camp with your servant Purah and listen to what they are saying. Afterward you will be encouraged to attack the camp. So he and Purah his servant went down to the outposts of the camp.

—Judg. 7:10–11

Gideon was facing a huge battle. He had already obeyed God, but the battle was close at hand and God recognized his fear and doubt. God gave Gideon a plan that would give him the courage to face the battle. He told him to take a friend and go to the outside of the enemy's camp where he would overhear what it would take for him to attack and win.

I have faced many battles in my life. They were not always as physical as was Gideon's, but they were very real to me. But I have come to know God will always work out the fear in our lives if we will only trust and obey Him.

HOPE FOR YOU

God can give you the strength you need for anything you are facing. He knows your fear and doubt and has a plan for you. Are you willing to listen to God and take the first step, just as Gideon did?

Day 123

SHOW COMPASSION TO THOSE WHO FEAR

"Don't be afraid," David said to him, "for I will surely show you kindness for the sake of your father Jonathan. I will restore to you all the land that belonged to your grandfather Saul, and you will always eat at my table."

—2 Sam. 9:7

How many times have you been afraid to face someone because of what they would say or do to you? In this situation, David was king and Saul was defeated. It had been a long struggle. Mephibosheth, the grandson of Saul, was afraid to face David. He did not know how he would be accepted by the new king. He was a cripple, and he was not sure he would be allowed to live. David shows him love and mercy and he even went beyond what this boy could ever have dreamed of receiving from him.

Isn't that just like God? He has so much more for us than we can ever imagine if we would just face our fears and come to Him. He will show us how to approach those we fear the most and receive the benefits for doing so. I am so glad that I took the risk and trusted God to face those I feared the most and let Him work it all out for His glory and for my good.

HOPE FOR YOU

Do you need to be a David in someone's life? Do you need to reach out as Mephibosheth did, and find out what is waiting for you? God will show you how.

Day 124

DON'T BE AFRAID, YOU ARE WORTH IT TO GOD

So don't be afraid, you are worth more than many sparrows.

—Matt. 10:31

Do you know and feel the value God places on you? Jesus was showing us that God the Father loves and cares for us much more than for those little sparrow birds we see every day. The fact is, they trust Him and He takes cares of them, as we should do.

God was willing to send His only Son, Jesus, to die for you. Don't you think He knows how special you are?

I have had issues understanding that, based on my background and the choices I made in my life. Once I saw the light of God's love and care and value of me, I understood that I do not have anything to fear.

Nothing can take away God's love or rob me of His Spirit in my life. Do I still face troubles and many issues of everyday life? Yes, I do, but now I want to face them God's way, and with that comes joy, peace, and contentment.

HOPE FOR YOU

Do you know and feel worthy because of who Christ is in your life? That belief will then lead you to face and defeat all your fears and receive His true peace.

Day 125

DO NOT BE AFRAID

David also said to Solomon, his son, "Be strong and courageous, and do the work. Do not be afraid or discouraged, for
the Lord God, my God is with you. He will not fail you or
forsake you until all the work for the service of the temple of
the Lord is finished."

—1 Chron. 28:20

David's advice was encouragement to his son, Solomon, who was
facing the biggest undertaking of his life. David knew how God
had helped him overcome his fears and that nothing was too big for
God to handle. David also knew what it would take for Solomon to
face his fear over the size of the job, the risks involved, the pressures
around him, and then be able to resist the temptation to let his fears
stop him from doing the work.

I have learned that I can put off the important things I need to do
first and focus on the ones that are easier and take less work to do. Just
as David wanted his son to become the best he could be, God also
wants the same thing for each one of us.

HOPE FOR YOU

Getting started is probably the hardest part of doing anything, isn't it?
Are there things God has for you to start right now? What is keeping
you from doing what God is asking you to be and do? Don't delay, get
to work now.

Day 126

ADMIT AND SPEAK OPENLY ABOUT YOUR FEAR

> So the king asked me, "why does your face look so sad when you are not ill? This can be nothing but sadness of heart." I was very much afraid, but I said to the king, "May the king live forever! Why should my face not look sad when the city where my fathers are buried lies in ruins, and its gates have been destroyed by fire?"
>
> —Neh. 2:2–3

Nehemiah had no trouble admitting his fear to the king because he refused to let his fear keep him from doing what God had called him to do. Nehemiah knew he had been called by God to go to Jerusalem to rebuild the city. He also knew it was a big task and he needed the king's permission and help to do so.

Nehemiah knew he needed to admit his fear as the first step in committing it to God. Do we think God doesn't know we are afraid and why? Since God knows, why doesn't He just handle it? That is not God's way for us. He wants us to come willingly and openly and pray and ask Him to help us overcome anything to accomplish His work. That way God gets all the glory and credit and not us.

I have been hard-headed and stubborn about admitting my fears to anyone, most of all God. But God knew one day would come when I had no other choice if I was to have the joy, peace, and contentment that I so longed for in my life and relationships.

HOPE FOR YOU

What is it you need to admit and face and bring to God so you can accomplish the work He has for you to do?

Day 127

JESUS ASKS, "WHY ARE YOU SO AFRAID"?

Jesus was in the stern sleeping on a cushion. The disciples woke Him and said to Him, "teacher don't you care if we drown?" He got up, rebuked the wind and said to the waves, "quiet be still." Then the wind died down and it was completely calm. He said to His disciples, "why are you so afraid? Do you still have no faith?"

—Mark 4:38–40

When the storms of your life come, and it is guaranteed that they will, what do you do first? Do you panic and act as if Jesus doesn't care about your storms, or do you trust Him, confess your need to Him, and believe that He cares for you?

If He allowed the physical storm to come to His chosen disciples, don't you think He will allow your storms to come as a test to reassure you of your faith and trust in Him? Trials also teach you to grow when He handles them, as only He can.

In looking back, I can see many times when I was so fearful and I did not understand how God would let this happen to me. I was failing to see He was at work all along helping me to see my need of depending totally on Him for everything. I did not always pass His tests the first time, but He never failed to give make-up ones to me.

HOPE FOR YOU

Where are you now? Are you like the disciples in a storm and not sure God is there? I can assure you that He is, and now wants you to have faith in Him alone to calm the storms.

Day 128

IT IS I, "DON'T BE AFRAID," SAYS JESUS

But when they saw Him walking on the lake, they thought He was a ghost. They cried out, because they all saw Him and were terrified. Immediately He spoke to them and said, "Take courage! It is I. Don't be afraid."

—Mark 6:49–50

The disciples were afraid. In the same circumstances I imagine we would have been too. They saw a man walking on the lake towards them. They did not recognize Him till He got to them and spoke. Then Jesus calmed their fears and calmly climbed into the boat. Soon the storm was gone.

Do you recognize His presence is the only antidote for fear? Only He can calm the storms of your life and show you the reality of truth that He has for you to be and live. Do you recognize that He is the only answer to your fear?

I lived in fear and doubt the majority of my life. I did not allow Jesus to be in complete control. I always held back certain parts, until one day I was left with no choice but to let go of it all to Him. Since then the storms still come, but I know who can calm them, and I run to Him first.

HOPE FOR YOU

Are there parts of you that you have never let Jesus come into completely? Fear will reside there until you do. Turn it all over to Him today, and see the peace He wants to provide for you.

Day 129

BE STILL AND WAIT PATIENTLY FOR THE LORD, DO NOT FRET

> Be still and wait patiently for Him, do not fret when men succeed in their ways, when they carry out their wicked schemes.
>
> —Ps. 37:7

David was telling us to relax and not to get ahead of God. Fear, worry, and doubt will not help you in any way. David's message is always to trust in God first. David knew that is what God wants and requires from us. We know as believers, trust is how we can receive all the blessings God has for us, and also to be able to help others through this life.

Fretting, worrying, doubting, and fear all stem from the lack of faith, trust, and dependence on God alone. When I take my eyes off His Word, and when my mind wanders into my own understanding, I soon begin to live in a world of fear and all that comes with it.

I spent many years wandering in and out of total trust in God. I am so thankful He waited on me when I wasn't still and waiting on Him. He never gave up on me.

HOPE FOR YOU

God never gives up on any of His chosen children. Have you given up on Him? Are you still and waiting patiently for Him? He is waiting for you and wants you to come back to Him.

Day 130

TRUST, DON'T DOUBT, AND GOD WILL HEAR YOU

But when he asks, he must believe and not doubt, because he who doubts is like a wave of the sea, blown and tossed by the wind.

—Jas. 1:6

James was a half brother of Jesus and grew up with him. James did not believe until after Jesus died on the cross and rose again. James knew what it meant to doubt and fear first hand. God showed James that Jesus and all He preached was the truth, and that the prayers of those who do not doubt (or try to outguess) God would be heard and answered.

I now see why some of my prayers in the past were not heard or answered as I thought they should have been. I would ask and pray, but my mind was focused on human and worldly reasoning. I was not totally committed to receiving His answers. God cannot accept both. You must cooperate in His plan for you.

HOPE FOR YOU

Are you totally committed to God, or are you still allowing yourself to be tossed about by the ways of the world? Have you asked and prayed to God, but did not receive an answer? You can begin again and truly believe and trust. God is ready to show you His answers. Are you ready to receive them?

Day 131

DO NOT BE AFRAID, LET'S EAT

Elijah said to her, "Don't be afraid. Go home and do as you have said. But first make a small cake of bread for me from what you have and bring it to me, and then make something for yourself and your son."

—1 Kgs. 17:13

God always promises to take care of us, even when we least expect it. In this story, Elijah was a great prophet of God in Israel. It was a law to take care of the prophets. God sent Elijah to a widow who was taking care of her son, to ask her for food.

When Elijah told the widow to provide him food, he knew she was afraid. The truth was that she only had enough food for one more meal for herself and her son. She was resigned that it would be their last meal.

Have you ever faced life-threatening circumstances and then trusted God and He worked them all out in ways you could never have imagined? Faith in God overcomes fear every time. I thank God that I am learning to trust and seek Him first, and not live life independent of Him.

HOPE FOR YOU

What are you facing? Is God asking you to trust Him totally and not work it out independent of Him? Listen and answer His call to you.

Day 132

DON'T BE AFRAID OF THE PROJECT AT HAND

After I looked things over, I stood up and said to the nobles, the officials and the rest of the people, "Don't be afraid of them. Remember the Lord, who is great and awesome, and fight for your brothers, your sons and your daughters, your wives and your homes."

—Neh. 4:14

Nehemiah was sent to the people in Jerusalem to help them remember the goal of rebuilding the wall surrounding the city. It was a big job, and they were doing well, but had gotten tired, discouraged, and faced much opposition. Nehemiah prayed and then reminded them of why they were involved in the project to begin with, and what it was going to accomplish. Focusing on what God has in mind will always overcome fear.

I can easily get as tired and discouraged as these people were. There is not much encouragement around us to choose otherwise is there? But I have learned I am called to be an encourager to others to not lose hope and become discouraged about what they are called to be and do. It is the purpose of our churches to build one another up in the faith of our Lord, and to mature and complete the job He has for each of us together in Christ.

HOPE FOR YOU

Even if you have uncompleted areas in your life, now is the time to get back to them and finish the plan. God is willing to show you how to be energized and focused on Him to the end.

Day 133

WHY LIVE IN THE SIN OF
FEAR AND WORRY?

"But blessed is the man who trusts in the Lord, whose confidence is in Him. He will be like a tree planted by the water that sends out its roots by the stream. It does not fear when heat comes, its leaves are always green. It has no worries in a year of drought and never fails to bear fruit."

—Jer. 17:7–8

Jeremiah was sent to Judah to help them see it was all about God and not about their own sinful ways. They had turned from God even though they had seen all He had done for them. Their hearts had turned to the world and not to Him.

Jeremiah assures us that those who trust in the Lord and depend on Him, need not fear or worry. He used the example of a tree and the elements because we all can relate to nature in our everyday lives.

I remember many times when I have strayed and then looked around me at the wonder of nature and directed my heart back to Him. God is the only way to live a victorious life full of joy, peace, and contentment, regardless of the circumstances.

HOPE FOR YOU

Have you strayed from God and lived your own way? He is not far from you. Get up and look around you and see His wonderful work and what He has for you. He is waiting for you to come back to Him right now.

Day 134

DO NOT WORRY BECAUSE OF THE EVIL OF MAN

Do not fret because of evil men or be envious of those who
do wrong.

—Ps. 37:1

David shows us we are not to be spending our time being concerned with those who are living evil lives and yet seem to be winning in this life. God's ways are different from ours, and His supreme authority will always win out.

It can be very tempting to feel sorry for ourselves because we live the right way and still seem to struggle in this life. We have to keep focused on why God created us in the first place. God did not promise us an easy life here, but He will reward in eternity, based on all that we have done for Him here.

God has shown me that I can be content without all I thought I needed, because He has so much more for me than the things and people of this world could ever offer me.

HOPE FOR YOU

Are you living as God shows you to live, or are you attempting to compete with others who seem successful? Are you caught up in the stress and frets of this world? It is a choice to make, and I can assure you God is all you need to live a peaceful and joyful life.

Day 135

DO NOT BE AFRAID OF THOSE THE LORD BRINGS TO YOU

The Lord said to Moses, "Do not be afraid of him, for I have handed him over to you, with his whole army and his land. Do to him what you did to Sihon king of the Amorites, who reigned in Heshbon."

—Num. 21:34

Do you believe God can conquer your fears before you even face them? God wants to give us victory over our enemies, but God does have some requirements we need to meet to receive victory from Him.

First, we must believe that only He can help us. Is that hard when you can't see, feel, or touch Him physically? Then we must completely put our trust in Him to help us. Last, we must do the action steps He shows us.

Sounds like a lot? I have learned that the longer you resist His ways and will, the more fears you will have and the longer it will take to overcome them.

HOPE FOR YOU

So why wait? Let's just "do it." I recently experienced a unique way of expressing it from a dear friend who showed us to just snap our fingers and say to the Lord, "Happy to do it," and mean it. Practice that now.

Day 136

GOD KEEPS SHARING, DO NOT BE AFRAID

The Lord said to me, "Do not be afraid of him, for I have handed him over to you with his whole army and his land. Do to him what you did to Sihon king of the Amorites, who reigned in Heshbon."

—Deut. 3:2

The Israelites once again faced big problems. They were no match for the army of King Og of Bashan. But when they went to battle they won because God took care of it. He fought for them and just as He helped them then, He will help us now to face whatever the battles are in our lives.

Does He have to keep reminding you, just as He did Moses, not to be afraid in each battle that comes? Looks like He does. I don't know about you, but He has to remind me constantly. I am a weak and needy person. How about you?

HOPE FOR YOU

Just remember today that no matter how impossible the situation looks, no matter how afraid you are, God is sovereign, and He will keep His promises to you. Are you keeping the conditions He requires of trusting and depending in Him only?

Day 137

DO NOT BE TERRIFIED BY THEM, OUR GOD IS AMONG YOU

Do not be terrified by them, for the Lord your God, who is among you, is a great and awesome God.

—Deut. 7:21

Moses told the Israelites that God would destroy their enemies, but not all at once. He encouraged the people by telling them it would be a steady process, and God was in charge. Moses also told them how great and awesome God really is.

I can get overwhelmed and terrified when I forget that God is a great and awesome God who has a plan and process for me that doesn't always all happen at one time.

I am a microwave gal. I want it done in an instant. I am learning that God's timing is much better than mine, and I must not get terrified in the process of waiting and following His plan one step at a time. His peace is worth much more than my instant pleasure every time.

HOPE FOR YOU

Are you at peace, or are you living a terrified life? God is a great and awesome God and His ways are so much better than we can ever imagine. Follow Him, not yourself.

Day 138

SIN CAN SOMETIMES BRING FEAR

If you put away the sin that is in your hand and allow no evil
to dwell in your tent, then you will lift up your face without
shame, you will stand firm and without fear.

—Job 11:14–15

Zophar, a friend of Job, was explaining here the principles of God. He just had the wrong man and situation. Job had endured so many bad things in his life, one right after the other. We can see how his friend might mistake Job's sin as the cause of it all, can't we?

God sees and knows everything about our lives. He is the one we are accountable to for our every thought that can lead to sin. However, this was not the case with Job. He was going through a test that God had allowed, and even though he listened to all the advice that came his way, he was relying on God alone for the answers.

I have learned I can hide secret sins from others and even myself, but never from God. Hiding them only causes me to fear more, and to feel the pain of sin and separation from the one true lover of my soul. I have also seen God will send tests to me just to see if I am truly His. Staying in close contact with Him is how we can know the truth of our situation.

HOPE FOR YOU

Are you living an honest life before God and yourself? Or are you hiding secret sins that you think no one knows about? God knows and still loves you very much. He wants you to come clean before Him and give up your life of fear and torment.

Day 139

GOD HAS THE PLAN, DO NOT BE AFRAID

> Last night an angel of the God whose I am and whom I serve stood beside me and said, "Do not be afraid, Paul. You must stand trial before Caesar; and God has graciously given you the lives of all who sail with you."
>
> —Acts 27:23–24

Are you in a crisis in your life as Paul was at this time? Are you working hard planning your own escape instead of asking and letting God be in control? Do you listen for God? Once you realize that no matter what your circumstances are, God is in control, then you can have freedom from any fear.

It is a matter of focusing on the big picture and plan of God, instead of our limited vision. That is what overcomes fear because then we will trust, obey, and pray first to God, not after our plans have failed.

I have let myself get into many crisis situations because I lost sight of the big picture of God and His plan for me. But God has never failed to bail me out and let me begin again on the right path with Him.

HOPE FOR YOU

Are you regularly spending time with our Lord and Savior? Do you know you are living in His will and plan for you, and do you really care? Or do you have it all figured out and you just hope He blesses your plan and goes along with it? True life in Him is to be joyful, peaceful, and contented, no matter what is going on around you. You can know that now.

Day 140

FEAR NOT IN THE NIGHT OR DAY

> You will not fear the terror of night, nor the arrow that flies
> by day, nor the pestilence that stalks in the darkness, nor the
> plague that destroys at midday.
>
> —Ps. 91:5–6

When are you most afraid, day or night? Doesn't it make sense that most of us fear more in the night or those days that seem as dark as the night? The exact writer of this psalm is not known, but the message is very clear. God doesn't promise us a world free from terror, but He does promise His help and protection when we face danger.

To receive and know His protection, God requires a few basic things from us. We have to trust and obey who He is and what He is able to do for us. Then we have to allow Him to be in complete control of our lives and make Him first daily in our lives.

I have to learn and remember these basic things of life over and over again. I have made many choices in my life that did not take these things into account, and that is where fear and doubt had the opportunity to step right in. But God keeps reminding me in so many simple ways to keep focused on His ways for true life in Him.

HOPE FOR YOU

What are your nights and days like now? Do you rest well and enjoy the journey? Do you know the Lord Jesus as your personal Savior and Lord? Only He can change your days and nights into what He has for you, and give you His protection and love through them all.

Day 141

EVEN WHEN AFRAID OF GOD, CAN YOU FACE HIM?

Then I would speak up without fear of Him, but as it now stands with me, I cannot.

—Job 9:35

Job, at this point, had been through many tragic events in his life. He had never thought of himself as sinless, but he could not see any reason why God was allowing him to go through these terrible times. He did not feel himself a match for God, nor could he find any help from his situation from God. He was at the point of sinning and feeling sorry for himself, all the while wanting to know God's plan in all of his misery. He wanted to ask God, but he wasn't quite sure how to go about it.

I have been through many situations where I just couldn't see the big plan of God, and I felt it must all be a punishment for me. In these times, I failed and made wrong choices instead of faithfully following God and allowing Him to work it all out.

Job got to this point, but the good news is that God stepped in and showed Job that His ways are best and that it will work out. God did the same for me, even after I had made some pretty bad decisions.

HOPE FOR YOU

Are you at a "Job" point in your life? Are you questioning and even fearing to ask God about it? There is no fear with Him. He wants to show you that right now. Come in true faith and see His plan for you.

Day 142

I SHALL NOT BE IN WANT

The Lord is my shepherd, I shall not be in want.

—Ps. 23:1

David knew the Lord was his Shepherd. Is the Lord your Shepherd? Do you believe He can provide and take care of all your fears and doubts? Just as the Lord is our Shepherd, we are His sheep. If we follow and trust as good sheep normally do, there should be no fear. Only by living obedient lives will we be led into the right places and the right ways. This takes discipline from us and discipline by God to keep us in His will.

Until I learned to give up my will and let God be in total control, I was an out of control sheep. I followed all the wrong people, ended up in the wrong places going the wrong ways, and was anxious and fearful about all of it. But God is the great Shepherd and following Him is the only way to live the life He has for me.

HOPE FOR YOU

Are you an obedient, willing sheep, following the Lord wherever He wants you to go? Or are you still a frightened sheep working at doing it all yourself and following the wrong shepherd? Look up and give it all to God right now. He will lead you and you will not be bound in fear.

Day 143

DO NOT BE AFRAID TO SHARE GOD

You who bring good tidings to Zion, go up on a high mountain. You who bring good tidings to Jerusalem, lift up your voice with a shout, lift it up, do not be afraid, say to the towns of Judah, "Here is your God."

—Isa. 40:9

I saiah was sent on a mission to tell the people of Judah not to be afraid to share God and to tell others what blessings He had for them. God has a plan for each of us. He blesses us so that we can be a blessing not only to Him, but also to others. How can we accomplish the plan and purpose God has for us if we live in fear? What we will end up doing is sharing our fear and making others fearful too. We will rob them and ourselves of the love and care God has for us.

Being afraid is a waste of the precious time God has for us. It took me longer than I would have ever wanted to find that out. The good news is I am so glad I have found it out now, and God can still use me to accomplish what He had planned all along.

HOPE FOR YOU

Where are you in God's plan for your life? Are you living and sharing His good news in your life or are you afraid He is no longer in charge of it all? Make the choice that Isaiah did. Believe and tell others about our God without fear.

Day 144

WHERE IS YOUR TRUST?

When I am afraid, I will trust in you.

—Ps. 56:3

Over and over again David says not to be afraid of anything, just trust in the true God. Why then do we still fear? Are we not listening? Or do we have a hard time believing it is true? The world around us does not teach this nor does our culture pay any attention to the Word of God.

When I lose sight of God's plan and fail to focus on Him first, fear takes over. But isn't it great to know we can change right now and begin again?

I love to read God's Word because it shows me God is forgiveness, change, and is the one who will never leave me. It is we who move from Him, not He from us. That is great news of hope, and I am so thankful and grateful that He cares so much for me and that I can share that truth with others.

HOPE FOR YOU

Right now you can make this easy. Trust Him, and say over and over—as many times as you need to get that mind-set and belief in place—"I trust in you God, and I am not afraid."

Day 145

DO NOT BE AFRAID OF RUMORS

Do not lose heart or be afraid when rumors are heard in the land; one rumor comes this year, another the next, rumors of violence in the land and of ruler against ruler.

—Jer. 51:46

Jeremiah told the Israelites not to lose heart and not to be afraid of what they heard and saw around them. Not much different from what we see all around us, is it? Our news system is faster at getting rumors to us than Jeremiah's was, but still rumors will come with each day.

Rumors are nothing more than living in the "what ifs" of life. We are good at doing this when we take our minds off of what God tells us. We listen every day to those who do not have a clue about who God is. We believe them and then begin to fear, worry, fret, and doubt, and then we pass our fear on to others as well. That is how we keep those rumors alive, and forget who God is.

I have had to learn to focus on what God says first, and not be overly concerned about what those who don't know Him have to say. I have found I can live in the "what ifs" as if they were true, instead of just the rumors that they are.

HOPE FOR YOU

Where are you living today? Are you like the Israelites, living in fear of rumors, or are you living as God intends, living in the truth of His Word? It is time to choose.

Day 146

DO NOT BE AFRAID, THE BATTLE IS NOT YOURS

> He said: "Listen, King Jehoshaphat and all who live in Judah and Jerusalem! This is what the Lords says to you: 'Do not be afraid or discouraged because of this vast army. For the battle is not yours, but God's.'"
>
> —2 Chron. 20:15

Jahaziel, son of Zechariah, was instructing Judah as the enemy approached not to be afraid—that the battle was not theirs but God's.

I have not faced vast armies, but my battles seemed pretty big to me. I haven't always remembered that even though I am facing them, they are not mine to fight. God is within me, and He wants to be in charge and fight my enemies for me. That can only happen when I give all my fear and discouragement to Him and let Him fight through and for me.

How do I do that? I must realize the battle is not mine. I then allow His strength to work by making sure the battles I choose are His plan for me. And I ask for His help. There is nothing too big for God. He is ready to be in charge.

HOPE FOR YOU

What battles are you facing? Are they yours or God's? How have you chosen to face them, God's way or yours? Begin now to see God's plan in everything, and let Him face it all for you.

Day 147

BE STRONG, DO NOT BE TERRIFIED

"Have I not commanded you? Be strong and courageous, do not be terrified, do not be discouraged, for the Lord your God will be with you wherever you go."

—Josh. 1:9

God showed Joshua how to successfully lead the people and have prosperity as well. It goes against what we have been taught in our lifetime, doesn't it? We think if we achieve power, are influential to others, and strive to continue to get ahead we will be successful and certainly have no fears or be discouraged, right?

But God's plan is different than our own. He has commanded us as His children to be strong and courageous by depending on Him, not ourselves. He commands us not to fear or be discouraged because we can depend on Him. We are to be assured and trust that God will be with us always, wherever we go.

I haven't always chosen His ways, and in looking back I can't undo what I chose to do. But I know now that His way is best, and I can begin again right now to follow Him, and not myself or others.

HOPE FOR YOU

Whose opinion of success do you seek—the world's or God's? Our way brings fear and discouragement. God's way brings His strength to us and gives us the courage to face fear and discouragement by knowing He is with us always.

Day 148

DO NOT BE AFRAID OF WHAT YOU HEAR

> Isaiah said to them, "Tell your master, 'This is what the Lord says: Do not be afraid of what you have heard—those words with which the underlings of the king of Assyria have blasphemed me.'"
>
> —Isa. 37:6

Isaiah was assuring King Hezekiah not to be afraid or listen to what he had heard, but to continue to trust God, and Jerusalem would not be taken by the king of Assyria. King Hezekiah continued to pray knowing God was already taking care of the situation. He wanted to keep strong and not let anything get in God's way.

Many times we can listen to those around us who do not even profess to know God. We become frightened by what they say.

For many years I made bad choices because I listened to the wrong people. I felt they knew better than God. But I have learned to listen to those who bring the truth and want to face life God's way and not by their own opinion of the truth.

HOPE FOR YOU

Are you listening to God or others? Are you praying expecting, or not knowing? God has all the answers, we just need to trust and believe them as truth.

Day 149

DO NOT FEAR MEN OR BE TERRIFIED BY THEIR INSULTS

Hear me, you who know what is right, you people who have my law in your hearts: Do not fear the reproach of men or be terrified by their insults.

—Isa. 51:7

Isaiah encouraged those who followed God and gave them hope in facing others. He wanted them to know that God is the truth, and even those who do not believe will one day see the truth. Our first concern should be loving and obeying God, not men. He is to be first, and we are not to fear those who would make fun of us or dislike us because we believe in God.

I was raised to be a people-pleaser first, and it has been a hard journey to put God first, and not others. I always wanted people to like me, and think well of me, and I did a lot of things that God was not pleased with to obtain that end. But the good news is that God sees our heart, and He can help us see the truth, and we can change.

HOPE FOR YOU

Are you as faithful to God as He is to you? Are there unbelievers you want to please more than God? God alone demands all of our faithfulness. Put your trust in Him and do not fear what others think of you. God's truth will take care of all of it.

Day 150

DO NOT LEARN OR BE TERRIFIED BY THE SIGNS IN THE SKY

This is what the Lord says: "Do not learn the ways of the nations or be terrified by signs in the sky, though the nations are terrified by them."

—Jer. 10:2

Just as we do now, the people of Judah wanted to know the future. They sought to know it through listening to what other nations had thought they found through the reading of signs in the sky. Jeremiah's answer was not to learn the ways of other nations or be terrified as they were of what they had found.

God alone should be worshiped. He promises to guide you. You are not to depend upon the made-up charts of God's stars. He may not always reveal the entire big picture of your life at one time, but He will go through it with you as it unfolds. We are to trust not in the stars, but in the one who made the stars.

I once thought there was not much harm in looking at a newspaper or magazine for the daily horoscope. Most of it was for fun, and very seldom did any of it come true. I have friends and relatives who still do this. But I have come to see how this can make us very afraid and we can begin to trust in it and stray from the truth of God. He wants us to follow and obey His Word, and He will take care of our future.

HOPE FOR YOU

Are you as I was? Do you run to God's Word, or do you depend on someone else's knowledge of it? What do you think of horoscopes and all the other things we have let become part of our everyday lives? Are you involved?

Day 151

IT IS I, DON'T BE AFRAID

> But Jesus immediately said to them: "Take courage! It is I.
> Don't be afraid."
>
> —Matt. 14:27

J esus had not gone on the boat with His disciples. He had stayed behind to minister to others. He sent the disciples out on the lake without Him. When He was finished with His ministry He chose to walk to His disciples on the water. When they saw Him they were afraid. He knew they would be because this was not normally how they saw Him, and this was not His usual means of travel.

But Jesus, being all God and all man, recognized their fear. He told them to take courage and not be afraid. He does the same with us today. He wants each of us to know that with His power living inside of us, once we have believed and trusted in Him alone, we have no reason to fear anything.

I sometimes simply forget that I have the power of Jesus Christ living in me, and that I can call on the Holy Spirit at any time to overcome the fear that comes my way. I am sorry for this, and the more I keep focused on Him and His Word, the less it happens—but it can still happen. The good news is that I recognize it so much more quickly now and know that I do not have to give into those negative emotions of fear. It is a choice.

HOPE FOR YOU

Where do you turn first in times of fear? Learn to turn to Jesus, and you will see how He wants you to live.

DO NOT BE AFRAID OR DISCOURAGED, HIS POWER IS WITH US

Do not be afraid or discouraged because the king of Assyria and the vast army with him, for there is a greater power with us than with him.

—2 Chron. 32:7

King Hezekiah was preparing to face Sennacherib, King of Assyria. He had been a good ruler for the people of Judah, and he loved God. That is why he could confidently tell the people not to be afraid or discouraged. As they prepared their plans, King Hezekiah knew where he stood with God. God saw his faithfulness and against all human odds Assyria was defeated.

I have not always confidently known where I stood with God. Therefore, fear could attack and I would give in. I see now that you can know God personally and know where you stand with him.

Even though I have not had to face great battles with vast armies, my battles have seemed pretty big to me. With God's strength, I have learned He can win the battles. Now I can encourage others that He can win theirs as well.

HOPE FOR YOU

What battles are you facing today? God is the greater power over them, and He wants to give you His strength to win. Do you know where you stand with God? You can seek Him with all your heart and He will show you the way.

Day 153

DO YOU TRUST IN GOD?

> In God I trust, I will not be afraid. What can man do to me?
>
> —Ps. 56:11

Today our country and its people are not so sure about trusting in God. David assured us that we can and should trust always in the one true God.

We see all around us, "In God We Trust," but do we really? Will it truly matter if those who oppose that phrase get their way and have it removed?

Our forefathers knew there would come a day where we would have to make a choice as to whom and in what our trust really would be. They were wise to imprint their faith in God on our coinage in 1864, so that we would not forget Him and how He helped the people who established our country. Then in the 1950s our leaders added it to our paper currency and also added to our Pledge of Allegiance, "under God." Also at that time "In God We Trust" became the official motto of our United States.

Just as our country has forgotten to trust in God today; I have failed many times to trust God first in my life. I have let fear override my faith and trust in Him. That is not what God wants of me, but He will not force Himself on me. He is faithful, and will forgive me when I fail to trust Him.

HOPE FOR YOU

Where do you place your trust? Is it in God or someone or something else? We need more than ever to trust in God so that our country will never forget Him, and all the many blessings He has given our country and to us personally.

Day 154

WHY ARE YOU AFRAID?

He said to them, "Why are you troubled, and why do doubts rise in your minds?"

—Luke 24:38

The disciples of Jesus were afraid, troubled, and had many doubts after the death of Jesus. Even though He had explained it all, they still had not seen the entire picture. Jesus knew this, so He appeared to them to once again encourage them and get them on the right path He had for them.

Today with so much more information and the means to communicate it, do you ever wonder, doubt, or fear what was and what is to come? Our minds can become so cluttered with the world and our life that we fail to focus on Jesus first. Jesus is still assuring us of His plan and what will come, but are we listening?

I have not always lived putting the Lord first. I can let everything totally overwhelm and consume me. But now I know God has plans for me, and they will never cease until I do. But I must spend time with Him so that I can know and live in them.

HOPE FOR YOU

Are you living in the truth of God and His facts or are you tuned into only the world's message? Now is the time to know where you stand with Him. Do not be troubled, afraid, or doubtful, God is in control and wants to show you so much more.

Day 155

DO NOT BE TERRIFIED BY THEM, OR I WILL TERRIFY YOU

> Get yourself ready! Stand up and say to them whatever I command you. Do not be terrified by them, or I will terrify you before them.
>
> —Jer. 1:17

Jeremiah's message was for the people of Judah and Israel. Just as we do now, the Jews strayed from God. They had sinned by worshiping other gods. Jeremiah told them not to be terrified by what they were facing. God was still with them and was giving them another chance. The time had come that they must obey or they would fail.

Not an easy message to bring, is it? I had to realize in my life that I had let other gods creep in, and when I faced a major crisis, I tended to fall apart and be terrified inside. On the outside, I played the fake and blame game, but I was living a lie.

God heard my cry and assured me I could still stand up and He would be there to help me face anything as long as I did it His way. I could begin again. He still has lots of work to do in my life, but I am so thankful He listened and I heard Him.

HOPE FOR YOU

Are you like the Jewish people and other people of today? Have you let other gods creep in and now you are in a real mess? I assure you God is still there. He wants to hear from you. Cry out to Him today and live.

Day 156

DO NOT BE FRIGHTENED, THE END WILL NOT COME RIGHT AWAY

> When you hear of wars and revolutions, do not be frightened. These things must happen first, but the end will not come right away.
>
> —Luke 21:9

Jesus wanted to prepare us for what is to come, so He showed us that even though false messiahs, natural disasters, and persecutions would come, it was not yet the end. Even now we are looking at a lot of events going on in our world. To us they seem unusual and we could wonder if the time of Jesus' return is at hand. Will we be the ones to see it?

At times in my life, I was very unprepared for the coming of Christ, and I could get easily frightened about events that looked as if it could be the time of Jesus' return. Why was I afraid? I knew I had not been living as He wanted, and I was afraid to face Him.

I finally was put in a position where I had to confront my fear and get it settled. Once I did, I now look forward to His coming with joy. It could be that just as I am writing these words, He might come. Whenever it happens, it will be a blessed event, and in God's perfect timing.

HOPE FOR YOU

Are you living in fear of all that is going on around us? Are you ready and excited about the return of Jesus? You can be. He is willing to show you how.

Day 157

YOU NEED NOT FEAR

You will laugh at destruction and famine, and need not fear
the beasts of the earth.

—Job 5:22

Job was going through awful things and he didn't know why. He had
friends who thought they had the answers and could help him. One
was Eliphaz. His message to Job was that pain can help us grow in faith
of God. Not bad advice, but the one thing he focused on was that Job
must have done something bad to have so much pain to go through to
grow in his faith.

I am thankful God does not work as we think, but as He wills. When
we follow Jesus, there is no assurance we will not have to face great
pain. Also, there is no assurance we will be rewarded here for the good
we do either.

I have had some friends like Eliphaz. I even listened to them, and did
as they advised. But I realized I was not being wise in putting my trust
in man, rather than in the one true God. He alone had all the answers
I would ever need.

HOPE FOR YOU

Do you have friends like Eliphaz? They think they know God's will for
us, and tell us any time they can? I want to be an encourager to point
you to the truth found in God's Word. I don't have all the answers,
but He does. And you can find them personally for your life in Him
alone.

Day 158

FEAR NO MORE, GOD WILL SAVE YOU

So do not fear, O Jacob my servant, do not be dismayed, O Israel, I will surely save you out of a distant place, your descendants from the land of their exile. Jacob will again have peace and security, and no one will make him afraid.

—Jer. 30:10

Jeremiah was sent to assure the Jews that God would save them. Are there conditions on that promise? There always are. God who created us, wants us to glorify and honor and praise Him above all else. He completed that plan by sending His only Son, Jesus, to die and be raised again as payment for our sins. Our part is to believe and trust Him only.

I know I have let fear rule because I did not believe I could ever measure up to what God expected of me. I accepted that lie based on my background and on people constantly reminding me I would never amount to anything. What a prison I allowed myself to dwell in for many years. But God is in the saving and freeing business. He rescued me, and shows me daily I never have to go back.

Hope for You

Are you chained in the prison of fear? Do you know that God wants to free you? He loves and cares so much for you. He sent His only Son Jesus to die for you. Come now, believe, trust, and be freed forever.

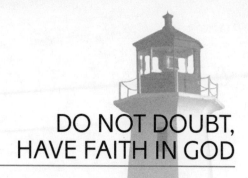

DO NOT DOUBT, HAVE FAITH IN GOD

"Have faith in God," Jesus answered. "I tell you the truth, if anyone says to this mountain 'Go throw yourself into the sea,' and does not doubt in his heart but believes that what he says will happen, it will be done for him."

—Mark 11:22–23

Jesus was speaking to His disciples about how to pray. He knew they would need definite instructions so that as believers they could communicate with Him, and understand how to do that.

I have found there are four conditions we must meet to have great communication with God. We must believe and trust in Him alone, and believe in His Son, Jesus Christ as our Savior and Lord, hold nothing against anyone, do not pray with selfish motives, and what we pray for must be for the good of the kingdom of God.

I have failed many times to meet these conditions and have wondered and doubted why I did not see my prayers answered. I then began to be thankful and grateful for the way I could communicate with God. I want to do it His way, not mine.

HOPE FOR YOU

Do you see your prayers being answered? Do you doubt God? Have you met His conditions? Today, begin again; He is listening.

Day 160

SEE TO IT HE HAS NOTHING TO FEAR

If Timothy comes, see to it that he has nothing to fear while he is with you, for he is carrying on the work of the Lord, just as I am.

—1 Cor. 16:10

Paul was sending a young man, Timothy, on ahead to Corinth. Paul respected him and wanted to make sure he was taken care of and encouraged. We all need to be encouragers of others and also be encouraged by others.

We never know where God is going to use us, and when He will call us to use the gifts and talents He gives us to serve Him and others. Many can be fearful and discouraged while serving.

I have lived in fear of the many limitations that I allowed to be placed on my life. Through those times, I have learned from those sent to encourage me how to overcome fear. This is a double blessing for me. When I am encouraged, I then want to encourage others too. Only God can work and do that in our lives. He takes the evil intended, and turns it into a blessing!

HOPE FOR YOU

Do you need encouragement in facing your fears? God will send someone to you. Then, are you ready to share with others the encouragement they need? You are missing the blessings God has for you by not obeying and letting Him show you His plan for you.

Day 161

DO NOT WORRY ABOUT
WHAT TO SAY

But when they arrest you, do not worry about what to say or
how to say it. At that time you will be given what to say.
—Matt. 10:19

Jesus told his disciples that when they were arrested for preaching
the gospel, not to worry about what they were going to say in their
own defense. He had prepared His disciples to present His message,
and He wanted them to continue to do so.

Today we cannot even imagine what it would be like to share the
message of Jesus and face true persecution for doing so. In a lot of
countries our fellow brothers and sisters in Christ face this as a daily
part of life. You may know some who face this every day.

It is good to be reminded that should we be faced with this situation,
we are not to worry about it because the Holy Spirit will take care of
our words, and He will also guide us through whatever we have to go
through. We can encourage others in this situation that they are not to
worry either, and that God will take care of them.

HOPE FOR YOU

Are you strong in your faith to face true opposition? Do you worry
about what to say and do should you face those who would persecute
you? Just as Jesus assured His disciples that the Holy Spirit would be
with them, He is here today with us as well.

Day 162

DO NOT WORRY WHEN YOU ARE BROUGHT TO TRIAL

> Whenever you are arrested and brought to trial, do not worry beforehand about what to say. Just say whatever is given you at the time, for it is not you speaking, but the Holy Spirit.
>
> —Mark 13:11

Jesus was not advising His disciples to quit studying the Scriptures to gain more insight of Him. He wanted them to have the right attitude when they shared the gospel and not to worry or be fearful and defensive about their faith. The Holy Spirit would be there and they would have all the right words to say.

I love sharing the gospel now, but I used to be very worried and frightened about doing so. I did not feel I would be arrested, but I did feel the threat of others, especially as to how it could affect my work in corporate America.

I also felt unworthy to do so because I did not have the knowledge and background I felt was worthy enough of the call of the Lord. I have missed many opportunities to share Christ, but God is faithful to forgive.

HOPE FOR YOU

Do you worry about being called on to share Jesus with someone and what the outcome might be? God says we are not to worry or fear because the Holy Spirit is our defender. Be prepared at any time to share and see God at work in you.

Day 163

DO NOT FRET BECAUSE
OF EVIL MEN

> Do not fret because of evil men or be envious of the wicked.
>
> —Prov. 24:19

S olomon was a very wise man and he wrote to teach others how to live godly lives based on God's instructions. Did he always follow his own teachings? His life proved he did not, but in the end, he knew God's forgiveness and he changed his ways.

We need to ask ourselves if we are living godly lives. Do we fear and worry about keeping up with those in influence who are living wicked lives? We are called to be different and not to be caught up in this world, but is that the way we live?

I got caught up in seeking the success of this world—of man's way—instead of God's. It is easy to do. I thought I was a good person and not an evil one for doing it. I wanted for myself and my family what I saw others have. I did not even consider how they achieved it.

God has shown me how to be content to live on less than I earn, so that I can give and help those in need; and also be able to save so that I can live debt free.

HOPE FOR YOU

Do you need to make a change? Don't wait as long as Solomon or I did to do so.

Day 164

I WILL RESCUE YOU, SAYS THE LORD, FROM THOSE YOU FEAR

"But I will rescue you on that day," declares the Lord, "you will not be handed over to those you fear. I will save you, you will not fall by the sword but will escape with your life, because you trust in me, declares the Lord."

—Jer. 39:17–18

The Lord showed Jeremiah to tell the people not to be afraid of those around them because He would save them. He also told them not everyone will receive His rewards in this life. Jeremiah had faithfully served God at this time for forty years and had endured much with very little rewards.

Why do we trust God at all in this life? Is it for His rewards, or is it because we love Him, and are not concerned whether we receive His rewards or not?

I, for one, said I loved God, but I know I have served Him out of selfish motives many times, instead of true love and honor. I wanted it easy and comfortable.

God does not promise us that at all. He will take care of us, and we are not to fear, but we must learn He is still in control and sees the big picture. It is His timing and strength that brings us through hard times and it is His faithfulness to us that makes it all possible in the first place.

HOPE FOR YOU

Do you love God and are you willing to serve Him no matter what? Or have you put conditions on how He is supposed to reward you?

Day 165

DO NOT WORRY ABOUT WHAT YOU EAT OR DRINK

And do not set your heart on what you will eat or drink, do not worry about it.

—Luke 12:29

J esus commands us not to fear or worry. He tells us that it is pointless because only He can fill our need and only He knows what we truly need. Jesus knew this was a big area of understanding we would need to possess. So He made sure it was plain and clear by giving the same message to many writers of the Bible to share with us.

I know in my head not to worry, but how can I avoid it? I have found that I want to out-plan God. I waste precious time working at figuring out what could go wrong instead of trusting God for the outcome.

His ways are better than mine, so I have learned to trust Him and not myself. Another way I have learned to avoid worry is to pray for those around me who are also worriers, and make sure my time with them is spent not worrying.

HOPE FOR YOU

Are you caught up in worrying? What has it gotten you? Can you renew your mind to not do it? Yes, you can, and you must before it claims your physical health and also the health of those around you.

Day 166

DO NOT WORRY ABOUT YOUR STAGE IN LIFE

Were you called while a slave? Do not worry about it, but if you are able to become free, rather do that.

—1 Cor. 7:21 NASB

Paul was sharing with the church at Corinth not to worry about the stage of life we are in when God chooses us to become His own. We can get caught up in so wanting to do what we feel led to do that we miss being and doing right where we are.

We must realize God has placed us where we are, and looking back or ahead can get in the way of what God is trying to do through us. Many times, I have made choices I thought would be God honoring and the right thing to do, only to find out they were not my calling at all. I ended up worrying and working at them in my own strength and not the Lord's. Then I would get discouraged, defeated, and give up.

Staying in close touch with God is the key to knowing when we should continue on in His way or make a change in life. I have made some wrong choices simply because I did not ask and wait for God to answer.

HOPE FOR YOU

Do you dwell on regrets and the "what ifs" of life? Are you content with who you are, and where you are in relationship to the call of God? Paul is telling us we must learn not to fear or worry about anything but to trust and depend on God.

DO NOT BE AFRAID TO TELL THE TRUTH

"It's all right," he said. "Don't be afraid. Your God, the God of your father, has given you treasure in your sacks, I received your silver." Then He brought Simeon out to them.
—Gen. 43:23

Joseph's brothers were afraid because on their first trip to Egypt they paid for the grain they purchased and went back home to Jacob. When they got there, they found their money, along with the grain, as if they had not paid for it. God knew the truth, and Jacob knew his sons. So when it was time to buy more grain, Jacob sent the money back as well as more money for the current purchase. He told his sons to tell the truth. Jacob was teaching a great lesson in integrity and trusting God to take care of us.

From a very early age, my life was filled with fear and not living the truth. When faced with admitting and telling the truth about anything, I would lie to cover up the error so I would not be punished.

That became the pattern of my life, and I constantly had to defend myself from one lie to the next. It was when I finally realized that God defends me and works it out when I tell and live the truth; life changed for me. Now I have true joy, peace, and contentment.

HOPE FOR YOU

Are you living in integrity and the truth? If not, God wants you to admit it, and He will forgive you and show you how to live and walk in His truth for life.

Day 168

DON'T BE AFRAID, I WILL PROVIDE FOR YOU

So then, don't be afraid. I will provide for you and your children.

—Gen. 50:21

J oseph not only forgave his brothers for harming him, but as God had blessed him greatly, he promised to provide for them and their children too. He showed how God forgives us; even though we don't deserve it, He is willing to do so.

Is it hard for you to forgive yourself and others? This was not taught to me as a child, and it was a hard lesson to go through. But the good news is, God can bring good from evil and redeem the time that was lost because of it.

I have seen God at work in taking care of my family, and because I have, I want to share with others how it is possible for them too. God can be trusted and depended on for everything.

HOPE FOR YOU

Are you afraid to step out and forgive yourself and others? Do you want to bless the ones who harm you, or do you want them cursed? God's way is one of blessing. Choose His way and He will provide for you.

Day 169

DO NOT BE AFRAID WHEN THE UNGODLY PROSPER

Do not be afraid when [an ungodly] one is made rich, when the wealth and glory of his house are increased, for when he dies he will carry nothing away, his glory will not descend after him.

—Ps. 49:16–17 AMP

These words were written by the sons of Korah to show the people that the wealth and success of this world will not bring freedom from fear at all. Wealth cannot be taken with anyone when they die. It stays here. All that is taken is what has been sent on ahead for the glory of God.

Why then are we afraid and concerned when we see those who do not believe in God seem to prosper and look successful? The truth is, most people of great wealth who are not believers are some of the unhappiest people we could ever know.

I thought for the majority of my life that my success was based on how well I did financially. The truth was, I didn't know how to successfully handle the wealth I had, so how could God bless me with more?

Since I have let Him show me the message of success in Him, wealth is not the issue. I want to use the resources He gives me for His glory and kingdom and then trust Him to provide all I need.

HOPE FOR YOU

Are you afraid of the rich ungodly people? Do you want to be one of them? Wealth is not what life is all about. It is not your measure of success, only God is.

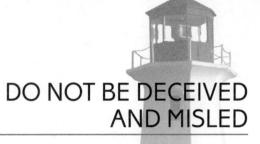

DO NOT BE DECEIVED AND MISLED

Do not be so deceived and misled. Evil companionships (communion, associations) corrupt and deprave good manners and morals and character.

—1 Cor. 15:33 AMP

Paul was telling the church at Corinth and all believers that it is easy to become like unbelievers when we keep company with those who are unbelievers. Then we have the same fears in the world of an unbeliever because we are led astray from the truth of the Lord.

Have you met those who appeared to be great believers when in fact they were not at all? I have. I married one, and what happened was that I let it break my fellowship with God and the trust that I had built up in His Word. Then the result was that I became more fearful of this world than ever, and I did things that were not in the character of God.

Paul is urging us to consider every relationship before we enter into it. Don't be misled, and make sure to consult God in everything.

HOPE FOR YOU

Are you associated with those who have deceived and misled you? There is a way out. Ask God to show you the way back to Him, and He will take care of you.

Day 171

YOU WHO FEAR MAY TURN BACK

"Anyone who trembles with fear may turn back and leave Mount Gilead." So twenty-two thousand men left, while ten thousand remained.

—Judg. 7:3

The Lord showed Gideon he was about to face a major battle and that he needed less and the right men to win. He told Gideon to ask the men who were afraid to turn back. That would be the condition of their faith. Gideon obeyed God, confronted his men, and many admitted their fear and left.

I am sure that many times we have wanted to be in that number. We've wanted to recognize our fear and just quit. God knew that to win this battle, He did not need those supporting Gideon to be afraid. He also wanted to show Gideon that He would help him win and not the vast size of an army. What do you think happened to those that quit and left Gideon?

Many times I have put my trust in myself instead of God, and then when fear came, I quit before He could show me His plan for it all. I am learning that I no longer have to live that way. God has special plans for each of us, and we are not to fear, but trust and obey. That way quitting is not even an option.

HOPE FOR YOU

Have you ever been tempted or actually quit something you knew was right for you, because of your fear? You can begin again with God and let Him show you His plan.

Day 172

DO NOT BECOME WEARY DOING RIGHT

> Let us not become weary in doing good, for at the proper time we will reap a harvest if we do not give up.
>
> —Gal. 6:9

Paul was giving a challenge to the early churches in southern Galatia, not to become weary in doing what the Lord had called them to do, even though right now they may not see any results. But Paul wanted them to know that God cares and He sees, and that is all that matters.

At times I have found that fear can set in easily when I don't see the results of what I am doing. In the corporate world we are rewarded for achieving results in a short period of time. That thinking has taken over our culture.

I have done many shortcuts that I thought would bring about the results I believed I needed only to see that God had a better and bigger plan for me. God's timing is different from mine. It is hard to keep going without seeing the big picture as He does if we let fear come ahead of our trust in the Lord. I missed out on God's blessings in doing so.

HOPE FOR YOU

Are you growing weary of doing right and good things because you don't have any results to show for your efforts? Remember, God is in control and true contentment comes from Him. So do not be discouraged; He is right here with you.

GOD DOES NOTHING WITHOUT LETTING US KNOW

The fact is, God, the Master, does nothing without first telling His prophets the whole story. The Lion has roared— who isn't frightened? God has spoken—what prophet can keep quiet?

—Amos 3:7–8 THE MESSAGE

God clearly gives us His Word and the people to bring it to us. So why are we frightened and afraid? Is it because we want to still the voice of God as the people of Israel wanted to do with Amos? Do we want to live as we please and not as God wants?

Living as God intends is not seen as our first choice or option is it? Even as believers, we can get far away from His plan and choose to live as we want. In a day where pleasure rules and hard work is not seen as success, is it any wonder we are living in such fear and despair?

I chose to go about my own way, only letting God in at times, but not all the way. I thought He would understand and help me out. I have learned that He wants total commitment to Him, not just for the rewards and blessings, but because we love Him more than anything or anyone else, and we desire His way more than any other.

HOPE FOR YOU

Are you living a lie? Are you totally committed to God? Today face Him, and see the joy, peace, and contentment He has waiting for you.

Day 174

NO LONGER WILL YOU FEAR OR BE LOST

"I will place shepherds over them who will tend them, and they will no longer be afraid or terrified, nor will any be missing," declares the Lord.

—Jer. 23:4

Jeremiah was speaking to those who were in charge of the people. He was telling them the judgment God had declared against them for the poor job they had done. God will hold our leaders accountable for those He places in their path. God promises to protect those who are left, and will send good leaders to take care of them and show them not to be afraid or terrified.

I was raised in a family without responsible leaders to guide me. I cannot blame them entirely as they did not grow up with great role models either. This is how fear is passed from generation to generation.

I made the same mistakes my family did when I didn't trust God completely. I worked to figure it out on my own. I lived independent of God. I then influenced my family into those same beliefs. Finally, God changed me, and gradually my family can see that change and also want to seek some different meaning in their lives as well.

HOPE FOR YOU

How are you leading those God has placed in your care? Do they trust God totally, or are they wandering? His change can come at any stage. It is never too late.

DO NOT FEAR THOSE
IN AUTHORITY

> For rulers are not a cause of fear for good behavior, but for evil. Do you want to have no fear of authority? Do what is good and you will have praise from the same.
>
> —Rom. 13:3 NASB

Paul is telling us what we do does matter to those over us. When we choose to do what is right, we have nothing to fear from them. Do you know those who are afraid of laws and the lawmakers who govern them? I realize this world does not always have good leaders, but is that a reason to fear them?

I have always wanted people to like me. I have gone the extra mile to get people to do so. I found out the only one I need to be concerned about pleasing is God. When I am on the right track, He will take care of everything else that may come up. I no longer have anything to fear from people; I know God will take care of me.

HOPE FOR YOU

Do you fear those in authority? Do you have reason to do so? God has a plan for you to do good. Are you operating His way? Those who are, have nothing to fear.

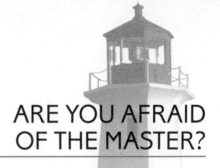

Day 176

ARE YOU AFRAID OF THE MASTER?

> "So I was afraid and went out and hid your talent in the ground. See, here is what belongs to you."
>
> —Matt. 25:25

Jesus told us why we are not to be afraid of Him or anyone else. Jesus uses what we can understand, that of a master and his servant. This is our relationship to Him. Jesus is our Master, and we are His servants. But the relationship goes much deeper to that of friendship, not slavery.

In this story, one man was given a talent by the master. We can think of it as money or we can think of it as skill and ability. The Master wanted to see what the servant would do with what he had been given. The servant did nothing except play the blame game for disobeying. The master was not pleased and made him leave. He gave his talent to others.

I can see myself in this picture at different times in my life. I wanted to please the Lord, but my fear and insecurity prevented me from wanting to do anything about it. I did not ask for help from anyone, certainly not God, and I was very defensive and critical of others. God showed me this is not the way to please Him. Now He has given me so much. If I had kept choosing as this servant did, what I would have missed!

HOPE FOR YOU

Are you living as this servant did? In fear of God and all He represents? Do you know what God wants of you? Are you willing to find out? God will show you how to please Him and not live in fear.

Day 177

ARE YOU WORRIED AND UPSET ABOUT MANY THINGS?

"Martha, Martha," the Lord answered, "you are worried and upset about many things, but only one thing is needed. Mary has chosen what is better and it will not be taken away from her."

—Luke 10:41–42

Jesus was concerned about Martha. She was upset about the situation in her household and had asked Jesus about it. I am sure the solution she got from Him was not what she had expected. Jesus knew Martha loved Him and wanted to serve Him, but it was the way she chose to serve that caused Him to show her what would be even better.

I can relate so well to Martha because for most of my life I have been just as out of balance as she was! She was gifted with many skills and wanted everything to be in perfect order at all times at the expense of missing out on the main priorities of life. This is a perfect description of me up until ten years ago.

Just as with Martha, Jesus showed me that taking time to get to know Him was more important than focusing on all the busywork that would only give me credit and make me feel good about serving Him.

HOPE FOR YOU

Are you a Martha or a Mary? Jesus focused on the women, but men, it could just as easily have been a Mark and a Matthew. I am sure we all know people who are so busy serving Jesus for all the wrong reasons. The question is, do you want to be what Jesus said is better? I assure you, He will show you how to be just that!

Day 178

ARE YOU CHOKED BY LIFE'S WORRIES?

The seed that fell among the thorns stands for those who hear, but as they go on their way they are choked by life's worries, riches and pleasures, and they do not mature.
—Luke 8:14

The church I now attend has a "Vision" statement of why our church exists. It is "to develop mature followers of Jesus Christ." When I first heard it I thought it was unique to our day and age. I also did not really know whether I was a mature follower or not.

Jesus, in this story, related the people to what they could understand and what they were familiar with in their lives. We all see seeds and soil and we recognize them. He described several kinds of soil, but this particular one shows us what happens when we become caught up in the world, are overcome with the worries of this life, and are lured by the materialism all around us, resulting in leaving no time to become mature followers of Jesus Christ.

I can certainly say, "Been there, done that." How about you? It is so easy to fall into this type of Christianity. I am thankful God showed me I do not have to stay this way, and neither do you. He showed me I can become the kind of follower that can allow Him to develop me into maturity.

HOPE FOR YOU

What kind of follower are you for Jesus Christ? I want you to know that Jesus is the answer to change, and He can grow you into the type that matures and follows Him alone.

Day 179

MAKE UP YOUR MIND AHEAD OF TIME NOT TO WORRY

But make up your mind not to worry beforehand how you will defend yourself.

—Luke 21:14

Jesus told His followers they would face persecution, but not to worry about it. Since He died, we have had to handle the trials of life. But He is showing us how to choose day by day to live victoriously, without worrying about it.

Right now we don't live in a country that is keeping us from following Jesus and sharing Him with others. There are some countries that focus on doing that, and we may be in that situation at some point in time. Are you ready to still follow Jesus and not worry about it?

At times in my life, I thought I did not have any choice of how to live it. The truth is we always have a choice. Jesus wants us to choose Him. He wants us to make the choice and not to fear and worry about it. He is promising us one day a life more glorious than we can ever imagine. But until then, we can begin living the wonderful life He has for us right now.

HOPE FOR YOU

Are you living a blessed life or do you feel defeated and worried? Jesus wants to show you how to live a wonderful life right now in spite of your circumstances. Are you willing to follow Him and not worry?

Day 180

ARE YOU OBEDIENT TO CHRIST, EVEN IN YOUR THOUGHTS?

We demolish arguments and every pretension that sets itself
up against the knowledge of God, and we take captive every
thought to make it obedient to Christ.

—2 Cor. 10:5

Is your life a battle? Do you feel you are always the loser? Do you find it hard to see God's plan and His will for you? In our own way, we all struggle day to day with life. The truth is, God has made the way already; we are just not in on it yet. So how do we get in on it?

Paul advised the Corinthian people that they must be willing to give up all to God. He must be the Commander in Chief of your life, not you or others. Then we are to commit our every thought to Him, so we can allow Him to live through us. I know that sounds hard, doesn't it? I tell you from experience that until you do, your days and life will be a battleground without the peace, hope, joy, or contentment you seek. You will continue to be controlled and you will not see a way out. Fears and doubts will become a reality, even though they are not real.

HOPE FOR YOU

Become a friend of Jesus Christ by giving Him every thought to take captive; and live a life full of hope and peace that only He can bring. This is the most important decision and choice you will ever make.

Day 181

ANXIETY IN THE HEART OF MAN CAUSES DEPRESSION

Anxiety in the heart of man causes depression, but a good word makes it glad.

—Prov. 12:25 NKJV

Solomon and his staff recorded most of these wise sayings early in his reign as king. God used him to share how to live godly lives. Just as Solomon had problems living God's way, so do we.

It is said that depression is the leading emotional disorder in America. We take more medication and seek treatment for it more than any other ailment. Why is that? In my life I faced the choice of being glad or sad many times. I found it is our choices that let the cares of this world weigh heavily in our hearts that can become depression. What can overcome that feeling and emotion? I have found it is the Word of God planted firmly in our hearts and minds.

These words are found in His love letter to us, The Holy Bible, and also from other people around us. Stay clear of those who will not bring you His good words, and stay in the Book that always has the words to help us face our lives, no matter the situation.

HOPE FOR YOU

Are you living in anxiety and fear to the point of depression? God has a plan for you, and He is ready to show you. Get into His good words to you, and surround yourself with those who will bring you His good words.

Day 182

JESUS DOES NOT FALTER NOR IS HE DISCOURAGED, WHY SHOULD WE BE?

He will not falter or be discouraged till he establishes justice
on earth. In His law the islands will put their hope.

—Isa. 42:4

Isaiah was speaking about the second coming of Christ when this
earth will be under His complete rule and all will live in justice
under Him. This shows us that when we hit those times in our lives
when all seems hopeless, Jesus is there to pick us up.

Just as God knows He will not falter or be discouraged, He shows us
how we do not have to either. This shows the real character of God to
us, and through His Spirit living in us, we can help others around us
see it too.

In my life I have messed up and allowed discouragement to overwhelm me many times. But I know God never left me. He is here when
I am at my best for Him, and when I fail too. This gives me the hope to
see the best and help others see it too, no matter what we face.

HOPE FOR YOU

Have you failed? Are you discouraged? Jesus is here and He wants to
show you that He will help you reach the hope you need, and one day
it will be fair and just.

Day 183

DO NOT BE DISCOURAGED BECAUSE OF OTHERS SUFFERINGS

> I ask you, therefore, not to be discouraged because of my sufferings for you, which are your glory.
>
> —Eph. 3:13

Paul was telling the believers that they were not to be discouraged because of the pain they saw him going through to get the message of the Lord to all. He was willing to suffer and even die for the cause of Christ. Why would he do that?

We should value and honor those who were willing to sacrifice so that you and I can hear the message of the Lord without fear and suffering. What a price they paid, and many are still paying today! The next step for us is to face whatever comes so that others may know the wonderful God we love and serve.

For a long time I wanted life to be as easy as I could have it. I could achieve it, I thought, by doing lots of hard work the world's way, getting the credit for it, and then resting and doing what I wanted. Pretty selfish reasoning, isn't it? But once the Lord showed me my life is not about me, but all about Him, that plan changed!

HOPE FOR YOU

Is your life focused on you and your plans or on the Lord and His plan for you? Are you discouraged because life is not going your way, or are you encouraged by the sufferings of others, so that you can have a life in Jesus Christ?

Day 184

HOW ARE YOUR DAYS?
ANXIOUS OR CHEERFUL?

All the days of the desponding afflicted are made evil [by anxious thoughts and foreboding], but he who has a glad heart has a continual feast [regardless of circumstances].
—Prov. 15:15 AMP

Solomon knew what it took to have a happy life, regardless of the circumstances, and he shared it with us. It is said, "our attitude determines our altitude," and we can see that very clearly in this message.

The key to having a happy attitude and life is to keep focused on that which is good and right, and not to allow any thoughts that would rob our day from being a joy for us. We can't always choose what happens to us, but we can choose how we face it.

I have always wanted to keep an attitude that others would see Jesus through me. I can let my thoughts rob me of joy. I know the right attitude is a choice, and by His Word, I can choose to dwell on the right attitude.

HOPE FOR YOU

How is your daily attitude? Do you choose the good thoughts and reject others? You have the choice to do so. Let God show you the way to a happy life, regardless of the happenings in it.

FATHERS, DO NOT PROVOKE OR FRET YOUR CHILDREN

Fathers, do not provoke *or* irritate *or* fret your children—
do not be hard on them or harass them; lest they become
discouraged *and* sullen *and* morose *and* feel inferior *and*
frustrated; do not break their spirit.

—Col. 3:21 AMP

Paul, in writing this from prison, knew what was going on in the
families of the early church. It is still going on today. Where do
we as parents miss the mark? In sharing this concept with fathers, Paul
knew it was the children who would keep the message of Jesus real
in the generations to follow. So it was important that they be cared
for with discipline handled in love. He wanted to make sure that the
children would not become discouraged and give up on the plan God
had for their lives.

Growing up without a father in my life made it very difficult to see
how my heavenly Father, God, loved and cared for me. Sadly I did not
do any better with our children than my parents had done with me. I
put other things and seeking success in this world ahead of their many
needs. But God has shown me I can begin again.

We now work at letting each one of our children and grandchildren
know how much we care and value them as gifts from God, so that
they will not be discouraged and will want to seek the Lord and His
plan for them in their lives.

HOPE FOR YOU

Do your children know they are loved and are special gifts from God? I
encourage you to be real and honest with them, admitting you are not
perfect, but that God is, and that He loves them very much. God can
mend and change any relationship; let Him handle it through you.

Day 186

DO NOT WEAR YOURSELF OUT TO BE RICH

> Do not overwork to be rich; Because of your own understanding, cease!
>
> —Prov. 23:4 NKJV

Solomon was considered the richest man who ever lived. His wealth was vast, and he knew it was easy to lose it as well. He knew where his riches came from. He wanted us to know that life is not about working to get a lot of wealth here, but about what it takes to have the treasure that can never be lost.

I can relate to this message so well. I was a "workaholic," and I viewed work and wealth as my security. That brought on a lifestyle where fear and worry were constant in my life and I was driven to keep working.

God has shown me that money is to be used to give, save, and spend—in that order. God always shows us the right way to use our resources, and then gives us the choice to follow it or not. I have learned this is His plan for us, and it is so much easier than the merry-go-round I used to be on.

HOPE FOR YOU

Are you in fear and panic because of overworking to make money? This is not what God has in mind for you. Seek His help now, and see His plan for you. You can enjoy the joy, peace, and contentment He has waiting for you.

Day 187

DO NOT GET DISCOURAGED BY WHAT YOU ARE CALLED TO DO

Therefore, since we do hold and engage in this ministry by the mercy of God [granting us favor, benefits, opportunities, and especially salvation], we do not get discouraged (spiritless and despondent with fear) or become faint with weariness and exhaustion.

—2 Cor. 4:1 AMP

Paul urged the people at Corinth that the cause of Christ is too great a ministry to become discouraged or to fear the attacks they may face. Whatever calling God has placed on us, have we settled for less than what God has for us? Are we willing to make a move to change the situation or make the most of the opportunity He has given us?

It is said of U.S. workers; that 59 percent are unhappy with where they are working. The biggest reason given for that dissatisfaction is the pay range in the age group of 35–44. Is this a shock to us—to be in the prime time of your calling and to be discouraged and unhappy because we feel we are not getting paid enough?

I know I stayed in a profession that was not the one God had for me. I missed out on a family lifestyle and becoming the person God wanted me to be. Why did I continue to do it? It was my selfish pride, and the money was great. The good news is, God can still work it out. He has given me a new vision and the ability to enjoy the work He has for me at this time of my life, and I trust and depend on Him to provide for all my needs.

HOPE FOR YOU

Are you doing the work God has prepared for you to do? Do you enjoy it regardless of the income? God has a plan. Seek Him and see what He has for you.

Day 188

DO NOT BE DISCOURAGED

The Lord Himself goes before you and will be with you; He will never leave you nor forsake you. Do not be afraid; do not be discouraged.

—Deut. 31:8

Moses knew he was about to die and he wanted to make sure that his successor, Joshua, understood that God would be with him. Moses wanted to assure Joshua and all the people not to be discouraged because God would never leave them.

What a great promise, and what a wonderful gift to give to those you care about and love the most. I am so thankful that I know God is faithful. He has never left me. Even when I want to get discouraged, I know it is not the choice God has for me.

I have not always listened to God or made the right choices in life, but the good news is, I am listening now, and that is what counts when you face life head on and want to make a difference, God's way.

Life is not to be lived in the past or the future, but right now. God has everything ready for you to be able to face today. He has taken care of yesterday, and He is ready to face your tomorrows with you.

HOPE FOR YOU

Can you encourage someone today that God is faithful and is there for them? Are you facing great challenges, and could you become discouraged in them? God says, do not fear and do not be discouraged.

Day 189

DO NOT LOSE HEART, EVEN THOUGH WE ARE DYING DAILY

> Therefore we do not become discouraged (utterly spiritless, exhausted, and wearied out through fear). Though our outer man is [progressively] decaying and wasting away, yet our inner self if being [progressively] renewed day after day.
>
> —2 Cor. 4:16 AMP

Paul faced many trials and sufferings, but he knew one day he would receive the rest and rewards God had for him. Because of that truth, he encouraged all of us not to quit, but to keep going no matter the cost.

I have come to learn that weakness is the key to experiencing God's greatest gifts to us, the renewing of our mind, and the strength to go on. I am a very weak person even though I pretended for many years to be the strongest. I worked at being strong in my own strength, and then one day there was no strength left.

Once I faced my true self and was able to admit to God that I needed Him and wanted Him to change me; He was able to begin a new work in me that allows me to overcome the fear and prison of the past, and help others do the same—His way.

HOPE FOR YOU

Are you living a defeated life? Do you want to quit? God has a plan, and He wants to show you how to begin again and carry on to the end. "Don't forsake your eternal reward because of the intensity of today's pain" (Author unknown).

Day 190

DO NOT BE DISCOURAGED

Then the Lord said to Joshua, "Do not be afraid; do not be discouraged. Take the whole army with you and go up and attack Ai."

—Josh. 8:1

Joshua and the people were just recovering from some trouble within their own nation. Joshua knew that he had faced this same battle before and lost. This time he wanted to win, and the Lord assured him that he would.

The Lord wanted Joshua, his people, and us to know we do not have to fear and be discouraged about anything we are facing. God is true and keeps His promises when we obey the conditions He places on us.

I have not always realized that God wanted to be in on my every moment. I have let the fear of discouragement come over me so that I did not want to obey and go on with Him on this life journey. I am thankful that I did not let fear paralyze me forever, as some have done, and I can walk right through anything daily with the Lord.

HOPE FOR YOU

Are you living in your fear and unable to move past the problem? God wants you to know that He is close and that you no longer have to live independent of Him. Come to God now and be encouraged.

Day 191

DO NOT LOSE HEART

Say to him, "Be careful, keep calm and don't be afraid. Do not lose heart because of these two smoldering stubs of firewood—because of the fierce anger of Rezin and Aram and of the son of Remaliah."

—Isa. 7:4

Isaiah was not predicting the best future for Israel. He wanted them to know not to be afraid or lose heart. God was with them, and they would be able to handle whatever they were facing.

I have faced many things in my life, and I must admit I didn't see the big picture. I lost heart and I was afraid. But instead of bringing it to God, I chose to run away from those situations. I have caused pain to others by losing heart and giving up.

God still has a plan, and now instead of running from Him and my problems, I run to Him first and let Him handle my problems. His promises are true, and He shows up to help me every time.

HOPE FOR YOU

Has life handed you a turn you don't want to make? Have you lost your hope and let fear overtake you? God has so much waiting for you. Come and let Him show you now. Don't run.

Day 192

DO NOT BE TROUBLED

And you will hear of wars and rumors of wars; see that you are not frightened or troubled, for this must take place, but the end is not yet.

—Matt. 24:6 AMP

Jesus wanted to make sure that we trusted Him and did not let signs try to predict what would be coming in the future. We know He is coming back, but until then we are not to be frightened or troubled about it or anything else. Jesus told the Jews as a nation that they would be hated for believing in Him, and that many will choose to turn away from Him.

Do you live in the "chicken little" theory of fear when things happen all around you? Do you think the sky is falling and the world is coming to an end? In the past I would think my world was coming to an end just because some event happened in the world, and was reported by non-believers.

I let that cloud my decisions on how to handle the news. I lived that way for many years until I realized what Christ had done for me. He died so that I would not be fearful or troubled. All I have to do is keep my mind and heart focused on Him and not the world, and He will take care of me.

HOPE FOR YOU

Where is your focus today? Are you worried and upset about wars, rumors, finances, and all the many issues we all are facing? Do not be troubled; God is still in control, and He will show you His peace to endure it all.

Day 193

DO NOT BE AFRAID OF THEM

Then I said to you, "Do not be terrified; do not be afraid of them."

—Deut. 1:29

M oses was reliving the story of when God's people had reached the Promised Land and they had sent twelve spies to go in first, and what they had found. Then he reminded them that even though they were not to fear, they had done so. They had rebelled against God. They were not allowed to go into the Promised Land.

This is a reminder to us that when we let our fears control us, we are rebelling and sinning against God and the result will be that we will miss out on the blessings God has for us.

I admit I did not consider that I was living a life of sin when living in my fears and letting them, instead of God, control me. I justified them and I led others with me on that journey too. But God showed me the result of my sin, and now I live in the freedom and joy Jesus had for me all along.

HOPE FOR YOU

Do you consider being fearful, worried, doubting, dreading, and discouraged as sin? I realize now, anything that is living independently of God is sin in His eyes. I am glad He is narrow and demands my obedience. His ways are the only ones I want to choose. Be free today and not a prisoner of fear any longer.

Day 194

DO NOT GIVE WAY TO HYSTERICAL FEARS AND ANXIETIES

> It was thus that Sarah obeyed Abraham [following his guidance and acknowledging his headship over her by] calling him lord (master, leader, authority) And you are now her true daughters if you do right and let nothing terrify you [not giving way to hysterical fears or letting anxieties unnerve you].
>
> —1 Pet. 3:6 AMP

Peter was helping both women and men in a marriage setting learn how to live together as godly people. He was married, so I am sure God had shown him and his wife how to live as godly disciples of Jesus.

Today, it seems we have lost sight of the importance of commitment and putting the Lord first in our relationships. There is little difference in the divorce rate between non-Christians and Christians in America.

I have contributed to that divorce statistic. I no longer want to be a part of it. It is a choice, and Sarah, the wife of Abraham, showed us how we can avoid it. Here is the truth of how we as women are to live with our husbands, and Peter's message to husbands as well.

HOPE FOR YOU

Ladies, do your fears bring you to the point of being hysterical and anxious with your husband? Fellows, how do you handle it when she gets to this point? Face this today and come together God's way.

Day 195

PEACE IN YOUR HEART, NOT FEAR

Peace I leave with you; My [own] peace I now give and bequeath to you. Not as the world gives do I give to you. Do not let your hearts be troubled, neither let them be afraid [Stop allowing yourselves to be agitated and disturbed; and do not permit yourselves to be fearful and intimidated and cowardly and unsettled.]

—John 14:27 AMP

J esus is telling us not to allow ourselves to be without His peace in our lives. When we fear and doubt and have a troubled heart, we are not allowing the Holy Spirit to be in control.

We can all seek peace, but true peace only comes from the Lord. By our relationship with Him, we can see the difference in His peace and the peace this world can offer us.

We have a daily choice to depend on Him instead of ourselves and the world. The Holy Spirit is here to help us make the right choice. I can still remember seeking peace and not finding it until I fully committed and trusted Jesus for it all. We cannot find peace anywhere or in anyone else.

HOPE FOR YOU

Do you have God's peace, or are you still seeking it from the world and others? God is the only way to true peace, and it is a gift for you to choose. Choose Him and see the plan He has for you.

Day 196

DO NOT BE TROUBLED

And who is he who will harm you if you become followers of what is good? But even if you should suffer for righteousness' sake, you are blessed. And do not be afraid of their threats, nor be troubled.

—1 Pet. 3:13–14 NKJV

Peter is sharing with us that we do not have to be troubled about what others may say of us for being followers of Jesus Christ. Even if we have to suffer, we are still honored to be among His chosen.

I have spent many years living in fear and being troubled by what others thought of me, both as a follower of Jesus and as a person. The freedom from living that way lies in having a clear belief of my identity in Christ, so that I can trust Him to handle anything that may come before me, and not be upset or fearful of it.

HOPE FOR YOU

Do you know who you are in Jesus Christ? Is He worth going through anything you face as a blessing, not a curse? True fellowship is allowing God to be in charge of all of our thoughts and emotions so that fear has no place to live.

Day 197

DO NOT FEAR DISGRACE, YOU WILL NOT BE HUMILIATED

> Do not be afraid; you will not suffer shame. Do not fear disgrace, you will not be humiliated. You will forget the shame of your youth and remember no more the reproach of your widowhood.
>
> —Isa. 54:4

Isaiah cared so much for the people; he wanted them to know God still loved them even though they had disobeyed Him. He wanted them to know God forgave them, and the future will overcome the past.

Do you know your future can be so great it will overshadow your past failures? It has taken me a long time to take God at His Word on this topic. I knew God had forgiven me, but I still lived in the guilt and self-condemnation of it all.

But God's grace is so amazing. He will continue to give us new beginnings and keep us on His path to total dependence and trust in Him alone. That is the only way to truly live now and forever.

HOPE FOR YOU

Are you living in your disgrace or God's grace? Be free today to live as God says who you are and can be. Do not let the past trap you into not forgiving yourself, and receiving the freedom from all the guilt and self condemnation of it.

Day 198

DO NOT BE DEPRESSED

Then [Ezra] told them, "Go your way, eat the fat, drink the sweet drink, and send portions to him for whom nothing is prepared; for this day is holy to our Lord. And be not grieved and depressed, for the joy of the Lord is your strength and stronghold."

—Neh. 8:10 AMP

Nehemiah was not the official religious leader of the Jewish people at the time. Ezra was. Ezra told the people about their sin and they were very upset. They wept and wanted to go into mourning. They became very depressed about the entire mess. Ezra told them not to do that. Ezra, along with Nehemiah, assured them this was a new day. They were to rejoice and enjoy the food provided and send some to those who did not have anything.

Isn't this just like our God? He wants us to know He forgives and forgets and we are to begin a new day in His joy and strength. I have learned this life is not about what I do or don't do, but who I am in Jesus, and the relationship He wants from and for me. It is truly all about Him.

HOPE FOR YOU

Is it all about God in your life, or are you living in depression and the fear of your life? Have you lost His joy and given up on His strength and power in your life? Just as it was for the Jewish people, today is a new day for you. Take the time to celebrate and give the gift to someone else.

Day 199

HAVE NO FEAR, THE LORD IS YOUR CONFIDENCE

Have no fear of sudden disaster or the ruin that overtakes the wicked, for the Lord will be your confidence and will keep your foot from being snared.

—Prov. 3:25–26

In the world where we live, just as Solomon experienced many generations ago, we see many sudden disasters. We see major companies fall. We see people losing their jobs. Men die needlessly. The weather seems out of control. Many things are happening and we just can't seem to be able to understand or explain them.

Do you let all these fears scare and frighten you? Are you struggling between living in what you see, hear, and know, and living confidently in the Lord? Do you believe and share with others that He is in control and will keep all believers safe?

I can lose my confidence in the Lord when I listen, see, and hear too much of the bad that is going on around me. I can forget to focus on the good He wants me to experience, because the good news is very seldom presented to me.

HOPE FOR YOU

Now is the time we let the media know we are people who do not thrive on horror, violence, and the evil of the world. We can choose not to listen or pay attention to the news reporters' misguided reporting. Then we can choose to honor the Lord in our home, families, and relationships. We do not have to be like the world, and God will show us how to be different.

Day 200

DO NOT FEAR THEM

> Only do not rebel against the Lord; and do not fear the people of the land, for they will be our prey. Their protection has been removed from them, and the Lord is with us; do not fear them.
>
> —Num. 14:9 NASB

Moses was doing his best to urge the people to go on into the Promised Land God had for them. But their fear was greater than their trust in God or in Moses as their leader.

Are we any different today thousands of years later? I fulfilled the same plan and direction and chose fear instead of loving the one true God who had everything under control for me. But God, even when I didn't deserve it, made a way for me to see once again who He is and who I am in Him.

The normal opposite of fear should be faith in the one true living God. The truth is, love is the opposite of fear, and once we see that and begin to love and care for our God, He will lead us back into the places He had for us all along.

HOPE FOR YOU

How is your love relationship with God going? He is waiting for you to make Him first and see the plan He has for you as you walk daily with Him.

Day 201

DO NOT BE SILENT

> One night the Lord spoke to Paul in a vision: "Do not be afraid, keep on speaking, do not be silent."
>
> —Acts 18:9

The Lord came to Paul in a dream, knowing his fear, to tell him not to be silent. How many times, living in fear, do we become silent? When we are silent, we have let our fear overpower us and paralyze us from the very things God has for us to say and do.

I can see in my life that when I have let my fears overwhelm and disable me from functioning in my normal ways, I become silent.

Paul could have kept silent, and we would probably have agreed with his choice. He was in a very evil place, and he did not see what good he could be to these evil people. But God knew the plan, and showed him he was to keep speaking and that he was not alone as there were other believers around him. He obeyed and while there, a church was established, and he wrote more letters for all of us to hear too.

HOPE FOR YOU

Are you silent for the Lord because your fear has overpowered you? Go find those who will encourage you and help you once again to get on the path that God has for you. Paul ended up finding other believers in this wicked place, and started a church. Do not live in silence; others need to hear what God is doing in your life.

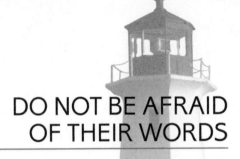

Day 202

DO NOT BE AFRAID
OF THEIR WORDS

And you, son of man, do not be afraid of them or their words. Do not be afraid, though briers and thorns are all around you and you live among scorpions. Do not be afraid of what they say or terrified by them, though they are a rebellious house.

—Ezek. 2:6

God had given Ezekiel the responsibility of speaking with ungrateful and unkind people. Do you know any of them? God prepared Ezekiel by telling him not to be afraid of their words.

We have all heard this old English proverb of "sticks and stones may break my bones, but words will never hurt me." But it doesn't keep us from fearing other people's words, does it?

I used to get offended when kids would call me names for being fat or make fun of me because I did not have a father in my home. Those words can stick if we allow them to be forever in our memory.

God told Ezekiel many times in this situation in his life not to fear speaking or living around abusive and unkind people. I have learned these people are all around me and I cannot avoid them. How I prepare to face them God's way is the key.

HOPE FOR YOU

Are you living around people who hurt and abuse you? God has a way for you to handle this situation. Ask Him, and let Him take you through the hard times to victory.

DO NOT BE DISCOURAGED

See, the Lord your God has given you the land. Go up and take possession of it as the Lord, the God of your fathers, told you. Do not be afraid; do not be discouraged.

—Deut. 1:21

M oses was telling the people again how they had let fear and discouragement overcome them so that when they had the opportunity to go into the land that God had for them, they did not go.

This is a good reminder of the many times when God has prepared things for me, and because of my fear I chose not to follow through on His plans. I could have chosen to let those bad choices control me for the rest of my life. But God had another plan for me. He let me see that I do not have to let my fears and bad choices of the past become a way of guilt for me to live in for the rest of my days.

But just as Moses knew God was still with them, and eventually led those who believed into the land He had for them, God will do the same for us today. He is a God of forgiveness, and the one who loved us so much that He was willing to give us His Son, Jesus, to die, so that we could live forever.

HOPE FOR YOU

Are you living in the failures of your past? Do you fear the future? Are your past sins still controlling your life? Jesus has His peace and a new beginning waiting for you. Step out of your fear and into His plan of peace for you.

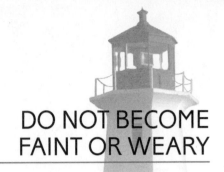

Day 204

DO NOT BECOME FAINT OR WEARY

Therefore, since we do hold and engage in this ministry by the mercy of God [granting] us favor, benefits, opportunities, and especially salvation, we do not get discouraged spiritless and despondent with fear, or become faint with weariness and exhaustion.

—2 Cor. 4:1 AMP

Paul was encouraging the people at Corinth not to become tired and overworked because of what God had called them to be and do.

How hard in today's world is it to avoid being overworked and over-tired? I know now that without God, I cannot overcome it. I have fallen into the trap (and can still go there) of feeling I have to work to please God and that He has to help me do it. I have been on the Christian "merry-go-round" of guilt and self-condemnation and feeling I having to do more and more or else I am not a good Christian.

I have learned now that God's grace is a free gift and that my works have nothing to do with it. I am so thankful it is all about the work of Jesus first, and then He will direct me into what He has for me to be and do.

HOPE FOR YOU

God's plan of priorities and rest is for all of us. I have learned God's order is Himself first (not doing for Him, but being with Him), then our families, (with our husband coming before the children or relatives and friends), and then comes the work He has called us to do. When we get out of that order, the "merry-go-round" is activated. You will never be able to get off of it until you choose to do so. God wants to show you His plan of living; are you willing to seek Him and believe and receive it?

Day 205

DO NOT BE DISCOURAGED

> Joshua said to them, "Do not be afraid; do not be discouraged. Be strong and courageous. This is what the Lord will do to all the enemies you are going to fight."
>
> —Josh. 10:25

Joshua encouraged his people to face what they had to, knowing God had provided for them in the past and He would continue to do so in the future.

It is hard to keep from being discouraged when it seems that as hard as we live and work, we still feel there must be something more than this. I have been there many times, and have let the spirit of discouragement overwhelm me into giving up and quitting.

I know there is so much more than we can ever begin to understand about how God works in our lives. And because of that, I know He has the way out of living a fearful, discouraging life for each of us.

There is something more, and I know how to find it and share it with you. It is not a secret. It is not magical. It is the absolute truth of the living God, and it is available for all who will believe and trust in Him and in His Word to us.

HOPE FOR YOU

Are you one who is living a life of fear and discouragement thinking that this is all there is? Choose God's way and let His Word be the truth for you to live and be. God is personal and real and available right now. He does not give us feelings of fear and hopelessness; but those of encouragement and true joy, peace, and contentment. Let Him show you now.

Day 206

BEING ANXIOUS WILL NOT ADD TO YOUR LIFE

And who of you by worrying and being anxious can add one
unit of measure (cubit) to his stature or to his span of life?
—Matt. 6:27 AMP

Jesus told us clearly that worrying and being anxious would not add anything to our lives—either to the length or the value of it.

When your fear leads you to be a worrier and an anxiety-driven person, you are setting yourself up for problems that are far worse than the ones you allowed to take control in the first place. God designed our bodies so uniquely that they react when we do not use them according to His plan for them. It shows up in our physical health, it consumes our thoughts, it cuts down on our ability to work, and it has a negative impact on the way we treat and react to others. It eventually leads to reducing our ability to trust God.

I did not even stop to think what I was doing to God, myself, or others, when I allowed myself to be so anxious and worry ridden. I let my fear take control rather than God. I even blocked the way for God to help me. But God can redeem those times and use them for His glory.

HOPE FOR YOU

Is being anxious better than trusting God? How can you stop? Confront it now that you are anxious, and that you are worry ridden. Ask God to forgive you for not trusting Him to take care of you. Then daily seek Him, and He will show you how to live without fear, anxiety, or worry.

Day 207

DO NOT BE UPSET

"Martha, Martha," the Lord answered, "you are worried and upset about many things, but only one thing is needed. Mary has chosen what is better, and it will not be taken away from her."

—Luke 10:41–42

Jesus was a personal friend to these two sisters, Martha and Mary, and their brother Lazarus. Later he raised Lazarus from the dead. But in conversation with Martha on this visit to their home, He made her face the person she had become. He showed her what He wanted her life to be.

I understand becoming fearful to the point of worrying and then ending up totally "bent out of shape." Ever been there? I can relate to Martha easily. It is not who I want to be, but my personality can lean toward her view of thinking. It has taken me many years to let the Lord confront me on these same issues, and let Him change me into who He wants me to be, just as He did Martha.

HOPE FOR YOU

In the same situation would you react as Martha did? Is that who God wants you to be? Jesus showed her that getting involved with the details and ignoring the guests was not His plan for her or for us either. He showed her there is a right time to work for Him, and also a right time to be with Him. She was out of God's balance as we can so easily be as well. Are you living in God's balance?

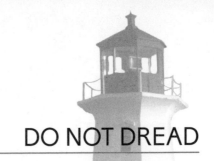

Day 208

DO NOT DREAD

I will give you peace in the land; you shall lie down and none shall fill you with dread or make you afraid; and I will clear ferocious (wild) beasts out of the land, and no sword shall go through your land.

—Lev. 26:6 AMP

Moses shared God's promise for living unafraid and without dread. Dread is another word for fear. We fear others and what they can do to us.

I have found God can use our dread for His glory and our good. I was fearful of my Mom. When I could, I left her and stayed far away for 26 years. During those years I dreaded even thinking of her. When she would call, it took all I could do not to retaliate and be ugly to her as she was to me. I had nightmares of her, and I dreaded the thought I might grow to be like her.

Then one day God showed me that if I was ever going to have the relationship He wanted me to have with her, I had to face my fear and dread of her. I first faced her on the telephone and then in person. I found her to be a woman working on her own fears to become what God wanted her to be. Before she died I got to pray with her for the very first time in our lives. It was a precious moment and it erased all the fear, anger, and dread I ever had of her. I know she is in heaven and I will see her again. I no longer dread looking or acting like her.

HOPE FOR YOU

Are you living in dread and fear of someone or something in your life? I encourage you to confront it now and receive the peace of God and His leading as to how to erase it.

Day 209

DO NOT BE AFRAID OF SUDDEN TERROR AND PANIC

Be not afraid of sudden terror and panic, nor of the stormy blast or the storm and ruin of the wicked when it comes [for you will be guiltless].

—Prov. 3:25 AMP

Solomon was telling us that when we trust in the Lord and believe what He said, we are not to fear any sudden terror or panic of anything we may face.

Being from Oklahoma, I cannot begin to tell you of the fears I have had when faced with terrible storms and the fear of upcoming ones. Did I ever have to go through one full scale? No, but they have certainly been all around me, and as quickly as they came, they were gone.

I am thankful that I did not let those fears consume me because I still live in an area that can see major storms, but I am not afraid. Facing that fear of weather has also shown me that I can help others confront their fear of it and learn to prepare and do all they can and then let God take care of the rest.

HOPE FOR YOU

Are there areas of your life where you experience terror and sudden panic and you know this is not a great way to live? Do you know God does not want you to live in fear? Come and let Him show you how to overcome your terror and panic.

Day 210

DO NOT MAKE OTHERS AFRAID OR DREAD

Do not call conspiracy [or hard, or holy] all that this people will call conspiracy [or hard, or holy]; neither be in fear of what they fear, nor [make others afraid an] in dread.

—Isa. 8:12 AMP

Isaiah did not go along with Judah's national policies. He called the people to commit first to God and then to the king and the government. He knew that this type of government was going to be overthrown.

This is where, as a nation and as a people, we are today. We are living in what others fear, and by doing so we pass that fear and dread to others. We are not committing to God first. We are not letting Him control how we think and act.

For many years I have given in to the control and fear of others rather than committing first to God. I know how that looks and feels. It is not as God intends. We have nothing to fear and dread when we place our faith and trust in Him alone. Then we can be the people He wants us to be.

HOPE FOR YOU

Are you faithful to God? Have you placed your trust and commitment in Him first—or in this world? These are very important questions that need an answer before you can learn to live without fear and dread in your life. God is willing to show you how to live in the answers He has for you.

Day 211

SERVE WITHOUT FEAR

> The oath He swore to our father Abraham; to rescue us from the hand of our enemies, and to enable us to serve Him without fear in holiness, and righteousness before Him all our days.
>
> —Luke 1:73–75

These are the first words Zechariah spoke after months of not being able to speak. In his words he told the story of the coming of Jesus for whom his son John was to prepare the way. He also gave us the purpose and plan for our lives that Jesus would fulfill.

God does not promise us an easy life when we chose to trust, obey, believe, and follow Him. But He does promise that we can know how to live without fear when we put Him first and keep Him in the center of our lives. Then nothing can interrupt His plan for us.

I have had many "centers" in my life that I have allowed to take God's rightful place. Some of them are: food, career, family, friends, church, money, and pleasure. These are all good things in their proper place. But they cannot replace God at the center of your very inner being and life.

HOPE FOR YOU

Rick Warren says in *The Purpose Driven Life*, "None of these things are strong enough to hold you together when life starts breaking apart. You need an unshakable center." Do you have the unshakable center of God in your life?

Day 212

DO NOT LET YOUR HEART
BE TROUBLED

> Do not let your hearts be troubled. Trust in God; trust also in Me.
>
> —John 14:1

J esus was facing death at the time He was telling His disciples not to be distressed or fearful. When they should have been comforting Him for what He was going to do for all of them, He was telling them all they would ever need to overcome anything they might face.

Believing, trusting, and obeying God are the keys to overcoming anything. Are there any other ways? This world would tell you so, and I have tried many of them. But I am certain now, and can forever proclaim, there is no other way but God, and we must come through His Son, Jesus, to receive it all.

The world would have us believe there are many ways to our God of choice. For many years I bought into that assumption. Sounds nice and inoffensive doesn't it? But the truth is, it is a lie. Jesus is the only One who paid the price for us and the only Way to reach God the Father and live forever in Heaven. Jesus knew we would face having to confront these lies, and He wanted us not to let our hearts become fearful about it.

HOPE FOR YOU

Is your faith founded and grounded in the truth of Jesus Christ? I skimmed over that belief for many years. I knew it, but telling someone else sounded narrow and I would leave myself open to fear and dread. But once I asked God to show me what I really believed and why, all the fear and dread faded away.

Day 213

DO YOU DOUBT, AND ARE YOU TROUBLED?

Why are you troubled, and why do doubts rise in your mind?

—Luke 24:38

Jesus was asking His disciples, once He had risen from the grave as He had promised, why they were troubled and doubtful. He had prepared them for His resurrection. He wanted them to know He saw their fears and doubt but that He was the truth that would take away all their concerns.

Have you ever had doubts and fears about your belief in Jesus? I have, and for many years I was not willing to be honest to seek Him to find out why. I knew and believed enough in Him to get me into heaven; but not enough to let Him live each and every day through me until that happened. I realized I did not know my true identity in Christ and that was why the fears, worries, doubts, discouragement, and depression could overtake me so easily. I let them have complete control over me instead of the Lord.

Once I came to the knowledge of who Jesus is personally to me, and established that daily relationship with Him, fear and doubt had no place in my life.

HOPE FOR YOU

What does Jesus mean to you? Is He *in* your life or *is* He your life? There is a difference and by knowing for sure comes the freedom from fear and doubt.

Day 214

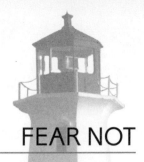

FEAR NOT

And shall say to them, Hear, O Israel, you draw near this day to battle against your enemies. Let not your [minds and] heart faint; fear not, and do not tremble or be terrified [and in dread] because of them.

—Deut. 20:3 AMP

M oses knew there would be many tough battles to face as the leader of his people. But he knew God was the answer and that none of them were to fear. He shared and lived this way.

This is a good reminder to us to not fear, whether we are in military battles or the everyday battles of life we all face. How closely we let God come to handle these fears is our choice.

I used to think that I was doing a pretty good job of handling my fears because on the outside I felt confident. But underneath I was as fragile and at war with myself as many of you are experiencing right now. I felt as if God had enough on His hands without me bringing my little insecurities to Him.

How ungrateful and unthankful I was for what He had done for me. I now realize He wants all of me so that I can trust and depend on Him and not in myself. Then, whatever wars and fears may come, He will take care of them. And then, by allowing Him to do so, I can help others see He wants to do the same for them. There is nothing that is too little for Him to handle for us.

HOPE FOR YOU

Is it God you trust and depend on for everything, or is it yourself and others? Can you see that He wants you to come and learn to run to Him first with everything?

Day 215

DO NOT BE AFRAID OF EVIL PLOTS OR SLANDER

You shall not be afraid of the terror of the night, nor of the arrow [the evil plots and slanders of the wicked] that flies by day.

—Ps. 91:5 AMP

The author of this psalm is not known, but the message is very clear concerning not being afraid of what we are facing today. How many times in the news do we hear about evil threats, plots, and unkind words? But God has said we are to not be afraid or let these messages and people control how we live.

Many times I have allowed myself to be controlled by what was happening in the world or what was predicted to happen or what people said concerning me. This led to focusing on them more than on my relationship to God. How I must have hurt God. I have come to know that He is a forgiving God. He knows and sees my heart and my love for Him, and He allows me once again to establish that faith and trust in Him alone.

HOPE FOR YOU

Are you caught up in the world and what others think of you? I urge you to look at the big picture. Come to God and let Him know how you feel. He alone wants to help you face this fear and live differently in this world.

Day 216

DO NOT LOSE HEART AND GIVE UP

> Also [Jesus] told them a parable to the effect that they ought
> always to pray and not to turn coward (faint, lose heart, and
> give up).
>
> —Luke 18:1 AMP

The story Jesus shared was about a widow who went to a judge for protection from those who opposed her. This judge was not a believer in God or a respecter of persons; but because she kept bothering him and was wearing on his patience, he agreed to help her.

Jesus said this is not the way God treats us as believers. He assures us we are heard and that help is on the way when we have faith enough to wait for it and not try to figure it out. He urged us to not give in to our fear, but to let faith, through prayer, be in charge.

God has always been faithful to me, but I have not always been faithful to Him. I have let other things and people come first. Then when I got caught up in the fear of it all, I expected Him to answer when I prayed. I have learned that He still loves and cares for me even in those times. He showed me I could surrender and come back and put Him again in first place in my life. Now that is the only place I want Him to be. I think of Him continually, and my prayers are heard and answered in His timing and in His will.

HOPE FOR YOU

What is in control of your life today? Is it faith in God, or is it giving in to fear and doubt? Have you given up on God and feel He will not answer your prayers? Don't give up on God; He has not given up on you.

DO NOT BE DISCOURAGED

Have I not commanded you? Be strong and courageous. Do not be terrified; do not be discouraged, for the Lord your God will be with you wherever you go.

—Josh. 1:9

God was telling Joshua what life in Him would be like and what he needed to do to be able to face it well. His first command to be followed was to be strong and courageous.

Then God said not to be terrified of what would come. Just as then, there are lots of evil and terrible things going on; but we are not to let them keep us from following the Lord. God knew Joshua would be tempted to get discouraged and that could lead to letting fear be in control. How often do we let things discourage us from living as God intends? How often do we miss what He has for us?

I have let the fear of discouragement come into my life so many times that it became the way I normally reacted to any situation. What a sad way to live. I knew God had a better way, and once I chose to allow Him to change me into a courageous and encouraging person, life changed for me. Can I say I never get discouraged? No! But I can say I refuse to allow it to become my normal way of thinking.

HOPE FOR YOU

Are you living with discouragement as your friend instead of God? Today is the time to change that. How can that happen? You can allow God to reign once again as King, and by reading His Word written for you.

• 217 •

Day 218

DO NOT BE DISMAYED

So do not fear, for I am with you; do not be dismayed, for I am your God. I will strengthen you and help you; I will uphold you with my righteous right hand.

—Isa. 41:10

Isaiah assured the people that even though they had disobeyed God and were in captivity, God was still with them. They were His chosen people and God was with them.

Many times I have lost sight of the fact that as a believer, even when I have disobeyed, I am still His chosen and that He will keep me from being frightened by what is going on around me and in my life.

When that happens, I know I must allow God to direct my thoughts. I do not have to give in to feeling dismayed and frightened, even when I have made bad choices that affected many lives.

HOPE FOR YOU

Are you in a situation where you are feeling disappointed and overwhelmed by paralyzing fear and anxiety? Come to Jesus, He values you and wants to show you the way through and out of it.

Day 219

"DON'T BE AFRAID," HE SAID

When the disciples heard this, they fell facedown to the ground, terrified. But Jesus came and touched them. "Get up," He said. "Don't Be Afraid." When they looked up, they saw no one except Jesus.

—Matt. 17:6–8

Before his death, Jesus took three of His disciples, Peter, James, and John, with Him to the mountain top. He wanted to show them who He really was—God's own Son.

After seeing everything Jesus had to show them, they were terrified. Jesus, in His compassionate nature, touched them and told them not to be afraid. He knew what they would face in their journey of following Him; and wanted them to know they were not alone and had nothing to fear.

I have forgotten this message many times in my own journey of life. I have been afraid of the smallest things because I forgot to remember Christ's promise to all who believe. The more I spend time with Him, reading and rereading His Word, I find the stressful times of fear are less and less. I also know how to handle them better, as God promised.

HOPE FOR YOU

Have you forgotten the message of Jesus? Do you fear? You can know that Christ came, lived, died, and rose again so that we no longer have to be prisoners of our fears; we are to trust Him with them.

Day 220

YOU SHALL NOT FEAR OTHER GODS

> With whom the Lord had made a covenant and commanded them, "You shall not fear other gods or bow yourselves to them or serve them or sacrifice to them."
>
> —2 Kgs. 17:35 AMP

The writer of Second Kings is not known, but it probably was Jeremiah. The Israelites, in their fear of the many trials and troubles, often became involved in choosing to worship and serve other gods rather than the one true God who created them and loved them. They did this for the same reasons we do.

Here they are commanded not to let fear drive them into involvement with any other gods other than the true GOD Himself. Sound impossible? Nothing with God is impossible.

I once thought the measure of my success both to the world and to God was how much I earned, how hard I worked, and how many awards I received. The ultimate goals I set for myself were to have a Gold American Express card and a Mercedes convertible. I got most of my list—except for the convertible. But I realized I did not even know the God I thought I was pleasing. I was in fear because I was not sure He would forgive and forget my evil ways. The good news is, God understands and is willing to show us how to begin life with Him again, no matter what we have done.

HOPE FOR YOU

Are you living in the world's measure of success or God's? You can know for sure. Come, let Him show you how your fear and anxiety can be replaced by joy and peace.

Day 221

GIVE HIM YOUR ANXIETY, WORRIES, AND CARES, ONCE AND FOR ALL

Cast all your anxiety on Him because He cares for you.
—1 Pet. 5:7

We know that living independent of our one true God is sin. Peter assured the people that no matter what they feared, God cared for them. There were to give their fears to God to handle. That's a wonderful offer. So why do we choose to live fearful lives if God says give them to Him?

Is it possible we don't trust and believe that God really cares for us? Or is it we do not want to admit our need of Him? Also we don't want to be seen as having weaknesses, do we?

I have learned that giving Him all the things that would rob me of His joy, peace, and contentment is exactly the message of His telling me to "fear not." I do not have to fear because He is ready and able to handle everything I give to Him.

HOPE FOR YOU

Are you living in anxiety and fear? Do you believe He cares for you so much that He wants you give it all to Him and be free? That is His message of grace for you. Accept and receive it now.

Day 222

DO NOT BE DISCOURAGED

He will not falter or be discouraged till He establishes justice
on earth. In His law the islands will put their hope.

—Isa. 42:4

Isaiah is showing us a picture of the Lord and how we as believers can follow Him. Just as Christ, who died for us so that we can live, never quit or got tired of what His life's purpose was, we are not to do so either.

I have seen what discouragement can do in the lives of many. It can cause them to surrender the hope God has for them, and also it can influence others to do the same. It will then lead to living a life that is not meaningful without a desire to change.

There have been times when I have let discouragement come into my life to dwell. At those times, my personal relationship with God was at its lowest point. How did I get my life back on track? I didn't. I turned back to God, His Word, and acknowledged that He was the only way. Then He changed me.

HOPE FOR YOU

Are you in a sea of discouragement and sinking fast? There is help waiting for you. Admit you need the Lord of all and receive His love and grace. He will lift you out of the pit and set you on His solid ground.

Day 223

DO NOT BE DISCOURAGED OR AFRAID

"Do not be afraid or discouraged because of the king of Assyria and the vast army with him, for there is a greater power with us than with him."

—2 Chron. 32:7

King Hezekiah was a godly man and this is what he shared with his men before facing Sennacherib. He knew where he personally stood with God so he could confidently tell them not to be afraid or discouraged.

I know what it is to live with fear and have been easily discouraged in my lifetime. In facing my battles of life, I often chose to run rather than confront them. I lived in my own confidence instead of trusting and depending totally on God. But God never left or gave up on me. He knew at some point what would occur to turn me back to Him. My family and friends now see and receive the benefits of the change God has made in me. I am ready to help you know that He can make a change in your life too.

HOPE FOR YOU

Are you running from God or to Him? Have your battles made you discouraged and afraid? God is waiting right now for you to admit your need. Ask Him for His help. There is nowhere else to go. How long will you keep running?

Day 224

HAVE NO FEAR OF HARM

But whoever listens to me will live in safety and be at ease, without fear of harm.

—Prov. 1:33

Solomon wrote and collected many of these proverbs early in his reign. He wanted to share how to live godly lives through the wise thoughts of the Lord.

Are you listening to God today? Are you living in safety or fear? In such times as these we live in, we hear the world news and fear for our safety, don't we? Security the world's way will never be enough to make sure we are out of harm's way. Listening to God and obeying Him is the way to live free of fear no matter what is going on around you. He is your protector and the only one to whom we can listen.

I did not realize for many years that living in my fears was a choice—and a sin. I thought it was the only way of life for me. I just had to do the best I could. I missed the blessings that God had for me, and what Jesus died to give me. But God's forgiveness has given me back a changed life.

HOPE FOR YOU

Are you consumed and living in your fears? God has so much more for you. Trust Him, confront your fears, and God will give you the keys to freedom from them.

Day 225

DO NOT BE TERRIFIED

Hear me, you who know what is right, you people who have my law in your hearts: Do not fear the reproach of men or be terrified by their insults.

—Isa. 51:7

Are you being made fun of because you believe in God? Isaiah assured the people who were doing right and obeying the Lord, not to be terrified at what unbelievers said or thought of them. God will handle the unbelievers. You are to keep on doing what you should.

Today it is easy to give up on what we believe. Events make us uneasy and drive us to the point of being terrified, don't they?

At one time, I wasn't exactly sure what I believed and why. When tests came, I failed. I knew the basics, but I had not spent time with God understanding how other things came into play with those basics. But God knew my heart, and He made Himself available in all kinds of ways until I realized my need of completely becoming His and knowing more of Him. Then I could base my faith on His Word and know the truth. I could also then see the false teachers that are all around us, and help others see them too.

HOPE FOR YOU

Are you living one way in church and around church people and another way in your daily world? Be honest, God sees your heart and life, and wants you to know He still loves you and is waiting for you to come and let Him show you how to really live.

Day 226

DON'T FEAR WHAT THEY FEAR

> Do not call conspiracy everything these people call conspiracy, do not fear what they fear, and do not dread it.
>
> —Isa. 8:12

The Lord spoke to Isaiah, probably about 700 B.C., with this message, and it is valuable today. Isaiah was telling people to commit themselves first to God and then to the King of Judah. Isaiah was viewed as a traitor because he did not support Judah's national policies.

How does God want us to live? First, our minds need to be focused daily on God and the things of God and not on this world. We have a choice as to what we read, hear, and put into our minds. I want to focus on those things that report the goodness of God and not the evil of man.

I have to seek God to give me the balance of what I need to know and what is good for me to know. Too much of what is available can cause me to fear and dread, when I allow it to do so. I want something more God-honoring in the precious time He has given me.

HOPE FOR YOU

Do you fear what others tell you to fear? Have you taken on others' worries? God can show you how to overcome this in your life. Are you in balance with the things God has for you? It is a choice; choose God first.

Day 227

CONSIDER HIM WHEN YOU ARE WEARY AND LOSE HEART

Consider Him who endured such opposition from sinful men, so that you will not grow weary and lose heart.
—Heb. 12:3

We are not sure who penned the book of Hebrews, but the words are as clear to us as they were to the early Christians. We are not to grow weary and lose heart. Rather we are to remember what Christ did for us.

I find my faith weakens the most and fear can creep in when I allow myself to become physically exhausted. I have always been a 24/7 gal. I get up that way. I love life and people and I can fill up my hours very easily.

Then I learned God had more for me than just doing. He wanted balance in my life because He had things He wanted to teach me.

Recently I had a car accident, and it has taken me a long time to recover completely. It required surgery, and it has taken time for me to gain back the energy I once took for granted.

Through this I have learned to ask God—not others—to set the schedule and the pace, and the result is the publication of this book to honor Him and as a help for you in your personal walk.

HOPE FOR YOU

Are you just exhausted emotionally and physically? Have you lost your sense of balance and priorities? God wants to show you His scheduled priorities for you. Stop and listen, it will make all the difference in your life.

Day 228

DO NOT BE TERRIFIED OF THEM

I will make your forehead like the hardest stone, harder than flint. Do not be afraid of them or terrified by them, though they are a rebellious house.

—Ezek. 3:9

Ezekiel was being instructed by God to bring the message God had for these people. God knew Ezekiel would be afraid to the point of being terrified by the people he was sent to serve. He told Ezekiel to go and He would take care of him.

I have moved quite a few times in my life, and I can remember always being afraid and even terrified of the new people who would come into my life. I was not like everyone else. I feared having to begin again making friends and trying to find where I fit in. I didn't have the confidence of Christ to give me the strength I needed to overcome those fears.

Once I let God become a regular part of my life, I knew He would be there with me. I no longer had to let those old fears and thoughts keep coming back. He was ready to take me into the places He had chosen for me, and I was certainly ready to allow Him to do so.

HOPE FOR YOU

Are you in places with people you are terrified of being around? God wants to show you His plan for your being there and how to manage it all. Are you listening? Is God a regular part of your life so that He can show you His plan?

Day 229

DON'T FALTER IN TIMES OF TROUBLE

If you falter in times of trouble, how small is your strength!
—Prov. 24:10

Solomon knew that to be able to stand in the face of life, we must not falter, be afraid, or weak. No matter the trouble or how long it lasts, we must not get discouraged and give in to our doubts and fears. Solomon wrote this early in his reign as king. God gave him the plan, but just like we do, he failed the test.

Do you fall apart when troubles come? It doesn't matter how small or how large they are, when we fail to trust and depend on God's strength, we will end up afraid, discouraged, and we will fail the tests God has for us.

I know that when troubles come to those I care about and love, I must trust and depend on God, then He shows me how I can help them through their struggles. I have a gift of encouragement, and I love being able to share it.

But when those same troubles come to me personally, at times I have just collapsed. I can see God's plan for others, but when it comes my turn, I did not want to walk through those valleys to get to the mountaintop. God showed me that problems are good for me. I need to go through them so He can show me how to go through them His way, and then I can help others do the same.

HOPE FOR YOU

Have you thanked God today for your problems? They are your training for more to come, and also for helping others through theirs too. It is easy to be a Christian when everything is great, but what happens when it is not? Let God show you.

Day 230

NO LONGER BE TERRIFIED
OR LIVE IN PANIC

I will place shepherds over them who will tend them, and they will no longer be afraid or terrified, nor will any be missing.

—Jer. 23:4

The leaders who had gotten the Israelites into the destructive state they were in, were going to be dealt with very harshly. Jeremiah was sent to tell the people that a new leader would come and they did not need to be terrified or panic, but they should believe in him. This was a picture of how Christ would enter their future.

Did the people turn away from their false gods and listen to what Jeremiah was telling them? You can see what has happened to the Jewish people. Are they listening yet? How about our country, are we? Do we have leaders who please God?

I used to think that when I got into heavy, deep meanings in scripture I could just skip over those parts and only focus on what I felt was for me. Some of our church leaders are doing the same thing. They are leading us to a place where we think we want to be instead of teaching us where God wants us to be. I have learned life is not about me. It is all about God and what will bring Him honor and glory.

HOPE FOR YOU

Have you learned yet? As an influence and a leader of others, as we all are, we need to see the big picture. What are we teaching? Is it all about us and our needs and wants, or is it all about God and what He wants? When we learn the difference is how we will overcome our fears.

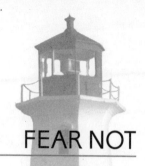

Day 231

FEAR NOT

> Then you will prosper, if you are careful to keep and fulfill the statutes and ordinances with which the Lord charged Moses concerning Israel. Be strong and of good courage; dread not *and* fear not; be not dismayed.]
>
> —1 Chron. 22:13 AMP

David learned from God that he would not be the one to build the temple, but that his son, Solomon would be the chosen one. David then tells his son what he needs to do to be successful and please God.

Isn't it amazing that some of the first things David tells Solomon are to be of good courage, do not dread, fear, or be dismayed? David knew the times would come when Solomon could let fear overtake him. How did David know that? Because he had let fear overwhelm him in his past, and because of it, he now was the advisor to his son and not the one actually involved in the mission to build the temple.

I have some of the very same patterns in my life. God has given me gifts and talents, but because of my fears, I missed out on the blessings He had for me. I let fear rob me of God's success plan for me. But God has been faithful to me just as He was to David. God has given me a new life and the hope to face it without fear getting in the way.

HOPE FOR YOU

Are you missing the blessings and success plan God has for you because of your fears? Now is the beginning of a new life. Be encouraged and fear not.

Day 232

IS YOUR MIND FREE FROM FEAR?

> But the wisdom from above is first of all pure (undefiled); then it is peace-loving, God courteous (considerate, gentle). [It is willing to] yield to reason, full of compassion and good fruits; it is wholehearted and straightforward, impartial and unfeigned (free from doubts, wavering, and insincerity).
>
> —Jas. 3:17 AMP

James, the half brother of Jesus, wrote words of wisdom and joy to the earliest churches. He also shows us how we can turn our fears into joy and how we can live without doubt and in the confidence of the Lord.

How do we get this wisdom from the Lord? Our fears block us from having this peace, joy, and wisdom. When fear comes, do you know you can choose not to go there? James is telling us this is what God has for us.

I know my fear and doubt have prevented me from keeping my mind focused on the Lord and having the peace and joy and contentment of Him in my life. But God is so gracious and caring and has restored me to the fullness of everything He can offer.

HOPE FOR YOU

Do you live in doubt of God and yourself? Do you have a relationship with Him so that you keep your mind focused on Him as you live without doubt and fear?

Day 233

DO NOT BE AFRAID

Do not tremble, do not be afraid. Did I not proclaim this and foretell it long ago? You are my witnesses. Is there any God besides me? No, there is no other Rock; I know not one.

—Isa. 44:8

I saiah assured the people about who God is, and how mighty He is. He would take care of them. Isaiah was sent to tell them not fear or be afraid of what would come. He also shared with them there is only one God; and they were to stay true and faithful to Him.

Can we lose sight of this great promise? God has given us so much and tells us we have nothing to fear. But are we listening?

I can see times when I got caught up in what was going on in and around me. I left God out of the entire picture. God never wants us to leave Him out. But He also will take us back when we desire to restore that relationship with all our heart.

HOPE FOR YOU

Have you left God out of your life? You may go to church or you may do good things, but does He have your heart? Do you let fear or God drive you? God is ready to help you face your fears His way.

Day 234

ARE YOU FREE FROM ALL ANXIETY?

> My desire is to have you free from all anxiety and distressing care. The unmarried man is anxious about the things of the Lord—how he may please the Lord; But the married man is anxious about worldly matters—how he may please his wife.
>
> —1 Cor. 7:32 AMP

Paul is telling the people to be content whether married or not, and not to let anxiety and cares rule them. God does not want us to have anxiety and cares about anything. It gets in the way of the plan He has for us. Paul shared his advice that, whether single or married, we each have a role to fulfill.

I have been both single and married, and in looking at my relationships, I can see where I let anxiety and fear of this world rob me of the plan God had for me in those situations. Whether single or married, we are to be free from anxiety and the cares of this world, and God is ready to show us how.

HOPE FOR YOU

Are you living in anxiety and distressing cares? It does not matter whether you are single or married. God has a plan for you to be free from your fears. Do not let your anxiety rob you of what God has for you. How do you do that? You have to confront your anxieties and not run away from them. Then God will show you how to deal with them.

Day 235

BE NOT DISMAYED

Therefore fear not, O My servant Jacob, says the Lord, nor be dismayed or cast down, O Israel; for behold, I will save you out of a distant land [of exile] and your posterity from the land of their captivity. Jacob will return and will be quiet and at ease, and none will make him afraid or cause him to be terrorized and to tremble.

—Jer. 30:10 AMP

J eremiah had the unique ministry from God of being able to speak to the people about the things they were facing and also to share what would come in the future as God revealed it to him.

He was such an encourager to them and to us. God wants us to know how to not fear or let any feeling of dismay and discouragement come into our lives. His promises are real. I have lived them. I have seen some pretty dark times in my life—loneliness, rejection, pain, and divorce.

But God, at those times, came and showed me from His Word and from others He sent into my life, that He was still in charge and was big enough to handle it all. My part was to let go of it and let Him take it.

HOPE FOR YOU

Do you believe God's promises as truth for you? Have you given God all your fears and cares? He is waiting to show you great and marvelous things that can only come from Him.

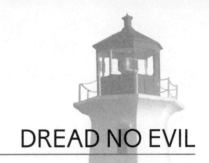

Day 236

DREAD NO EVIL

Yes, though I walk through the [deep, sunless] valley of the shadow of death, I will fear or dread no evil, for You are with me; Your rod [to protect] and Your Staff [to guide], they comfort me.

—Ps. 23:4 AMP

D avid had spent many years as a shepherd before he was a king. He wrote out of his experiences in that lifestyle. This psalm helps us understand that God is with us from our humble beginnings to our final outcome.

We see in this promise that we are not to fear or dread death. The fear of death is said to be one of the top fears of people today. God clearly does not want us to fear death. What relationship do we have with Jesus if we are still choosing to live in the dread and fear of death? How sad His heart must be that we are not trusting and believing that His promise of eternal life is real and possible.

I did not have much thought of death growing up because I did not have a loving and nurturing family that talked about it. As I have grown older, I have seen death come suddenly and when I least expected it. I chose to believe God is always there, and that those who trust and obey Him will live forever with Him. I have made it my life's mission to live and share God simply. I do not fear death because I know I will live forever with Him. I want others to know that certainty too.

HOPE FOR YOU

Are you living in the dread and fear of death? Choose God's simple way and overcome your fear today. Jesus died and rose again so that you may have life; trust Him, and live forever.

Day 237

LIVE WITHOUT DREAD OF EVIL

But whoso hearkens to me [Wisdom] shall dwell securely
and in confident trust and shall be quiet, without fear or
dread of evil.

—Prov. 1:33 AMP

S olomon wrote these wise sayings in the early beginning of his life.
He is said to be the wisest man who ever lived, and also the most
prosperous. Yet, even though he had all the knowledge and all the
wealth and God's attention, he still chose to follow his own ways. He
ended up realizing that finding true purpose and meaning in life only
comes from a personal relationship with God and living in obedience
to Him.

In my own life, God gave me many gifts, talents, and abilities. With
them came responsibilities that I chose to ignore. God in His faithfulness gave me many new beginnings so that I could develop and grow
my personal relationship with Him, which is the key to true contentment and being able to overcome the chains of my fear.

HOPE FOR YOU

Are you choosing to live as Solomon did? You have knowledge and
wealth but are still not content. You have to have more and more, and
with it comes more dread and fear of losing it. Let God give you a new
beginning now. Don't wait as long as Solomon (or I) did.

Day 238

STOP BEING ALARMED

> For they all saw Him and were agitated (troubled and filled with fear and dread). But immediately He talked with them and said, "Take heart! I AM! Stop being alarmed and afraid."
>
> —Mark 6:50 AMP

The disciples of Jesus were alarmed and afraid. The mere presence of Jesus calmed them. It was hard for them to believe who He was, but when He spoke the words "I AM," immediately all fear left them.

Can we experience the same thing today? Or are we trying on our own and with all the self helps available to overcome the fears we face? I know that many of my choices in which I have chosen fear instead of Jesus, the "I AM" in my life, have led me on destructive paths where I would not have chosen to go. But now I realize He is the only way and that recognizing His presence in my life is the key and the way to overcome my fears.

HOPE FOR YOU

Do you sense the presence of Jesus Christ in your daily life? Or are you running to other means to overcome or run from your fears? There is no other way, He is the "I AM" for all of us. Just as the disciples knew it and let Him be their "I AM" and overcome all their fears, so can you.

DO NOT BE AFRAID
OF THEIR WORDS

And you, son of man, do not be afraid of them or their words. Do not be afraid, though briers and thorns are all around you and you live among scorpions. Do not be afraid of what they say or terrified by them, though they are a rebellious people.

—Ezek. 2:6

E zekiel was given one of the most difficult situations we can face—that of being with ungrateful and abusive people. God had to reassure Ezekiel five times not to be afraid, and to keep obeying and sharing God with them, even though they were not listening.

How many times have I walked away from people who I felt were a threat to me, and have not shared the love of Jesus with them? I used to choose to ignore them or rationalize that they had the same opportunity as I did to overcome their evil ways.

The truth was that I let my fear of them trap me into walking away instead of sharing what God had for them. I no longer want to live in fear of anyone. I want to get to know them and I purposely ask God to show and prepare me how to do so. This is a big learning step for me, but the rewards far outweigh my fears, and once I am there, I am amazed how God works.

HOPE FOR YOU

Are you afraid of those people you know are ungrateful and abusive? Have you asked God for help in reaching out to them, or are you letting someone else do it?

Day 240

DO NOT BE AFRAID OF THOSE WHO WOULD KILL YOU

I tell you, My friends, do not dread and be afraid of those who kill the body and after that have nothing more they can do.

—Luke 12:4 AMP

Jesus was giving us a very powerful picture of our relationship with Him and God the Father. He was telling His disciples, in the midst of preparing to address large crowds of people, not to be afraid or live in dread of those who would kill you for sharing the truth of the gospel.

He told us that even though people, might want to kill us, and perhaps even do it, it is not those that we should fear. He wanted us to make sure our relationship with Him was first and not people because He had the keys to our forever life once this body is dead, by whatever way that happens.

I like watching good mystery shows on TV, which usually involve someone getting killed. I focus more on the characters and the story, rather than on the death of the victim. But in the end I always want justice. It's the same way with God.

HOPE FOR YOU

Are you more concerned and fearful of what men can do to your body in this world? Have you taken care of life forever with God by a true trust and belief in Jesus Christ so that what happens to this body does not matter? This is the true message of overcoming the fear of death and harm to our bodies.

DO NOT BE DISMAYED

Do Not fear, O Jacob my servant; do not be dismayed, O Israel. I will surely save you out of a distant place, your descendents from the land of their exile. Jacob will again have peace and security, and no one will make him afraid.

—Jer. 46:27

God punished His people for their unbelief, but He still cared for them. Israel, as a nation, has had a past of failures in obeying God, and so the result is His having to step in and take action. You notice, as Jeremiah tells the people, God still cared for them then, and He still cares for us today.

I love history. The Jewish people and nation certainly have an interesting history. Isn't it amazing that none of us ever seem to learn from the past? We repeat the same sins over and over again, and what do we get?

In looking at my past I can relate to the very same pattern. God gave me the plan and loved me deeply, but before I knew it, I made the same bad choices as before. I have learned that I can overcome the temptations of sin and learn to live His way. It is much easier than the revolving door of daily sin.

HOPE FOR YOU

Are you caught in the trap of fear and sin? Do you think you can't get out? God has a plan and can give you the strength and grace to do it. Life is all about Him, and now you can leave that past behind, never to return to it again.

Day 242

DO NOT BE AFRAID

And shall say to them, Hear, O Israel, you draw near this day to battle against your enemies. Let not your [minds and] hearts faint; fear not, and do not tremble or be terrified [and in dread] because of them.

—Deut. 20:3 AMP

Moses assured the Israelites that even though they faced great opposition, they were not to fear because God was with them. He reminded them what God had done and that He was willing and able to do it now for them.

It is easy when we face opposition to forget what God has brought us through in the past. We fail to remember the details of how He orchestrated it all for His glory and our good. I can see now that His hand was at work in my life, even when I didn't realize it and didn't depend on it. God never wants us to forget He is in control, and why.

I remember my childhood when I lived in fear because I didn't measure up to my Mom's expectations. I never managed to do enough or be good enough to please her. She reminded me that I was a failure over and over again until I really believed it. God is not like that. He wants us to know how special and valuable we are to Him and how much He cares for us even with all our faults and disobedience.

HOPE FOR YOU

Do you have memories that still remind you of what you are not? Let me assure you they are not from God, and He wants to erase them right now.

Day 243

OF WHOM SHALL I BE AFRAID?

The Lord is my light and my salvation—whom shall I fear?
The Lord is the stronghold of my life—of whom shall I be
afraid?

—Ps. 27:1

David uses these questions to help him come to the true understanding of his relationship with God. He knows that God is
His light and salvation, and keeping that in mind will show him how
to overcome any fear that may come.

Fear comes from the places of darkness in our lives. It comes to take
us prisoner with no chance of ever being free. This was the place I lived
in for the greater part of my life. I was born into it and it took God
years to show me I could be free from the chains that had held me
prisoner for so long. Nothing in the world of fear surprised me. I had a
list of fears, and they kept me from becoming the person God wanted
me to be.

I can easily relate to the life of a circus elephant. They are big and
strong, but are still under the control of a trainer whom they very
seldom hurt. How can that be? The truth is that an elephant is raised
chained to a stake in the ground. He becomes so used to it, that even
when the trainer no longer even bothers to put the chain on, the elephant still doesn't know he is free. Many people live their entire lives
that way. Jesus came to set us free, but we have to choose to believe and
trust that He can.

HOPE FOR YOU

Are you still in the chains of the prison of your fears? Do you know
Jesus came to set you free? Is He your light and salvation to lead you
out of your prison? Place your name in this psalm and be free today.

DO NOT BE DISTURBED BY OPPOSITION

> But even in case you should suffer for the sake of righteousness, [you are] blessed (happy, to be envied). Do not dread or be afraid of their threats, nor be disturbed [by their opposition]
>
> —1 Pet. 3:14 AMP

Peter was telling his people how suffering for Christ is for good, and they should be happy and feel blessed to suffer for the Savior. In looking at life that way, we have no enemies from others or from ourselves.

My mom always told me I was my own worst enemy and that I always chose to do things the hard way rather than the right way. When I met the Lord, I wanted to change, but I did not follow the ways I knew were right for me. It seemed too hard, and I didn't want to confront anyone along the way.

I conformed to this world, instead of letting God transform me to His world. God is faithful and He kept Himself in front of me until I finally believed Him more than I believed those who opposed me.

HOPE FOR YOU

Are you suffering for Christ or yourself? Do you fear your enemies or trust God to take care of you and be in total control? Do not let anything shake you from the arms of His love.

Day 245

FEAR NOTHING!

Fear nothing in the things you're about to suffer—but stay on guard! Fear nothing! The devil is about to throw you in jail for a time of testing—ten days. It won't last forever. Don't quit, even if it costs you your life. Stay there believing. I have a Life-Crown sized and ready for you.

—Rev. 2:10 THE MESSAGE

Jesus never promised us a life free from suffering and trouble. But He did promise us great rewards for staying faithful and true to Him. In the meantime, with that promise in mind, we are to fear nothing of this world.

One day in church I realized for the first time that those promises were for me. I no longer felt I needed to be good enough, do more than was ever possible, or be a part of a family that seemed to have it made in life. All I had to be was faithful and let God take care of the rest. God never gave up, and I really believe He has my crown sized and ready for me so that I can receive and give it back to Him in honor and praise.

HOPE FOR YOU

Do you feel the words of the Bible are for someone else? Or do you hope that someday they will be true for you? Today I want you to know that you no longer have to fear or be ashamed of what you have been. As a believer, you are God's child. He cares for you and His promises are for you. It is time to claim them!

Day 246

RECEIVE MERCY AND GRACE
WITHOUT FEAR

> Let us then fearlessly and confidently and boldly draw near to the throne of grace (the throne of God's unmerited favor to us sinners), that we may receive mercy [for our failures] and find grace to help in good time for every need [appropriate help and well-timed help, coming just when we need it].
>
> —Heb. 4:16 AMP

How do we reach God today? Since we cannot see Him in person, prayer is the communication link to a relationship with God. As the writer of Hebrews explains, we have access to God's throne of grace and mercy because of what Jesus did to give us that link. He has gone through everything we face here, but He did it without sinning. What then keeps us from that communication?

I didn't think I could ever be one who could pray out loud and expect God to listen and answer. I didn't have the right words. I wasn't as good as the person next to me or even if I was alone, why would God want to hear from me? But God showed me it is all about Him and not me, and when I am honest and come in faith believing and not fearing, He listens and He answers.

HOPE FOR YOU

Do you see fear as sin or just a result of who you are? God sees the real you and He loves you. He has made a way for you to be released from the grips of fear and be truly His. What are you waiting for?

Day 247

BE NOT AFRAID OF THE DARK

You shall not be afraid of the terror of the night, nor of the arrow (the evil plots and slanders of the wicked) that flies by day, nor of the pestilence that stalks in darkness, nor of the destruction and sudden death that surprise and lay waste at noonday.

—Ps. 91:5–6 AMP

The unknown writer here sounds as if he could be describing our world right now. He tells us we are not to be afraid of the dark, anything or anyone who could harm us, nor an illness that could come upon us even as we sleep.

Do you know we spend more money on security than any other single item in our budgets; but we are still afraid when darkness comes? We have insurance to cover everything, and we have triple-locked everything, yet we still have trouble sleeping well. It is said we are the most sleep-deprived country in the world. Why do we need 24/7 TV and radio Stations? Why do we need medicines to sleep? We are up and we are afraid.

Praise the Lord, I have never had much problem with sleeping at night. But when I do have problems, I realize I am letting the fears that stalk in the night rob me of the rest I need. God wants me to trust Him to take care of me while I sleep.

HOPE FOR YOU

Are you afraid, tired, and sleep-deprived? God is waiting for you to trust Him and let Him show you how to sleep in the presence of His peace.

Day 248

DO NOT BE AFRAID OF HIM

Do not be afraid of the king of Babylon, whom you now fear. Do not be afraid of him, declares the Lord, for I am with you and will save you and deliver you from his hands.
—Jer. 42:11

Jeremiah was assuring the people not to be afraid of the king who was out to harm them. God was able to take care of them. But did they listen? Even though they asked Jeremiah to get an answer from God, they had already decided to let their fears overtake them. They were running away.

How sad God must have been, and how Jeremiah must have felt when they did not trust God or his word either. I admit I have given God many a sad time as well. He has clearly shown me in His plan how to face life His way, and not to fear because He would be there to take care of me. I ran. It became a pattern until I realized I had nowhere to go. That was when He got my attention, and I knew I no longer needed or wanted to run from His care. My fears turned to love and faith in Him alone.

HOPE FOR YOU

Are you a runner too? Today is the day to stop, face God, face your fears, and let Him show you a new beginning. You will never regret it.

Day 249

DO NOT BE DISMAYED AT WHAT UNBELIEVERS THINK OR DO

Listen to me, you who know rightness and justice and right standing with God, the people in whose heart is My law and My instruction: fear not the reproach of men, neither be afraid nor dismayed at their revilings.

—Isa. 51:7 AMP

Isaiah encouraged those who followed God's law. It is the hope we all need to face those who are not believers, who make fun and try to legislate us out of existence.

Isn't it amazing there are still those who will not believe in the one true God? They want to make others just as fearful as they are by making fun, and even threatening their existence as believers. After all this time, we have not learned to trust God ahead of men and let Him handle it all.

Our world wants to teach us it is all about uniformity and looking the same. They want us to believe it is wrong to have differences and not to look alike. How sad. They are missing out totally on God's plan.

I have lived being fearful of those who would seek to take away what I thought was my security. I once based my security not in Jesus Christ, but on the people and a system that did not even believe in God. I found those can be lost quickly, but God never fails.

HOPE FOR YOU

Are you following and living God's way? Are you afraid of those who make fun of you and want to take away your freedoms? Trust in God and do not give into them; He will take care of you.

Day 250

DO NOT FEAR OTHER GODS

And the covenant that I have made with you you shall not forget; you shall not fear other gods.

—2 Kgs. 17:38 AMP

The writer tells us how the Israelites had given themselves over to idols and other gods, and how they wanted to worship them as well as the one true God. How sad God must have been after all He had brought them through. But God gave them His Word once more. They were to worship Him only, and just because all these other gods were around, they were not to fear them because of their belief in the one true God.

Are we so different from these Israelites? I would like to tell you they listened right away, but they had some other things to go through. I have worshiped and even been afraid of other people and things I allowed to become gods in my life. When I look around it is easier now than ever to get involved in the wrong lifestyle, even for true believers.

But God is always right here with us showing us how we do not have to let anything come ahead of Him and how He wants us to live and share Him with others. I am glad that He never left or gave up on me. He is still in control of everything, regardless of what other gods want to tell us. Learn to listen to the one true God of all.

HOPE FOR YOU

Do you have other gods in your life? Are you living in fear of them? Does anything come before the one true God in your life? Today is the day to leave them.

Day 251

BE NOT DISMAYED AND DISCOURAGED

Then you will prosper if you are careful to keep and fulfill the statutes and ordinances with which the Lord charged Moses concerning Israel. Be strong and of good courage. Dread not and fear not; be not dismayed.

—1 Chron. 22:13 AMP

David was with his son, Solomon, and the temple building was beginning. He had not been chosen by the Lord to build it. His son was the one to do that. David gave Solomon wise counsel from the Lord. He knew there were going to be many issues to face, and he wanted Solomon to be prepared for them.

I often chose to live in fear and not let God work it all out His way. I wanted to get ahead and God's way did not seem to get me there fast enough. I often fell into the trap of being dismayed and discouraged, and would give up and not complete the plan God had for me. But God never left or gave up on me. He still knew the plan He had for me—that of being able to encourage and help others overcome the same fears.

HOPE FOR YOU

Are you living in the trap of dismay and discouragement? There is nothing too hard for God, and He wants to help you out of your trap now. Trust and believe He is able and that He wants to help you be all you can be.

Day 252

DO NOT BE AFRAID OF THEM

And you, son of man, do not be afraid of them or their words. Do not be afraid, though briers and thorns are all around you and you live among scorpions. Do not be afraid of what they say or terrified by them, though they are a rebellious house.

—Ezek. 2:6

E zekiel was given a ministry that was not measured by the success of how well the people responded, but by how well he accepted and did what God asked him to do. That is why God knew it was going to be hard, and He told him five times not to be afraid or terrified of the people he was serving.

I can be very fearful of people around me. I grew up wanting to please everyone so they would reward and not punish me. What a hard way to live. I never felt I was able to do enough, and the rewards never lasted very long. I had missed God's message to me.

But God knew my heart and has shown me I only have to please Him and He will take care of the fear I have of others. Once I let Him show me, I was able to say no without guilt. I did not feel the need to defend or justify my existence.

HOPE FOR YOU

Are you afraid of others? Do you want to please them over anything else in your life? Does it stress you out, and you never seem to be able to keep it all going? Jesus is the balance in your life so that you can experience His joy, peace, and contentment, and not let others steal it away from you.

Day 253

DO NOT FEAR OTHER GODS

And the statutes, ordinances, law, and commandment which He wrote for you, you shall observe and do forevermore; you shall not fear other gods.

—2 Kgs. 17:37 AMP

The Israelites had been blessed by God, yet they continued to wander away from Him. He gave them all they needed, but they allowed other things, people, and gods into their lives as well. God knew when they did this, the other gods would come first in their lives and not Him.

I have let food, money, and the pride of pleasing people and receiving rewards from them, become my other gods. I can even treat them as real and see the power and control they have over me. I take my eyes off the Lord and they walk in, take over, and then I become afraid to leave them. Then I am afraid that God has left me, because I know I won't be able to leave them on my own.

What a way to live. God tells us we do not have to make those choices. He wants us to live by His ways and not let other gods get control. That way they will never be able to come in and we will not have to face being afraid of leaving them.

HOPE FOR YOU

What are your other gods? Do you know them by name? Are you afraid to leave them? Do you know they are in control and not God? God has freedom for you today.

Day 254

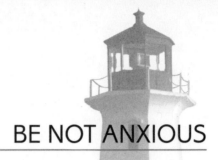

BE NOT ANXIOUS

[Most] blessed is the man who believes in, trusts in, and relies on the Lord, and whose hope and confidence the Lord is. For he shall be like a tree planted by the waters that spreads out its roots by the river; and it shall not see and fear when heat comes; but its leaf shall be green. It shall not be anxious and full of care in the year of the drought, nor shall it cease yielding fruit.

—Jer. 17:7–8 AMP

Jeremiah used a visual image in explaining God's message. He used what the people could see and what they could relate to in their lives. In previous verses he described a person who trusts only in man and not in God, and how he will not see succeed at all. Jeremiah shared how they were to live and not to fear or be anxious, even in times of extreme drought and trouble because it would prevent the fruit from coming in their lives and in the lives of others.

I have been through many drought times in my life. I became so self-absorbed that I feared and was anxious for the very existence of my life. I put my trust in man rather than in the Lord. Was I even a believer? I was, but a very weak one, and I did not realize the power and strength the Lord wanted to give me to face my life and fears. But the story is never complete until we take our last breath here on earth.

HOPE FOR YOU

Are you in a drought time? Are you anxious about it? In whom do you trust? Come to God and let Him show you the way through and out of it.

Day 255

DO NOT GROW WEARY

Those who hope in the Lord will renew their strength. They will soar on wings like eagles; they will run and not grow weary, they will walk and not be faint.

—Isa. 40:31

Ever feel like the world is caving in on you? Does fear have you so trapped that you are tired of facing another day? Isaiah brought a message of hope to the people about what was to come and how they could face it—God's way.

I have been in places where I felt hopeless. I was afraid of what was happening and what might happen as well. I had lost the hope that Jesus brings and had allowed my fears to control. I was sick and tired of it all. I was even serving and working in a church at the time. I looked good on the outside, but on the inside I was a mess.

What a bad place to be because it can paralyze you so that you think this is the best it will ever be. God in His awesome grace and mercy showed me this verse. It just screamed out to me. I do not have to be weary, but I can trust and depend on Him and get up and go running once again. He delivered me out of that dark place, and I don't want to go back, nor do I have to do so.

HOPE FOR YOU

Are you stuck in a dark and bad pit of a place? Have you taken your eyes off the Lord? Do you think this is permanent? Cry out right now, and the Lord will show you how to climb out to Him; and He will deliver you.

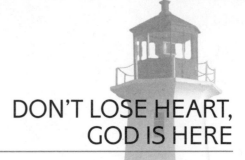

Day 256

DON'T LOSE HEART, GOD IS HERE

> And have you forgotten that word of encouragement that addresses you as sons: "My son, do not make light of the Lord's discipline, and do not lose heart when He rebukes you, because the Lord disciplines those He loves, and He punishes everyone He accepts as a son."
>
> —Heb. 12:5

Why would we ever want to talk about God disciplining us and punishing us? The writers were addressing the second generation of early Christians. They had, just as we can, forgotten what Christ had done and His love for them. Just as we as parents have to discipline our children because we love them and know what is best for them, so much more does God have to discipline us as well.

I can remember wondering if it was my fear causing me to lose heart, or was it the discipline of God that I did not want to face? It is never a fun time in either situation. But God had a plan for me to go through and learn valuable lessons I needed to know, so that I could have victory over sin, and help others have victory too. I am so glad I didn't quit and give up on God, thinking He was being too hard on me. God does love and understand me, and He wants to know you too.

HOPE FOR YOU

Does life seem too hard? Have you lost the joy and peace only God can give? Are you feeling sorry for yourself? Are you mad and angry at God? Has He gotten your attention? Now accept and learn what He has for you. It will be awesome!

Day 257

DO NOT BE TERRIFIED AND IN DREAD

And shall say to them, "Hear, O Israel, you draw near this day to battle against your enemies. Let not your [minds and] hearts faint; fear not, and do not tremble or be terrified [and in dread] because of them."

—Deut. 20:3 AMP

God gave Moses definite and detailed instructions about overcoming fear in the battles the Israelites faced. He wanted to make sure Moses and the people knew He was with them. He wanted to remind them what He had done for them in the past. We often face many trials and battles of our own. But God is faithful. He will allow struggles to come, but He has shown us how to face them when we listen and obey.

When I first met the Lord at an early age, I always knew what He had brought me through and what He wanted to be in my future. Isn't it easy to forget when we are not surrounded by other believers who keep us focused on what the Lord has done for us?

We can end up as I did, living on Sunday as the Lord wanted me to and spending the rest of my week in where my background, knowledge, and understanding led me. I am so glad God gave me a new beginning to the plan He had for me all along.

HOPE FOR YOU

Are you living in terror and dread every day? God has another way for you. Stop and let Him show it to you.

Day 258

DO NOT BE AFRAID OF THEM

> But the Lord said to me, "Do not say, I am only a child.
> You must go to everyone I send you to and say whatever I
> command you. Do not be afraid of them, for I am with you
> and will rescue you, declares the Lord."
>
> —Jer. 1:7–8

G od knows you and me as He knew Jeremiah long before us. Do
you really believe He thought about you and planned for you?
We are not accidents. We are valuable and God has a purpose and a
plan for each of us. God assured Jeremiah of the plan and purpose He
had for him, and not to be afraid to live it out where he was sent.

It took me a long time to come to this point in my life where I could
take God's Word for me personally. My background as an illegitimate
child raised by a single mom who was disappointed in herself and me
did not lead me to believe that God really had me in mind when I was
created. But I am so glad that He did create me and chose the perfect
details designed for me only.

HOPE FOR YOU

Are you living in God's plan and purpose no matter where you have
been placed? You did not just happen, and it is no accident where you
are right now. All the details belong to God because He personally
created and cares for you.

Day 259

DO NOT BE DISCOURAGED

> You will not have to fight this battle. Take up your positions; stand firm and see the deliverance the Lord will give you, O Judah and Jerusalem. Do not be afraid; do not be discouraged. Go out to face them tomorrow, and the Lord will be with you.
>
> —2 Chron. 20:17

Isn't it awesome that God chooses those whom He will speak through? In this situation He chose Jahaziel, a priest and son of Zechariah. He told the people of Judah not to fear or be discouraged in any way, because the battle was not theirs but the Lord's.

I have not always kept this in mind as I moved through my fear-ridden journey. I forgot the words that God wants us to keep in mind. In anything we face we must remember it is Him facing it through us, and we need to allow Him to do it His way. But how can we do this if we do not put Him first and seek His will and guidance to help us face it?

I failed many times in this area, but God always showed up so that I could ask His forgiveness for not letting Him handle it His way. Then He let me begin once more. If you have failed as many times as I have, you will get the message.

HOPE FOR YOU

Are you facing your battles and fears alone, or is God in charge of them? Always remember you have the Lord to handle everything. Don't waste your effort and time working it out in your own fear.

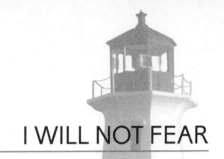

Day 260

I WILL NOT FEAR

> So we take comfort and are encouraged and confidently and boldly say, "The Lord is my Helper; I will not be seized with alarm [I will not fear or dread or be terrified]. What can man do to me?"
>
> —Heb. 13:6 AMP

The writer (some feel it was Paul, or at least one of his associates), was assuring the people that Jesus was the truth and that they did not need to return to their former ways. He is all we need, and we can live confident lives knowing that truth.

Just as the early church members, I can live independent of God when things are going good. But when the troubles and fears come (and they will come even faster when I choose that way of living), is when the fear sets in big time and I realize I cannot handle it by myself at all.

I have led a very insecure lifestyle and have not always depended on God for everything. I did not let the Scriptures become personal and real to me. But this statement of truth sums up what God had for me. Can you put your name and faith in this verse?

HOPE FOR YOU

Is the Lord your Helper? Are you comforted and encouraged by His truth? Then why do you fear man or anything else? What can they do to you?

Day 261

WHOM SHALL I DREAD?

THE LORD is my Light and my Salvation—whom shall I
fear *or* dread? The Lord is the Refuge *and* Stronghold of my
life—of whom shall I be afraid?

—Ps. 27:1 AMP

D avid knew dark days of fear. But when he let the Lord be his
light, salvation, refuge, and stronghold, there was nothing to
fear.

It took me quite a while to see this truth and let God be my life as
He wanted. I now see He is my light. He is my salvation. So whom do
I have to fear?

I grew up always fearing someone, mainly my Mom. She always
threw out statements that if I wasn't good and obedient, she would
lock me in my room. She also told me that I could be taken away and
committed to a mental institution. I don't recall being anything other
than just a curious child; but her threats sounded as if there must be
something seriously wrong with me. I believed she could and would
do exactly as she said.

I did get locked in my room a lot, but God was there in those times.
That was where I developed my love of reading and writing. Those
times were when I learned how to be obedient to Him, and He helped
me know how to deal with my Mom. She never kept the threat of
sending me away to be committed; but it took me a long time to trust
God would not send me away at some point in my life.

HOPE FOR YOU

Is the Lord your light and salvation? Are you living in dread of anyone
or anything? It is a lie, and God wants you to live in His freedom.

Day 262

DO NOT BE DISMAYED

But fear not, O My servant Jacob, and be not dismayed, O Israel. For behold, I will save you from afar, and your offspring from the land of their exile; and Jacob will return and be quiet and at ease, and none will make him afraid.

—Jer. 46:27 AMP

Jeremiah is telling the people because of their unbelief, what would happen and what they would have to go through. God has to make sure we understand His great love for us. He has to correct us so that we can become all He has for us to be and do.

I have received my share of correction and punishment from the Lord for my disobedience and unbelief. But through it all I see His plan and I am willing not to be afraid or dismayed by it. He is still guiding me to be and do what He had intended all along. This has been a great lesson for me. God is in control whether I want or allow Him to be or not. As a believer, this becomes the hope and fear chaser; that God loves us and He is in control.

HOPE FOR YOU

Is God your hope and fear chaser? Does He control your life? You are the one God loves, and He will not leave you.

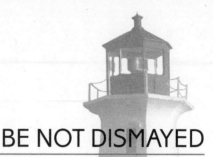

Day 263

BE NOT DISMAYED

Then David said to his son Solomon, "Be strong and courageous, and act; do not fear nor be dismayed, for the LORD
God, my God, is with you. He will not fail you nor forsake
you until all the work for the service of the house of the
LORD is finished."

—1 Chron. 28:20 NASB

D avid was instructing his son, Solomon, about building the
temple. Solomon was to build it instead of David. David accepted God's plan and offered to help and support his son. David told
Solomon not to fear or even live fearfully through the time it would
take to build the temple. God would not leave or fail to be with him.

What a promise God gives to us! Often in my life I forgot God's
promise and let a fearful, apprehensive attitude get in the way of what
God wanted me to be and do. I also did not do a great job of passing
God's joy and promises to my children. When they saw me become
afraid and out of control, they took on the same fears. God has allowed
me to show them now that His promises are true and real, and that He
can redeem the lost time we spent in fear together.

HOPE FOR YOU

Do you believe God's promises are true? Are you sharing them with
others? Don't let your fears rob you of the love and hope God gives to
you. Share His promises and see the fears disappear.

Day 264

DO NOT FEAR SUDDEN DEATH

> You shall not be afraid of the terror of the night, nor of the arrow (the evil plots and slanders of the wicked) that flies by day; Nor of the pestilence that stalks in darkness, nor of the destruction and sudden death that surprise and lay waste at noonday.
>
> —Ps. 91:5–6 AMP

The writer, probably David, tells us not to be afraid of anything—most of all death. God is our protector and we have His promises. The fear of death, as sudden as it can be, should not even enter into our minds.

Death used to be something I did not want to think about or discuss. I knew what the Bible said and I believed God, but I felt I had to keep doing good works so I could earn my way to be with Him. I was not grounded enough in what I truly believed to approach His understanding of the entire plan. I lived a fearful lifestyle because I did not want to face my fear of death.

But that is the part God wants us to do—face our fears and ask Him to show us the truth about them. Then we can live in His victory. Without some great Bible teachers and preachers, I might have gone on wandering around the topic and living in the fear of death until it came suddenly. Now I know that God has a place for me. I am the one He loves and I will live forever with Him. I no longer fear death and I share with others how they do not need to be afraid either.

HOPE FOR YOU

Are you afraid of death? Do you know the truth as described in the Bible? Begin now to study, and God will give you the assurance that you have nothing to fear.

Day 265

DO NOT BE AFRAID

Do not lose heart or be afraid when rumors are heard in the land; one rumor comes this year, another the next, rumors of violence in the land and of ruler against ruler.

—Jer. 51:46

Jeremiah was speaking to some very fearful people. Not so different from today is it? We have great ways of communicating. But do we always fill our avenues of communication with the truth or with rumors.

At one time in my life, I thrived on TV news and newspapers. I began and ended my day with them and watched and listened in between. I ate in front of the TV and it was the last thing I heard and listened to before I went to sleep. I spent more time with the TV and radio than I did with God. I also let what I saw and heard make me fearful.

Rather than letting God rule in my heart, the news ruled my thinking and the way I processed truth. I have learned that I am not to place my faith in what I hear from others. It is not how I am to spend my time. I need to make sure I have the balance of what I need to know from the news, and let God take care of the rest. I just had to let Him show me the plan He had for me.

HOPE FOR YOU

Are you so caught up in the world news that you forget God is in control? Do you realize that the ones bringing you the rumors aren't focused on the truth of the Lord? How distracted we can become. Begin today to seek God and what He has for you, and learn from Him, not the world.

Day 266

DO NOT BE DISCOURAGED

He said: "Listen, King Jehoshaphat and all who live in Judah and Jerusalem! This is what the Lord says to you: 'Do not be afraid or discouraged because of this vast army. For the battle is not yours, but God's.'"

—2 Chron. 20:15

Just as Judah faced her battles, we too fight our own daily battles of life. Jahaziel was chosen by God to tell the people of Judah not to fear or let discouragement come into their battles. The message is the same today.

When faced with many trials in my life, I have not always viewed them as God's battles. Rather, I took it upon myself to find my way through them. Sometimes I did not even ask for His help as I was working my own way through. How sad I must have made God. He saw me afraid and discouraged, just as the people of Judah were, and yet I did not come to Him. I did not trust and depend on Him to fight my battles.

But God in His grace and mercy has forgiven me for those times because I finally realized His way is the only way to have true joy, peace, and contentment. It's the only way to overcome discouraging thoughts or actions that come to me.

HOPE FOR YOU

Has the battle become too hard for you? Are you weak and discouraged and can't seem to find the way out anymore? Come to Jesus, He has the plan and He wants to take charge of those battles. He is the only way to victory.

Day 267

DO NOT BE TERRIFIED BY THEM

> And you, son of man, do not be afraid of them or their words. Do not be afraid, though briers and thorns are all around you and you live among scorpions. Do not be afraid of what they say or terrified by them, though they are a rebellious house.
>
> —Ezek. 2:6

Ezekiel was called to work right where he was. He did not have the best living conditions nor did he have a captive audience. But he was faithful to God and never gave up, and God never gave up on him.

I have always wanted the best out of life. I thought I deserved it. I was not raised in the best of circumstances and I felt I had to make up for that, both for myself and for my family. I often got terrified by those who did not believe in me—those who told me I would never amount to anything.

Other people also tried to convince me that God was not interested in me and was not my answer either. But after working so hard and thinking I was doing the right things, I realized I had missed God's message to me all along. God knew that one day I would get His message, and He waited for me. He was faithful when I was not.

HELP FOR YOU

Are you working for yourself without God's direction? Is it working for you? God has a plan and all He wants is for you to show up. He will do the rest. Show up today and begin to be His faithful one.

Day 268

RUN AND NOT GET TIRED

> Yet those who wait for the Lord will gain new strength; they will mount up with wings like eagles, they will run and not get tired, they will walk and not become weary.
>
> —Isa. 40:31 NASB

Isaiah was giving great comfort to the Israelites about what was to come when they were freed from captivity. He showed all of us that by waiting on the Lord we will be renewed and able to overcome all we will ever face.

To do this takes a lot of trust and faith in God alone. For me, this has been a long hard journey. No blame and no excuses; I chose to follow man's ways instead of turning totally to the one true God and letting Him handle it all. But God still waited for me. He let me travel those paths knowing that He would receive the glory once I came totally to Him. I am now renewed, changed, and I have received more of His promises than I could ever imagine.

HOPE FOR YOU

Do you wait on the Lord to handle your life? Or do you charge off on your own without asking or even thinking of Him? Are you tired of running your own race? God is waiting for you to come totally to Him so you will finish fresh and complete. Come now; don't delay.

Day 269

DO NOT BE DISCOURAGED

The Lord Himself goes before you and will be with you; He will never leave you nor forsake you. Do not be afraid; do not be discouraged.

—Deut. 31:8

Moses was in his last days and was turning over his leadership role to Joshua. He was 120 years old and wanted the people to know God's plan for himself and for them. He wanted Joshua to know that God would never leave them nor give up on them and that they were not to be afraid or discouraged about anything.

He also wanted to make sure they knew they must depend on God alone and not on anyone on earth. What a way to end one's life—being able to turn everything over to another and leave a legacy of hope and promise to all. Was Moses a perfect God follower? It is recorded that he was not. That was one reason he did not get to take the people into the Promised Land.

I cannot dream of living to be 120 years old, but I have lived long enough to realize the same truths. God is in control, and He will not leave any follower of His alone at any time. There is still hope and promise no matter how long we live.

I have not always been a great follower of Jesus Christ, but I know the hope and promises are true; and the legacy I want to leave is one of faithfulness and getting to know the one true God for however long He has left for me.

HOPE FOR YOU

What is your legacy? Do you care about what others know of you and your relationship to the one true God through faith in our Lord Jesus Christ?

STAND FAST, DO NOT
BE HELD ENSNARED

In [this] freedom Christ has made us free [and completely liberated us]; stand fast then, and do not be hampered and held ensnared and submit again to a yoke of slavery [which you have once put off].

—Gal. 5:1 AMP

P aul was confronting the very churches he had served. He showed the people they were not to let anyone convince them to become involved in keeping laws, being afraid, or living in slavery to men.

I admit that I have sometimes lost sight of what Christ did for me. I did not make sure I was grounded in what I believed or didn't believe about Him. In doing so, I got caught up in the winds of man-made religion instead of developing a deeper personal relationship with Christ.

I listened to what others said and not to what Christ personally said to me. This is a very frightening way of living in the Christian community of believers. Christ brought us freedom, and I was out there on the merry-go-round of working to live up to man's expectations and not God's. God showed me I can be released from the bondage of the slavery of fear of not meeting man's ground rules and once again come and know His plans, commands, and promises for me.

HOPE FOR YOU

Are you ensnared in God's plan or man's for you? Do you know the difference of God's grace and man's laws? Come today and be a friend to Christ not a slave.

Day 271

DO NOT GROW EXHAUSTED

Just think of Him Who endured from sinners such grievous opposition *and* bitter hostility against Himself [reckon up and consider all in comparison with your trials], so that you may not grow weary *or* exhausted, losing heart, *and* relaxing *and* fainting in your minds.

—Heb. 12:3 AMP

The writer wanted the second generation Christians to know that when they faced fear and discouragement they were to keep their eyes on Jesus and who He is in their lives. It is easy to focus on ourselves and our fears, but Christ gives us a better way.

I have an overabundance of energy and I can work and work until I get completely worn out, and then still think I should keep going. I have always wanted to depend on my own strength and not the Lord's, and the trap of fear and giving in to it then comes right on in. I set myself wide open to living for myself instead of for my Lord and Savior.

I had to face this as sin and that giving in to the traps of fear are sin as well. Jesus provided a better way for me, and He demands I follow Him. Every day I have a choice to follow Jesus or the world and myself. Too long I took the latter; now I choose Jesus, and He makes all the difference in how my energy is used for Him.

HOPE FOR YOU

Are you living for Jesus or yourself? How are you serving Him? Is it in your strength or His? Does fear have a big part in your life? Choose to live His way, letting Him control and see the difference in your energy level.

Day 272

DO NOT LOOK AROUND
AND BE DISMAYED

Fear not [there is nothing to fear], for I am with you; do not look around you in terror *and* be dismayed, for I am your God. I will strengthen *and* harden you to difficulties, yes, I will help you; yes, I will hold you up *and* retain you with My [victorious] right hand of righteous *and* justice.

—Isa. 41:10 AMP

Isaiah knew that God had chosen the Israelites as His people even though they did not deserve it. God wanted them to show Him off to the world, but they failed. Did He leave them? No, He just made the way so that we can all become His chosen people as well.

I had never thought of myself as chosen by God. I didn't think I was good enough or deserved to be chosen. I could easily become fearful and get alarmed and discouraged. Did I seek Him first? No. I thought I needed to figure it out and then if I could not, I would ask. What a waste of the precious time that my Lord gave me. I finally figured it out, that His Word is true for me as it was for the Jews, and that even though I don't deserve His love, care, and forgiveness, I am the one Jesus loves and died for.

HOPE FOR YOU

Are you wasting time living in your fearful and alarmed state? Do you want to know the joy, peace, and contentment that God has waiting for you? Stop, and let Him show you how you can know Him.

Day 273

DO NOT BE TERRIFIED OR TURN BACK IN BATTLE

He mocks at fear and is not dismayed *or* terrified; neither does he turn back [in battle] from the sword.

—Job 39:22 AMP

G od was sharing with Job what it meant to recognize and submit totally to Him. Job's friends did not have the right answers or advice for Job, but God did.

I have many times let my fears cause me to be so terrified that I ran from the battles of my life that God wanted me to stand and face. It seemed much easier to do so, but then I realized that God was not against me, but for me. He offered me His help. I just needed to choose to take and receive it. I am so glad that even though I had waited a long time to choose Him first, God was still there waiting for me.

HOPE FOR YOU

Are you running or staying and facing your battles? Do you think God has the way for you to be able to face them? He is waiting and is ready to help you now.

Day 274

DO NOT BE ALARMED OR STRUCK WITH FEAR

But Jesus, on hearing this, answered him, "Do not be seized with alarm *or* struck with fear; simply believe [in Me as able to do this] and she shall be made well."

—Luke 8:50 AMP

Jesus told Jairus, the leader of the synagogue, that his daughter was going to be made well. All he had to do was believe in Him. What reasonable person, when faced with that situation, could not see that Jesus was who He said He was?

I have seen many similar situations where physical as well as emotional and spiritual healing has taken place. Still, I had a hard time believing it could possibly be true for me. It just couldn't be as simple as believing, could it? Wasn't there something else that had to happen first?

I have found it is just that simple, and God wants it to be. How else can all people have a chance to know Him? We too have to make it simple for others to see and believe. When we try to outplay God with fancy words and interpretations, we take away the message and cause others to give up into the fears they already have.

HOPE FOR YOU

Are you working hard at becoming God? Do you take Him at His Word, or add yours too? Is God hard for you to know and believe? Come just as Jairus did and believe and see how God wants to work out all your fears.

Day 275

DO NOT BE ANXIOUS ABOUT HOW OR WHAT YOU ARE TO SPEAK

> But when they deliver you up, do not be anxious about how *or* what you are to speak; for what you are to say will be given you in that very hour and moment.
>
> —Matt. 10:19 AMP

Jesus assured the disciples that *when* they were arrested for teaching and preaching and following Him, they were not to be afraid of what they were going to say or how. It was taken care of already.

Today it does not seem we have much to fear about speaking or teaching and following our Lord here in America. But is that the truth? If so, we should have more influence than ever on our world. But the truth is most of us are afraid and anxious about saying anything to anyone about the Lord based on what they may think of us, what influence they have in taking away our livelihoods, and having to face any confrontation from anyone.

I know I used to be of the mind-set that "religion" was a private matter of choice, and I was not called to have to face any defense of my Lord and Savior. I have learned I have to know what I believe and at any time be prepared to share it His way.

HOPE FOR YOU

Are you ready and prepared to share Jesus Christ with anyone? Do you feel it is what He asks all of us to do? How accountable do you think He requires you to be in this area? Don't let someone else do what He has called you to be and do for Him.

Day 276

DO NOT FRET

> Do not fret *or* have any anxiety about anything, but in every circumstance *and* in everything, by prayer and petition (definite requests), with thanksgiving, continue to make your wants known to God.
>
> —Phil. 4:6 AMP

Paul knew it was hard not to worry and be anxious about daily life things. He knew God was in control of everything, and if we would face our worries and anxieties God's way, we could then turn them into prayers and God would help us through them all.

I have been through many worrisome and anxious times in my life. None of us can avoid them, but it is how we face them that counts.

I have learned everything starts in our mind through our thoughts; so that is where God wants me to focus all of my attention. God wants me to come in prayer and yes, even give thanks for the situations I don't see the point in having to go through. When I do this, it is amazing to see how clear God's message is to me and how His strength is so powerful to bring me to what He had planned all along.

HOPE FOR YOU

Are you going through things that are making you worried and anxious? How are you facing it? God has a plan that is customized and ready for only you. Ask Him to show you and thank Him for doing so.

Day 277

DO NOT BE IN TERROR BEFORE THEM

Be strong, courageous, *and* firm; fear not nor be in terror before them, for it is the Lord your God Who goes with you; He will not fail you or forsake you.

—Deut. 31:6 AMP

Moses was in the last days of his life and was addressing the people he loved and also Joshua, who was taking his place. He wanted them to know that God was with them and that God had not, nor would He, fail them. He was also letting them know he was not the only one who was in touch with God but that they could continue on in the strength and power of the Lord. What an encouragement he was to all of us.

In looking back, how great it would have been to have had someone to encourage and tell me that the Lord was with me and would never leave me. But I know God was still with me and now I can encourage others that He will be with them too. There is nothing or anyone we should be afraid or terrified of facing, because God is with us.

HOPE FOR YOU

Are you afraid or terrified by someone so that you cannot see God is with you first? Know now that God wants to be first in your life, and He will show you how to face those you fear.

Day 278

DO NOT BE ALARMED

Then Jesus said to them, "Do not be alarmed *and* afraid; go and tell My brethren to go into Galilee, and there they will see Me."

—Matt. 28:10 AMP

Jesus, even after being deserted by His disciples, still wanted to get in touch with them after He had risen from the grave. He used women, (Mary Magdalene and the other Mary [not His mother]), to deliver His message about where to meet Him. He also assured them they were not to be alarmed or afraid; He was alive and well.

I have spent many hours of my life being alarmed and afraid of many things and people. Jesus was always waiting for me to capture His message that I did not have anything to fear.

Just as the women were instructed to go and tell, Jesus had to assure me not to be afraid of anything. I was to do as He asked. Jesus is still assuring me not to be alarmed or afraid, but just go and tell.

HOPE FOR YOU

Are you afraid and alarmed to go and tell the message of Jesus to those who are waiting to hear? Do you need reassurance yourself of who He is and what He did for you? Jesus is waiting for you to come and find that assurance.

Day 279

DO NOT BE TROUBLED

And [Jesus] said to His disciples, "Therefore I tell you, do not be anxious *and* troubled [with cares] about your life, as to what you will [have to] eat; or about your body, as to what you will [have to] wear."

—Luke 12:22 AMP

Jesus wanted us to know plain and clear that we are not to worry or be anxious about anything. Is our faith in Him stronger than the sin of disobedience to Him?

I have failed the test of obedience many times in the area of worry and anxiety. I am blessed it has not robbed me of my health and that the Lord continues to forgive me when I am overcome with the temptation to worry or be anxious. He is building in me a strong faith so that I do not have to spend useless time in worry and anxiety.

HOPE FOR YOU

Do you trust in God alone to meet your every need? Or have your "wants" overcome the basic needs and become the source of your worry?

Day 280

DO NOT GROW EXHAUSTED

Just think of Him Who endured from sinners such grievous opposition *and* bitter hostility against Himself [reckon up and consider it all in comparison with your trials, so that you may not grow weary *or* exhausted, losing heart *and* relaxing *and* fainting in your minds.

—Heb. 12:3 AMP

Jesus wants to make sure we know that we are always to keep focused on Him and let Him handle everything that comes our way. The readers here were facing hard times such as we have never known, but they were able to walk through it all with Jesus in charge and first in their hearts.

I have to remember, always, that my darkest times and trials are nothing compared to what Jesus faced, and why He did it. I have always been that burst of energy; so much so that I can keep going until I get totally exhausted.

But when I get to that point, I know that is not the place God has for me. Everything will come crashing down, and I will say and do things that are not the real me in Christ. So I take care to plan and not become exhausted in my doings. My husband helps me because he has seen the ugly side when I go too far. He knows it is not best for me or anyone else either.

HOPE FOR YOU

Do you push the edge too much and end up totally exhausted? Are you of use to God at that time, and is He to you? In Jesus Christ there is balance and rest. Find it today, and plan on staying there.

DO NOT BE FRIGHTENED

But the angel said to the women, "Do not be alarmed *and* frightened, for I know that you are looking for Jesus, Who was crucified."

—Matt. 28:5 AMP

The women, Mary Magdalene and the other Mary, (not Jesus' mother) had not come expecting to find the tomb empty nor to meet an angel of God. How frightened and scared they must have been. But the angel showed them quite a few things. Jesus' promise had come true. They saw for themselves the tomb was empty and they had nothing to fear. Then they were instructed to go and tell. They hurried off, still a little afraid but filled with joy.

I can remember hearing and reading the story of Jesus' resurrection many times. But it finally became personal and real when I realized my life had not been about going and telling the good news of Jesus, but instead had been focused on all about me and what was happening and had happened to me.

Now, I knew and loved the Lord, but I kept Him a separate part of my life and did not invite Him into the parts that I thought were only mine. What a selfish way to live. No wonder life was hard and I made many bad choices. But God knew one day I would "get it" and then be able to go and tell of His love and mercy and grace extended to all who would but believe.

HOPE FOR YOU

Is Jesus Christ your life, or just in your life? Do you know the difference? Let Him show you today so you can go and tell and not be afraid.

Day 282

DO NOT GROW WEARY

And let us not lose heart *and* grow weary *and* faint in acting nobly *and* doing right, for in due time *and* at the appointed season we shall reap, if we do not loosen *and* relax our courage *and* faint.

—Gal. 6:9 AMP

Paul knew the Galatians were just like we can be. We get discouraged, fearful, and weary. Isn't it easy in that state of mind to want to give up?

I have missed many of the blessings God had for me by getting to the point of fear and doubt so that I gave up on God's dream for me. I didn't stop, listen, and ask God for the right directions. I just made up my own set of maps and took the turns I chose. But God never throws away His plans. He keeps them handy when you are ready to do it His way. You can come back and begin again as He has shown me to do.

HOPE FOR YOU

Paul challenged the Galatians many years ago, and his message is still clear to us today. Are you at the point of discouragement and fear, and letting your feelings and others convince you to give up the hope and go another path? You can't see results, and no one notices or even cares to thank you for what you are doing. Look up and see Jesus today, and let Him show you it is not about results and being thanked in this world that matters; it is all about Him.

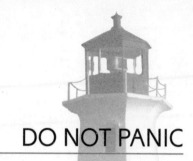

Day 283

DO NOT PANIC

And when you hear of wars and insurrections (disturbances, disorder, and confusion), do not become alarmed *and* panic-stricken *and* terrified; for all this must take place first, but the end will not [come] immediately.

—Luke 21:9 AMP

Jesus wanted everyone to know that He did not want us to be unprepared for what is to come. His disciples had plenty of questions and Jesus was ready to give them the answers they needed. This was before His death, and He knew they would need to be strong. He gave them clear instructions not to become stricken with panic.

I have known panic in my life because I took my eyes off Jesus and put them on myself and the world. My fears then had an open door and they walked right in to keep me in that mode of operation. I looked strong on the outside and talked a good positive message, but the truth was that inside I was operating in a panicked and fearful way.

Panic can take on many forms but the end results are the same. God is left out and fear is ruling. But God can use anything or anyone to bring us out of that state. I have lived in that state longer than I should have; but now I know I never have to return there again.

HOPE FOR YOU

Are you living in the panic mode? Is the news media causing you great fear and panic? Are you afraid to be living in the "last days" as some indicate we are? Jesus is speaking to you, and it is your choice to listen. You can choose to live in His hope and plan and not in your fear and panic.

Day 284

THERE IS NO NEED TO FEAR TERROR, IT WILL NOT COME

You shall establish yourself in righteousness (rightness, in conformity with God's will and order): you shall be far from even the thought of oppression *or* destruction, for you shall not fear, and from terror, for it shall not come near you.

—Isa. 54:14 AMP

I saiah was speaking to the Jews about what God was going to establish through them with the coming of His Son to rule. How marvelous is the church and its members who no longer have reason to fear within the church or be terrified by anything or anyone outside the church. What an awesome promise God has made to each one of us.

But I did not think God wanted this promise specifically for me. It was penned many centuries ago and applied to the Jews and Isaiah was chosen to tell them. Why would anyone want to take away the fear and terrors from within the church and outside the church for someone like me?

I had received Christ, but I had not received His forgiveness of my sins and my past, nor had I forgiven myself. I let them still control me. But God, in His detailed plan for me, knew I needed to hear His promises personally to me so that my life would never be the same.

HOPE FOR YOU

Are you living in fear from inside the church as well as from outside the church? Do you feel you are not valuable or special enough to receive God's promises? Have you truly received God's forgiveness? Have you forgiven yourself? God has a plan for you, and it includes every one of His gifts and promises. Are you ready to believe and receive them?

Day 285

HAVE NO FEAR OF BAD NEWS

He will have no fear of bad news; his heart is steadfast, trusting in the Lord.

—Ps. 112:7

What happens when you hear bad news, either personal or in the world around you? What do you say and do? Do you panic? Are you afraid? Or do you turn first to God?

The writer of this psalm is clearly showing us to put God first and then, when the fears come, we know He will take care of it all. Once we learn to live in that peace, joy, and contentment, anything that comes, even death itself, will not overcome or overwhelm us. We will be secure in God and nothing can shake us.

Can you put your name personally in these verses and believe them and live them? That is what the Lord is asking each of us to do. For many years I would not. I believed in God, but I also thought I had to perform for Him before I could receive His blessings. What a unhappy and unfulfilled life! But God showed me His truth and that I had lived in lies and fear long enough.

HOPE FOR YOU

Are you putting God first, and are you secure in the trust and knowledge He will take care of you? That is our only true security which cannot be found in people or things. It doesn't mean that we will not get bad news or face fears. But by trusting and knowing God is in control, we have a way to live life and receive His blessings and promises.

Day 286

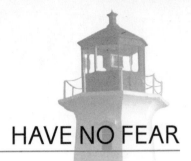

HAVE NO FEAR

His heart is secure, he will have no fear; in the end he will look in triumph on his foes.

—Ps. 112:8

Is your heart secure? The psalmist says when we trust completely in the Lord to take care of us, we can face anything without fear. This is not what the world teaches, but God is alive and well whether we want to recognize Him or not.

I have learned that no matter what comes, I need to face it through God's eyes and not my own. Confronting our fears is what God is showing us to do, and once we do it, then He will guide us into not letting them control our lives.

Fear is in this world, but it is how we face it that matters. Once I recognize fear for what it is and trust God for who He is, my fears go away. That is God's plan for me and for you too.

Hope for You

Are you living in God's plan or your own? Do you know your fears more than you trust God to take care of them? Is fear your friend or is God? They cannot reside as equals. At first, facing your fears can be a major event, but it is so necessary to let God help you overcome them. I urge you to let God show you how to do so now.

Day 287

I WILL NOT DREAD OR BE TERRIFIED

So we take comfort *and* are encouraged *and* confidently *and* boldly say, "The Lord is my Helper; I will not be seized with alarm [I will not fear or dread or be terrified]. What can man do to me?"

—Heb. 13:6 AMP

The writer of Hebrews is not known, but he knew fear was all around the Christians. He wanted to make sure they did not depend on themselves to overcome it, but call on the Lord for help.

I can live very independently and leave God out as long as things go well. But the first thing that comes along where fear can set in, I know I have really messed up. I can give into the world so easily instead of confidently and boldly letting God be in first place. But God still shows up faithful as ever, even when I am weak in my faith in Him.

HOPE FOR YOU

Are you living in your plan or in God's? Are things going as well as they could be? Now is the time to make the choice to trust God totally with everything; so that He can show you how to live boldly and confidently in Him.

Day 288

DO NOT BE SEIZED WITH ALARM

But [even] the very hairs of your head are all numbered. Do not be stuck with fear *or* seized with alarm; you are of greater worth than many [flocks] of sparrows.

—Luke 12:7, AMP

Jesus told His disciples then, and is telling us now, that our true value and worth is not measured by man, but by Him alone. The world measures us by our works and our appearance, but God cares for us just because we belong to Him.

It has taken me a long time to know that my identity in Christ is enough and that the world does not determine my success. It is hard to keep the picture and thoughts in my mind that I am a saint who sometimes sins. I am a work of art. I am accepted and forgiven and holy. This is what God says and sees in me, but I can get caught up in the world's ways and come up with a different picture. But God draws me back to Him by His Word and by those He sends into my daily life.

HOPE FOR YOU

Whose picture do you see and listen to in your life? Is it God's or men? Choose now to let go of what others think and what you might be deceived into feeling. Focus on your true identity in Jesus and what God has for you to be and do.

HE DELIVERED ME FROM ALL MY FEARS

I sought (inquired of) the Lord *and* required Him [of necessity and on the authority of His Word], and He heard me, and delivered me from all my fears.

—Ps. 34:4 AMP

God promises to deliver us from all our fears. Just as David learned, we too must know God requires obedience. To be delivered from all our fears we need to seek God and trust in His Word and promises.

I spent many years wanting to be delivered from my fears. I knew God could deliver me from them, but I was not willing to do what He required of me to receive His promises. I played the victim not the victor, and in it all, the enemy won.

But God did not leave me. He kept showing me that He was still faithful and loved me. Then once I made the choice to give my fears to Him, He showed me by trusting and depending on Him alone, peace, not my fears would win out.

HOPE FOR YOU

Are you ready to give God those fears? Do you believe He can deliver you without obedience to Him? Don't live independent of Him any longer. You are missing out on the blessing of His peace.

Day 290

BE NOT AFRAID OF
SUDDEN TERROR

> Be not afraid of sudden terror *and* panic, nor of the stormy
> blast *or* the storm and ruin of the wicked when it comes [for
> you will be guiltless].
>
> —Prov. 3:25 AMP

S olomon had faced sudden terror and had become fearful and panicked, but he knew that was not God's plan for him. He shared that to live as God intends takes a choice to trust God.

Life can be filled with sudden terror, but what do we do when it touches our lives personally? I have always been a follower of events locally and globally. Doing so can bring terror into my life.

I can find myself focusing more on the events than on what God has for me to do for Him. I have had to learn to exchange my time for what brings Him glory instead of filling my mind with terror.

HOPE FOR YOU

Are you living thinking that each day will bring sudden terror, or do you feel blessed to be living a God-filled life of hope and promise? It is a choice. Learn how God wants you to live, and give Him all the glory.

Day 291

CAST ALL YOUR ANXIETIES ONCE AND FOR ALL ON HIM

Casting the whole of your care [all your anxieties, all your worries, all your concerns, once and for all] on Him, for He cares for you affectionately *and* cares about you watchfully.

—1 Pet. 5:7 AMP

Peter knew it would be tough for the ones who are called to be leaders to handle the people they were called to serve. So he set down some basic things each of us must do so that others can comfort and help us. He knew we had to be humble and know we can do nothing on our own. Peter knew one of the things that can stand in our way is becoming very anxious about everything. When this happens we are not fully trusting God with our lives.

I was always so independent in my work and giving of myself to others. I had let my pride step in and I ended up overwhelmed, anxiety ridden, and a real mess. But God showed me that was not His plan for me. It is a daily choice to trust and depend on God only, but the blessings it brings to me is the joy, peace, and contentment of the Lord.

HOPE FOR YOU

Has anxiety taken over your life? Are you carrying it all on your own, or are you willing to confess to the Lord you need and want to change? Take the time now to trust God and let Him hear from you and gain the blessings He has for you.

Day 292

BE CAREFUL, DO NOT LET THE ANXIETIES OF LIFE OVERBURDEN YOU

Be careful, or your hearts will be weighed down with dissipation, drunkenness and the anxieties of life, and that day will close on you unexpectedly like a trap.

—Luke 21:34

Jesus wanted His disciples all to be on the watch for His return. And not to let anything come before the work He had for them to do. This means that we too have to make a choice not to let the anxieties of life overcome us. Jesus wants us to think of Him first and remember the plan He has for each of us.

I can remember when I did not think of Jesus first in my life. It was all about me and only about Him when I chose to let Him in. I could separate it all very easily. But then I came to the place where my way was no longer working, and I knew there had to be something else.

At that point I knew His Word was the truth for me personally, and I began to be able to put my name in the verses I read. Jesus told me to be careful and not become anxious or fearful about anything, and He keeps telling me that today.

HOPE FOR YOU

Is Jesus personal and real to you? Does He tell you to be careful and not become anxious? Do you listen? His way is the only one that works; join Him today and get in on the plan He has for you.

ARE YOU LIVING IN DREAD, WHEN THERE IS NOTHING TO DREAD?

There they were, overwhelmed with dread, where there was nothing to dread. God scattered the bones of those who attacked you; you put them to shame, for God despised them.

—Ps. 53:5

David knew that because of sin no one would choose God on their own. This is the most important fact each of us must find in our lives. We cannot save ourselves from anyone or anything. God has the plan and we have nothing to dread or fear when we accept it and believe and know only He can save us.

I used to believe that people could seek God if they wanted to, and when they chose not to do so, it really didn't affect me. I would pray for people to come to God instead of knowing the truth that He is in control of the seeking.

I know now there is nothing I can say or do to make a person believe in the Lord. But what God has for me to do is to live a life that can portray God to others, and then be willing to share what God has done that will point them to Him. Then when God approaches them they will want to let Him come in and save them.

HOPE FOR YOU

Are you waiting for some people to find the Lord, or do you want to help them see Him when He seeks them? Then live as God has for you. Share with those He brings into your path the marvelous things God has done for you and wants to do for them. I don't want anyone to miss God when He seeks them.

RESIST THE DEVIL, GOD'S WAY

So be subject to God. Resist the devil [stand firm against him] and he will flee from you. Come close to God and He will come close to you [Recognize that you are] sinners, get your soiled hands clean; [realize you have been disloyal] wavering individuals with divided interests, and purify your hearts [of your spiritual adultery].

—Jas. 4:7–8 AMP

James, the half brother of Jesus, tells us how not to let fear creep in, and when it does, what to do about it. Satan would want our fears to consume us, take over, and then when we give into them, make us feel guilty. But God is the answer and when we choose God and His ways, Satan has to flee along with all our fears. Victory is in Jesus alone.

I once thought that my sins were forgiven but that I would still have to struggle with their power until my physical death. Therefore, the trap of guilt and self-condemnation of my sins could shake my belief that I was really saved and a child of God.

I was right where Satan wanted me, and he did not even have to work hard at getting me to that point. I know now that Jesus died for every one of my past, present, or future sins. And when I daily confess my sins to God as He instructs me to do, it is not because I need to get back in good standing or fellowship with Him. It is because I love Him, and for what Jesus did for me on the Cross. Then, once I confess, those sins are forgiven and forgotten so that I do not have to live in the guilt and the self-condemnation of them. This is true "Amazing Grace" and available to all believers.

HOPE FOR YOU

Are you focused on Jesus first or on your sins? Are you living in the freedom He died to give you, or working hard to overcome sin in your own understanding? God's grace is now for you.

Day 295

RESIST HIM, STAND FIRM IN YOUR FAITH IN JESUS

But resist him, firm in your faith, knowing that the same experiences of suffering are being accomplished by your brethren who are in the world.

—1 Pet. 5:9 NASB

Peter warns us how fear can easily come in when we are alone, not involved with other believers, and focused on our troubles. Satan can see our weakness and take full advantage of it.

At times I have isolated myself from others, had my own pity party, and then wanted Jesus to join me. I found God is never going to accept an invitation to join me when I am not focused on Him.

He is a great and mighty God, and He will wait until we realize we can't handle the fear and pain of it any longer. The longer our pity party goes on, the longer it will take for relief from God to come. I recently had knee surgery, and I know that without trusting Jesus with the outcome and the pain, I would not be able to recover. He is the answer.

HOPE FOR YOU

Are you focused on yourself or on Jesus? What is the pattern of your life? Are you living in one big pity party with yourself as the only guest? Jesus is ready to help you overcome the suffering; reach out to Him now.

Day 296

HUMBLE YOURSELF
AND BE EXALTED

Humble yourselves [feeling very insignificant] in the presence of the Lord, and He will exalt you [He will lift you up and make your lives significant].

—Jas. 4:10 AMP

J ames realized after the death of his half brother, Jesus, that our worth is not found in us but in God alone. Jesus paid the price for us as believers to overcome any of our human fears.

Many times in my life, even though I was a believer, I did not hear and obey the words of Jesus. I tried to find and create my own significance (as the world teaches us to do), and found all the fear, hopelessness, and anxiety that come with trying to do it on our own.

I finally realized, even though I do not deserve it, nor can I earn it, God loves me and reaches out to give me dignity, worth, and value. Then I can live as He plans for me to do, once I humble myself and come into His presence knowing He is the only way.

HOPE FOR YOU

Are you seeking to overcome fear and find significance in this life on your own? Have you humbled yourself in the presence of the Lord lately or ever? You can come to Jesus now and know the truth.

Day 297

ARE YOU BEING TRANSFORMED?

And we, who with unveiled faces all reflect the Lord's glory,
are being transformed into His likeness with ever-increasing
glory, which comes from the Lord, who is the Spirit.

—2 Cor. 3:18

Paul wrote very personally to the people at Corinth about the glory of the Lord from the time of Moses until now. The church at Corinth was weak and easily gave into false teaching. Paul wanted them to remember and know the truth once more. He wanted them to know that being a committed Christian is a progressive experience, and the more we follow Christ, the more we will become like Him. That is His goal for us through the Holy Spirit.

We have more advantages over the early church and the Christians at Corinth. But have we changed because of it? I can honestly say that for many years I wasn't even thinking about who God was and about His transforming power in my life as a believer.

True faith in God and allowing Him to change us into His likeness through His Holy Spirit in us, is what overcomes fear and gives us the insight into the real plan God has for our lives. It is all about Him and not us, and when we don't live that way, fear comes right in and lives.

HOPE FOR YOU

Where are you living today? Are you on the progressive experience God has for you so that you will become transformed and more like Jesus? Or are you on your own path? It is fearful without Jesus in our daily lives. Now is the time to come and be changed into what God had for you all along.

Day 298

IF YOU CAN?

"If you can?" said Jesus. "Everything is possible for him who believes." Immediately the boy's father exclaimed, "I do believe; help me overcome my unbelief!"

—Mark 9:23–24

Mark knew much about fear and unbelief, yet he was chosen by God to write these precious words to the Christians at Rome. He shows the teaching of Jesus to all believers. Everything is possible for those who believe.

What a promise of God to show us that as believers we do not have to let doubt, fear, or anything else overcome us. I have been like this father many times. I would give the situation to God and then need help with believing God really could or would handle it.

But God has shown me that is not His way. I have to trust and depend and allow Him to handle it to completion. This takes spending time with Him and in His Word every day.

HOPE FOR YOU

Do you believe everything is possible with God? This does not mean it will happen and be answered as we want just because we believe. But we have to let God handle the outcome as this father did, and help us with our unbelief.

Day 299

CAST YOUR BURDEN UPON THE LORD

Cast your burden upon the Lord and He will sustain you;
He will never allow the righteous to be shaken.

—Ps. 55:22 NASB

David knew God wanted everything from him so that he would not have to carry it alone. Then God would work out all the details and handle it through him. But when we continue to fear, we can easily become shaken and give in to trusting ourselves to work it out and not God.

I know this truth, but I have failed many times in my life to trust God and let go of all my burdens, fears, doubts, and anxieties to Him. I can trust Him for most things, but somehow I think I am to be this "super-spiritual" Christian and as a martyr of the faith, carry all my own burdens.

How hurt God must be that I would assume that position when He sent His Son to die so that I would not have to do so. But God has shown me I no longer want my pride to cause any separation from receiving His love for me.

HOPE FOR YOU

Do you trust in God for everything? Are there fears, cares, concerns, doubts, and things you are fretting about needlessly? Are you playing the self-serving and prideful martyr? God is waiting for you to come totally to Him.

Day 300

HOLD FAST WITHOUT WAVERING

Let us hold fast the confession of our hope without wavering, for He who promised is faithful.

—Heb. 10:23 NASB

This was probably written to second generation Christians who may have been thinking of returning to Judaism. They were no different than we are. They soon forgot their roots and became self-sufficient. They forgot what Christ had done for them. They had given in to their fears and doubts and forgotten how they had come through persecution. They did not rely on Christ alone.

I can do the very same thing in my life. I can get so busy and want to do many things without remembering to ask if it is God's plan for me. Many times I have gotten off God's plan living life this way; but God is faithful and His promises are true for us as believers.

Hope in Him is the only thing that can complete my life, and knowing He will take care of me. It has been an awesome journey to this place, and He has it for everyone. We are the ones Jesus loves, and we must never forget that.

HOPE FOR YOU

Have you forgotten the hope of Christ that you first knew? Do you want to go back and live as before? Perhaps you have become disappointed in others and are allowing them to rob you of His joy, peace, and contentment. Remember God is faithful and His promises are true for you.

I WILL NOT BE AFRAID

> I lay down and slept; I wakened again, for the Lord sustains me. I will not be afraid of ten thousands of people who have set themselves against me round about.
>
> —Ps. 3:5–6 AMP

At this time in his life, David should have had many sleepless nights because his son, Absalom, was rebelling against him and had formed an army to kill him. But he made another choice, and God honored him. He lay down and slept.

I have spent many sleepless nights due to my insecurities and fears. I let my mind focus on me and not God, and I always ended up not sleeping.

I have found I require eight hours of sleep as God designed, otherwise I can fall into the traps of my own doing and listening to the enemy instead of my Savior. It is said our country is in need of peaceful, restful sleep, and most people don't know how to find it.

HOPE FOR YOU

Are you in need of God's peace so that you can have a good night of restful sleep? What is it you won't let Him take that keeps you from a wonderful place of rest in Him? Crisis can bring on unrest, but God is waiting for you to cry out and He will give you the peace, calm, and rest you need to handle any crisis.

Day 302

BANISH ANXIETY FROM YOUR HEART

So then, banish anxiety from your heart and cast off the troubles of your body, for youth and vigor are meaningless.
—Eccles. 11:10

Solomon was looking back on his life which, for the most part, he had lived apart from God. He knew the lessons now that he wanted others to know in their youth. He wanted to encourage others to live life fully, but live it always from the perspective of God's plan so that you will know how it will affect your life for eternity.

I know now that I should have been in the Word of God all my life and I would not have missed this truth of God through Solomon. I did not know I could overcome the anxiety, fear, and troubles which I let rob me of the peace of God in my life.

I made choices that were apart from God, and I did not view my life from His perspective. How much time I wasted living in my own fears and worry. But God is faithful to allow us to begin again at any time, and He will redeem the lost time. God has given me new meaning and purpose for the rest of my life and for eternity.

HOPE FOR YOU

How are you living day to day? Is it with God or apart from Him? Is it working for you or are your fears, anxieties, and cares getting to you? God has a different choice for your life. Make sure you find out now and not later.

Day 303

PEACE BE WITH YOU

On the evening of that first day of the week, when the disciples were together, with the doors locked for fear of the Jews, Jesus came and stood among them and said "Peace be with you!"

—John 20:19

This was the evening of the first day after Jesus rose from the grave. Jesus sought His disciples and found a group of fearful, doubting people who did not know what the next days would bring. He came into their midst through locked doors—certainly not the normal way to enter. He came to assure them about what had happened, and to show them that His promises were true. He came to give them His peace and assurance to overcome all their fear and doubts.

This was more than 2,000 years ago. Jesus is still the way to overcome any fear and doubt with His peace and His presence. I found I had lost sight of that. I knew Jesus was in me through His Holy Spirit, but I didn't allow Him to give me the peace and joy He had for me to overcome all my thoughts of fear and doubt.

I didn't spend time with Him in prayer or in studying His Word. I thought I could handle it without that close relationship. How wrong I was. Ten years ago I finally came to the place where nothing but Jesus could give me the joy, peace, and contentment I so wanted and needed. I had spent the greatest part of my life searching to fill the void in my life, only to find I had it all along, the peace and presence of God.

HOPE FOR YOU

Is your life at peace in the presence of the Lord? Only He can bring that to you. Today see how by spending time with God in His Word, you can have His lasting peace.

Day 304

ARE YOU IN TROUBLE?

The Lord is good, a refuge in times of trouble, He cares for those who trust in Him.

—Nah. 1:7

Nahum came upon the scene in the city of Nineveh. This is the same city where, 100 years earlier, Jonah had preached God's message to the people. They had listened to Jonah and obeyed and followed God. Now generations later, they once again had turned to their evil ways. Nahum was sent to bring the good news of the Lord to all who would listen and change, and also encourage those who were faithful.

I know I gave into fear and doubts and made wrong choices that impacted my life and others around me. I praise the Lord for sending those in my life who encouraged and helped me see I could change and have a new beginning in Christ.

Were my sins as evil as what the people of Nineveh had done? In God's eyes there are no measures on the amount or severity of sins, all have to be paid for and receive consequences. But God in His infinite wisdom knew I would come back from my wicked and wandering ways and then be willing to trust Him. He alone is my refuge at all times, and He takes away the fear and doubt of living. God also showed me I can seek His and other's forgiveness and be able to begin again in His grace and freedom.

HOPE FOR YOU

Is God your refuge at all times? Do you trust in Him alone, or are you still trying to make a middle ground with Him? He wants you to trust Him completely and depend on Him alone, and then He can be your only refuge.

Day 305

ARE YOU IN DESPAIR AND NEED STRENGTH?

The Lord gives strength to His people, the Lord blesses His people with peace.

—Ps. 29:11

D avid knew despairing times when only God could give him the peace he sought. David also knew he was a very weak person, and that without the strength of the Lord gave into fears and doubts and was easily influenced to live apart from God.

I have come to know I am a weak and prideful person. I have wanted to think I could handle anything and not give into despair, fear, and doubt. The truth is that the more I do it my way, the weaker I become.

I lived in my independent state apart from God for many years. But God never left me alone. He has shown me through my weaknesses that He is all the strength I will ever need. God willingly gives me His daily strength as I depend and trust only in Him.

HOPE FOR YOU

Are you depending on yourself and others for the strength you need daily to live? There is no other than God who can provide what you need. Don't spend needless time searching for another way, there is none.

Day 306

ARE YOU JOYFUL IN FEAR, PAIN, AND TROUBLE?

Consider it pure joy, my brothers, whenever you face trials of many kinds, because you know the testing of your faith develops perseverance.

—Jas. 1:2–3

Why would James (the half brother of Jesus) ever tell us to face all our fears, troubles, and the awful times with pure joy? Isn't God supposed to take care of us so that those times will never come to us? God knows what we need to go through so that we can learn the lessons He has for us. Why? So we will be encouraged and be able to encourage others as well.

I often used to consider myself the victim of bad stuff. I started my life as an illegitimate child and felt things could never be any better. I faced divorce, death, addictions, and relationships not as tests from the Lord, but as the fears and doubts from my past that would never leave me.

But God showed me that was not His plan for me at all. He wanted me to see beyond those circumstances and learn the lessons He had for me. God wanted me to grow in the knowledge of Him, and He wants that for you too. I learned life is all about His tests and how we react to them. True joy is in knowing that whatever may come, He is always with us.

HOPE FOR YOU

Are you a victim or a victor with God? Have you learned how to face your trials joyfully, or are you living in the fear and doubt of them? Be free today to face life His way.

Day 307

YOU HAVE AUTHORITY

Behold! I have given you authority *and* power to trample upon serpents and scorpions, and [physical and mental strength and ability] over all the power that the enemy [possesses] and nothing shall in any way harm you. Nevertheless, do not rejoice at this, that the spirits are subject to you, but rejoice that your names are enrolled in Heaven.
—Luke 10:19–20 AMP

Jesus knew as His children we would need to remember there is nothing to fear in this life. Not just because He could give it to us, but for the right reason—because He wanted us to trust and depend on Him alone. The most important part is having our citizenship in Heaven assured so that we can live forever with Him once our work on this earth is finished.

I have not always focused on the wonderful forever life God has assured for me as a believer and follower of Jesus Christ. In not choosing to do so, I have robbed myself of the peace of knowing that death holds no fear for me. I found I was not the only Christian to ever fear death. But that did not make it easier for me to face.

Today I live in the now God has for me. I know there is something better than I can ever imagine waiting for me, whenever God chooses to take me there. Death holds no fear for me, nor does it rob me of the urgency of living in the now.

HOPE FOR YOU

Are you assured of your place in Heaven? Do you know what it takes to have that peace? Find out now and live in the joy of knowing what God has in mind for you is better than you can ever imagine.

Day 308

DO NOT FEAR, BE STRONG

'But now be strong, . . . Be strong, all you people of the land,' declares the Lord, 'and work. For I am with you,' declares the Lord Almighty. 'This is what I covenanted with you when you came out of Egypt. And my Spirit remains among you. Do not fear.'

—Hag. 2:4–5

Haggai wrote to the Jewish people who had returned from exile and were returning to the worship of God. Do you know when fear, doubt, worries, and all your insecurities show up most? It is when we are not working or doing something. Haggai encouraged the people to be strong, not fear, and go to work.

A few years ago I hurt my left arm and just kept going. It was nothing major, but once I went to the doctor and found out the problem, I had to go through some painful and fearful workouts to get full use of it again.

A lady in our small group recently encountered the same problem and it was amazing how I was able to help her. I have encouraged her not to be fearful of the injury and to work through the difficult therapy knowing it will build the needed strength to recover completely. And she did.

HOPE FOR YOU

What is it you need to face and be strong and *work* through? What is stopping you right now from getting up and doing it? You have my permission to leave your chair and the reading of this book to go and do whatever the Lord is showing you to do. Decide now you want to overcome it, ask God how, then get up and go do it.

Day 309

I HAVE STRENGTH FOR ALL THINGS IN CHRIST

I have strength for all things in Christ Who empowers me [I am ready for anything and equal to anything through Him Who infuses inner strength into me; I am self-sufficient in Christ's sufficiency].

—Phil. 4:13 AMP

Paul saw his life was to be lived from God's point of view and not his own. He learned to be content in any situation because He knew the strength came from Christ alone.

This is a joyful and peaceful way to handle daily life. For many years I did not let Christ be my strength until I was absolutely out of my own. I have found it is better to come to Him first before I let my mind wander into thoughts that are not from Him.

God is interested in every little detail, and He wants to be involved in every area of our lives. It is a matter of getting our priorities, perspective, and our source of power in line with Christ.

HOPE FOR YOU

Where does your strength to overcome fear and doubt come from? Do you trust the Lord to get everything in proper balance in your life? Until you do, fear will be in control.

Day 310

HOPE IS THE ANTIDOTE FOR DEPRESSION

Why are you downcast, O my soul? Why so disturbed within me? Put your hope in God, for I will praise Him, my Savior and my God.

—Ps. 42:5–6

The writer of this psalm was discouraged and depressed because he was exiled to a place far from Jerusalem and could not worship in the temple. But he knew the cure for his depression and discouragement. He would dwell on the goodness of God and remember all he had in Him. It took his mind off of his present situation and gave him the joy and hope to know where he was would not last forever.

Depression is said to be the most common emotional ailment resulting from our fears and anxieties. We treat it in all kinds of ways without God being involved. I have found that our ways are only a temporary substitute for the real solution.

It is amazing that anytime I find my situation is not as I would like or think I deserve, it is usually night. Darkness seems to be able to hide the goodness of God from me. In the morning I can see clearly once again. I have learned that the darkness is also a gift from God so that I can see Him at work as well. I just have to place my hope in Him and remember all He has done for me at all times.

HOPE FOR YOU

Have you lost sight of who the Lord is and what He has done for you? Remember now to put your mind on Him, and let Him show you how to face where you are with the joy and hope that only He can bring to you.

Day 311

DO NOT WORRY OR BE ANXIOUS

And He said to His disciples, "For this reason I say to you, do not worry about your life, as to what you will eat; nor for your body, as to what you will put on."

—Luke 12:22 NASB

Jesus was very specific here about why and what not to worry about. He knew we would get caught up in the material things of life and fail to see the real meaning of faith in Him alone. He wanted us to know He loves and promises to take care of our every need.

This is not what Corporate America 101 teaches us, is it? Our world is focused economically on things, rather than on the one who provides them to us. We look out of place if we are not worrying with the rest of the world, or relying on God's plans rather than on our own.

I have spent many wasted hours trying to work out my life without even considering what God was teaching me at the time. But He never left me. He always brought me through it all because He knew one day I would see it through His eyes and not my own. Now I really want to focus on Him first, not last. It is a much easier, simpler, and fulfilling way of life.

HOPE FOR YOU

Do you worry about anything? Do you think of it as sin? What do you think you accomplish by participating in it? Admit you worry, confront it, and be free from it in Christ.

Day 312

DO NOT BE AFRAID

> Be not afraid of sudden terror *and* panic, nor of the stormy blast *or* the storm and ruin of the wicked when it comes [for you will be guiltless].
>
> —Prov. 3:25 AMP

Solomon wanted to assure us not to be afraid even when the unbelievers are in charge. We are not to be afraid of living in a world ruled by unbelievers because God knows and takes care of His own.

It is great for me to know that even though there are those who will never accept our Lord, I am not to be afraid of them. I am also not to turn away from them either. I have talked with many who, as far as I know, have not yet made the choice to trust and believe in Jesus. How sad for them and for God. But He still loves them, and so do I.

In our world today there are many different viewpoints of how to reach Heaven and live forever. I am viewed as being very narrow-minded in believing the truth of The Bible, which clearly states Jesus is the only way. We hear of attacks on Christianity throughout our country and the world, yet I will not fear. How comforting to know I have a Savior and Lord who cares and protects me from all fear.

HOPE FOR YOU

Does the nightly news frighten you concerning your faith? Is God in control of your life? There is no fear in God's truth.

Day 313

DO NOT WORRY OR BE ANXIOUS

Who of you by worrying *and* being anxious can add one unit of measure (cubit) to his stature *or* to the span of his life?

—Matt. 6:27 AMP

Do you worry, or are you just concerned? Do you know the difference? Jesus clearly tells us worry and anxiety is not good for us. Worry will not add time to our lives, and it can greatly shorten life.

I once thought I was only "concerned" with the issues of my life. But I finally had to admit to God and to myself that I worried and was anxious about everything. I felt so bad because I knew it meant I did not fully trust and depend on God with my life. But God is so gracious and forgiving, and He showed me there was another way to live without worry and being anxious.

Did I say you should never be concerned about anything in your life? *No*, but the difference is that worry will immobilize you and keep you from acting, while genuine concern will move you into action to God and trust Him to show you how to handle the issue His way.

HOPE FOR YOU

Are you a worrier and living an anxious driven life? You don't have to do so. God wants to show you a better way. Come and see the plan He has for you.

Day 314

ARE YOU ANXIOUS EVEN ABOUT YOUR CLOTHES?

> And why should you be anxious about clothes? Consider the lilies of the field *and* learn thoroughly how they grow; they neither toil nor spin. But if God so clothes the grass of the field, which today is alive *and* green and tomorrow is tossed into the furnace, will He not much more surely clothe you, O you of little faith?
>
> —Matt. 6:28, 30 AMP

J esus chose to compare what we wear to the lilies of the field. He wanted to show us since He takes care of the flowers, something we can see, He will take care of all our needs, including what we wear.

Isn't it easy to get caught up in our "wants" versus "needs"? I did. I even went into debt to have my "wants." I was out of God's balance and purpose for me by getting worried about the little things. I lost sight of God's promise to provide for me. I chose the way of debt that is so easy in our nation, instead of asking God how to handle the resources He gave me.

I am so thankful God showed me that debt is not an option to provide for the needs and wants of our family. He changed our way of handling the resources He has given us, and we share that with everyone who wants to have the same peace.

HOPE FOR YOU

Do you want to make a change to live God's way in the area of finances? He is willing to show you how right now. It is one of the best choices you will ever make.

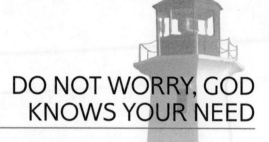

Day 315

DO NOT WORRY, GOD KNOWS YOUR NEED

So do not worry, saying, What shall we eat? Or what shall we drink? Or what shall we wear? For the pagans run after all these things, and your heavenly Father knows that you need them.

—Matt. 6:31–32

It seems we have allowed ourselves to be so concerned about us first that it is hard not to worry, isn't it? We have let our faith and our understanding of God and who He is pass from our minds and focus. Jesus Himself clearly told us we are not to worry.

Can you imagine what God feels when He sees how worried, scared, and insecure we have become by allowing ourselves to draw away from Him and all He wants to provide for us?

I have done my share of grieving and quenching the Holy Spirit in my lifetime, and I know now that is not the way to have true joy, peace, and contentment. God is clear on this issue—we are not to worry.

How do we overcome worry? God in His Word has all the keys. They are: to seek Him first, and to let Him control your thoughts and emotions. He will show you how. He is the Master teacher.

HOPE FOR YOU

Are you a great worrier, but call it something else? Today face it, call it what it is, and agree with God to let Him show you how to trust Him to not worry or fear.

Day 316

CAST ALL YOUR CARE ON HIM

Casting the whole of your care [all your anxieties, all your worries, all your concerns, once and for all] on Him, for He cares for you affectionately *and* cares about you watchfully.
—1 Pet. 5:7 AMP

Peter wanted to make sure we understood that we are to give everything to God, not just what we choose to give Him. We can get confused and feel that just because we have made a mess of things, and become caught up in carrying it all ourselves because we have sinned, that God is not concerned. He is and wants us to trust Him and change and give Him all of it.

I found myself quite often giving in to my circumstances rather than giving in to the Lord. Once I realized it was Him who controlled my circumstances, then I knew I had to cast it all on Him because it was for His glory and my good. This is not the way the world would have us believe, but God does.

HOPE FOR YOU

Are there things in your life you have been holding onto, either out of fear that God would not want to help you, or would not forgive you for attempting to handle it yourself? You can be free of it all. Give it to God, ask His forgiveness for not doing so earlier, and leave it with Him. The key is, once you give it to Him, do not get caught in the trap of wanting to take it back. Once and for all, leave it with the Lord. He can take care of it much better than anyone else.

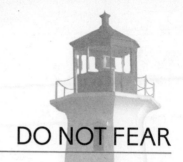

Day 317

DO NOT FEAR

> This is what I covenanted with you when you came out of Egypt. And my Spirit remains among you. Do not fear.
> —Hag. 2:5

Haggai was sent to the people living in Jerusalem to encourage them to keep working on rebuilding the temple. He reminded them how God had led them out of captivity in Egypt and even though they had sinned, He had never left them. It is also a reminder to us that even though we face many difficulties, and can get so upset with how things get handled, God's Spirit is with us.

I have been where these Jewish people were many times in life. When things got tough and it looked as if I was not getting anywhere, I wanted to give up. And I did give up many times. I would change and run from the situations only to get into even bigger ones.

Finally I realized God is everywhere and I cannot run from what He has for me to be and do. He even has all the details worked out. All I have to do is seek, ask, and obey.

HOPE FOR YOU

Are you discouraged and fearful of what you are facing? Have you lost sight of what God has done for you in the past? Will He not take care of you? Do not fear. God is here for you.

Day 318

THE LORD DELIVERS US

When the *righteous* cry for help, the Lord hears, and delivers them out of all their distress *and* troubles.

—Ps. 34:17 AMP

David knew very well how the Lord works with us. When we, as believers and righteous ones, cry out to the Lord, He hears and delivers us out of all our fears, doubts, and troubles. David had just been delivered from Abimelech after having to pretend he was insane to save his life.

I look back and I can see how the Lord delivered me out of some awful times into a life full of blessings. I am forever grateful and thankful to Him. Every time I cried out, He was there.

It took me a long time to be able to face my fears and troubles and trust Him enough to cry out. Once I knew the truth, it was easier to be able to depend and trust Him first.

HOPE FOR YOU

Are you in trouble? Do your fears and doubts have control over you rather than God? Now is the time to be sure you are a believer of the Lord Jesus Christ, and then to trust and depend on Him to hear you when you cry out. There is no other way. The sooner you find that out, the sooner your troubles will be handled once and for all.

YOU ARE CONQUERORS OVER THE WORLD

> For whatever is born of God is victorious over the world; and this is the victory that conquers the world, even our faith. Who is it that is victorious over [that conquers] the world but he who believers that Jesus is the Son of God [who Adheres to, trusts in, *and* relies on that fact].
>
> —1 John 5:4–5 AMP

John clearly tells us that we as believers are conquerors of this world. Included is everything that comes into our daily life that would rob us of victory. You cannot live in fear and be victorious in Christ at the same time. They do not mix, and it is up to each of us to see that we are living as Christ intended when He died for us.

I did not always see myself as being victorious and a conqueror in my life. My fears, and all that came with them, kept me bound in the prison I had let them create. That was not Christ's plan for me, but I just did not trust and believe that I was worthy and that He could forgive me of all I had become.

Then God came and presented Himself when I was at the very bottom of my life and showed me how important I am to Him. He told me He wanted to deliver me so I can live the life He had for me all along. Then He showed me I could be a help to others as well.

HOPE FOR YOU

Are you living the victorious Christian life that God has for you? Do you know you can be? Let go of all your fear to God now. See the marvelous plan of freedom He has for you.

Day 320

BE IN PERFECT PEACE

You will keep in perfect peace him whose mind is steadfast,
because he trusts in you.

—Isa. 26:3

David knew we can never avoid the trouble and fear that come to
us. But he knew that when our minds are focused on God our
fears do not have to take over. We can live at peace even when there is
no peace around us. Our attitude with the Lord determines how we
face life in living in a stable and steady way.

I know that when I take my eyes off the Lord, I can become very
unstable and unsteady and give in to my fears. When that happens, I
am not at peace and those around me are not either. What a sad way
to live.

On the outside I looked like everyone else, but on the inside it was a
very different story. God knew all along that I would finally accept His
truth and live at peace with Him and my environment. Why? So I can
be all He wants me to be and do for Him.

HOPE FOR YOU

Are you living in the peace of the Lord? Or are you still looking for it?
The way to do so is to trust and depend on Him alone. You must focus
all your being on Him to give you peace. Then, when fears come, you
have His mind alive in you and you can be at peace. This is the only
way to live.

Day 321

FEARING NOTHING FROM GOD AND BEING CONTENT

And God's peace [shall be yours, that a tranquil state of a soul assured of its salvation through Christ, and so fearing nothing from God and being content with its earthly lot of whatever sort that is, that peace] which transcends all understanding shall garrison and mount guard over your hearts and minds in Christ Jesus.

—Phil. 4:7 AMP

Paul was writing to the Christians at Philippi, thanking them for the gift they sent to him in prison. Paul wanted to assure them they had nothing to fear or be anxious about because contentment comes from the peace of Jesus Christ alone.

For many years I did not have peace. I was an active Christian and heard it preached and taught, but I thought because of my past I did not deserve it. I missed out on the personal meaning and message of Jesus Christ to me. But God did not give up on me ever finding Him and His true peace. It is meant for each of us who believe.

HOPE FOR ME

Are you daily living with Jesus Christ and in His peace? Are you living in your own fears and anxieties without Him? It is a choice, and now is the time to choose the way of the Lord.

Day 322

NO EVIL SHALL BEFALL YOU

Because you have made the Lord your refuge, and the Most High your dwelling place, There shall no evil befall you, nor any plague or calamity come near your tent.

—Ps. 91:9–10 AMP

The writer knew God doesn't promise us a world free from danger and fear, but He does promise His protection and help whenever we have to face it. God is our shelter when we are afraid, and God will carry us through all of them.

I spent many years not exchanging my fears for faith in the One and only Jesus Christ. I knew He would protect and carry me through them, but I didn't understand what He meant about dwelling and resting in Him alone.

I kept doing what I thought would work it all out, and when it didn't, then I would cry out. God heard me and delivered me, but I didn't feel I could ask Him to do that daily.

God, in His wisdom and knowledge of me personally, knew there would be a day where I could no longer work it out and would have to come totally to dwell and rest in Him alone. I am blessed and so grateful and thankful that day came.

HOPE FOR YOU

Are you still trying to work all your fears out yourself? Do you know what it means to dwell and rest in God? Let God show you now.

Day 323

DO NOT BE STRUCK WITH FEAR

Do not be seized with alarm *and* struck with fear, little flock, for it is your Father's good pleasure to give you the kingdom!

—Luke 12:32 AMP

L uke, as a writer of detail, was a companion of Paul. His style shows us how Jesus wants us not to be afraid or struck with fear. Come and know Him and allow Him to handle all the details of your life.

I am so blessed to finally know what Jesus actually meant for me concerning fear. I do not have to allow the spirit of fear to strike me at every point. In looking back, it hasn't been so very long ago that I allowed myself to be struck with fear at every turn.

What an awful prison to live in. It wasn't a real prison, but it felt like one. The Lord showed me how to come to Him first and let Him handle every detail before fear can strike at me.

HOPE FOR YOU

Does fear strike at you often? God has given us so much, but it does not include letting fear strike us. Let Him show you how to avoid it so that you can be free to do what He has for you.

Day 324

DO NOT FEAR OTHER GODS

And I said to you, I am the Lord your God; fear not the gods of the Amorites, in whose land you dwell. But you have not obeyed My voice.

—Judg. 6:10 AMP

The writer, possibly Samuel, recorded what the Lord sent a prophet to the Israelites to say. The Israelites disobeyed God and He wanted them to know how to get through. It was not by being afraid and being tempted to worship other gods which were all around them. He wanted them to know He was the only God and that only He could help them. It is not recorded how many of them changed, but Gideon was able to defeat the enemies around them.

Many times I have been just like these Jewish people. I disobeyed God and then became afraid and was tempted to get involved in other things that were certainly not of God.

I even gave in to those temptations. But God never left me alone. He was always willing to forgive and forget, and He helped me get on His path once more. He knew at some point I would finally come to Him first each day and live as He wanted.

HOPE FOR YOU

Are you living in disobedience to God? Is your life filled with joy or fear? He is ready to forgive and show you the way today. Won't you ask Him?

Day 325

TRADE ALL OUR FEARS
FOR FAITH IN HIM

He who dwells in the secret place of the Most High shall remain stable *and* fixed under the shadow of the Almighty [whose power no foe can withstand].

—Ps. 91:1 AMP

We are not sure who wrote this psalm, but the truth is very clear. God is our secret place to dwell, and when we dwell in Him, nothing can touch us. God wants us to trade all our fears for faith in Him, no matter how severe they may be. Trust Him. He can handle them all.

I once thought so lowly of myself that I could not see how God or anyone would want to pull me out of the mess and despair I had allowed to become my life. But God is our secret place and dwelling with Him is the only way our fears can be faced and overcome—His way.

I had been convinced that I was a nothing and that not even God could make something out of me. Do not allow anyone to convince you of that lie. There is always hope for the most desperate because God cares and loves us so.

HOPE FOR YOU

Do you need to trade in your fears for faith in God alone? He is waiting for you to do so. God will take them and show you how to handle them His way.

Day 326

COMMIT AND TRUST IN THE LORD

> Commit your way to the Lord [roll and repose each care of your load on Him]; trust (lean on, rely on, and be confident) also in Him and He will bring it to pass.
>
> —Ps. 37:5 AMP

David knew that life in God is about trust and commitment to Him. It means we have to personally know the Lord first. Then we have to believe that He will take care of us better than we could ever do for ourselves. In his life, David found this to be real. He lived believing in the goodness of God rather than dwelling on his problems.

In my life, I knew to trust and commit to the Lord, but I put certain areas and conditions on how much and how far I would go. What a confusing and messy life I lived.

God has shown me His way is the only way, and He even recently allowed a car accident to bring me to the point of realizing there were still areas and conditions where I had not totally trusted Him yet. Now I've given them to Him to handle.

HOPE FOR YOU

Are there areas of your life that you are withholding from God? Do you think He is not able, or does not care enough, to help you with them? God wants to show you now there is nothing too big or too small that He will not take from us. All you have to do is to trust God with them and commit yourself to Him to do so.

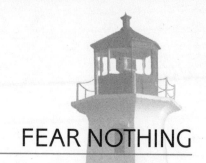

Day 327

FEAR NOTHING

> Do not fear anything except the LORD Almighty. He alone is the Holy One. If you fear him, you need fear nothing else.
>
> —Isa. 8:13 NLT

Isaiah was regarded, along with most of the prophets, as a traitor. He did not support Judah's national policies, and he called the people to commit to God and put Him first and then the government. He even went so far as to predict the overthrow of the government.

In looking back, I should have taken this message from Isaiah as truth in my life. Even though it was written many centuries ago to people in a different land and world, it still applies to us today. We can get caught up in the fears our world governments and others around us face because they do not trust in the Lord, nor do they view life from His perspective.

God does not want us to be afraid of Him as the word "fear" implies. He wants us to honor and hold Him in reverence first over everything else. When we do that, and continue to do so, we realize we have nothing to fear, because He is handling it all for us.

I have learned to trust and depend on the Lord first. Only then can I allow Him to control how I face life and handle the many blessings He gives me every day.

HOPE FOR YOU

Are you living in the fears of man and the world? Or do you honor and give reverence to God first? Men and the world will rob you of the peace that God has for you. Which way do you choose to live?

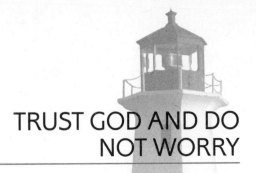

Day 328

TRUST GOD AND DO NOT WORRY

The Holy Spirit told me to go with them and not to worry about their being Gentiles. These six brothers here accompanied me, and we soon arrived at the home of the man who had sent for us.

—Acts 11:12 NLT

This describes the challenge Peter faced while obeying and going to and eating with the Gentiles. Peter was worried about how it would look and why was he called to go to them. But Peter trusted God to work it out, and he also took others with him. The story shows us the importance of the Holy Spirit living within us. Peter showed us how to listen and act knowing the power of God lives within us.

I am so thankful and grateful that Peter overcame his fear and worry and went to the Gentiles to share the message of Jesus. In his doing so, I am able to know the Lord today. God is not confined to one group of people, but He is for everyone. Also being of Native American decent, I am glad God knows no boundaries as man would place on others.

Hope for You

Are you still living in the fear of others? Is race, color, and influence part of your fear? Learn as Peter did to listen and trust the Holy Spirit living inside you as a believer, and overcome the fears that have been placed on you.

Day 329

WHO CAN BE AGAINST US?

What then shall we say to these things? If God is for us, who is against us?

—Rom. 8:31 NASB

Paul is assuring his people that God wants everyone to know Him. And trusting and believing in Jesus Christ is the only way to be able to do so. Paul also wanted to give the message of hope and that God will take care of everything that comes. We have nothing to fear when we face life God's way.

I lived for many years thinking I was not good enough for God. He couldn't possibly mean these words for me. I let the fears and influence of others rob me of what God had for me all along.

Not only is He willing to secure my future in heaven with Him, but He wants to make the journey there His plan for my life. It is such an awesome gift to me, and now I know I don't deserve it, but I am to just receive and live in true thankfulness to God for His gift to me.

HOPE FOR YOU

Are you working to earn your way to live in this life and in Heaven? Do you know that Jesus Christ already did the work for you? Today, believe, trust, and receive Him and know you are truly His, and there is nothing to ever fear again.

Day 330

DO NOT BE ANXIOUS
OR TROUBLED

And [Jesus] said to His disciples, "Therefore I tell you do not be anxious *and* troubled [with cares] about your life, as to what you will [have to] eat; or about your body as to what you [have to] wear."

—Luke 12:22 AMP

Jesus commands and demands us not to worry about anything. What is the key to getting out of the trap of fear and doubt? First of all, it comes with putting Him ahead of everything else. Nothing is more important than our relationship with God and living the plan He has for each of us.

Once I got this message into my mind, I would like to tell you I never feared or worried again. But the truth is, I have to make a daily commitment to spend time with God so that fear, worry, and doubt have no place in my life.

I have faced some tough times in the past, some are here right now, and I know there will be others that will come my way. But when fear and worry wants to creep in, it is then I know I need the Lord more than ever.

It is then that the Bible has to be my constant companion. It is then that I have to avoid those who would want to draw me into the same fears and worries they are in. It can come quickly, but God is ready to pull me right out of it and on to victory in Him.

HOPE FOR YOU

Are you stuck in a pit of defeat? Have you let your fears, and the fears of others, rob you of the peace of the Lord and the ability to overcome those fears? Today be free, rest, and abide in the Lord and see the plan He has for you.

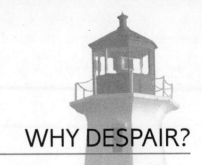

WHY DESPAIR?

> Why are you in despair, O my soul? And why are you disturbed within me? Hope in God, for I shall praise Him, The help of my countenance and my God.
>
> —Ps. 43:5 NASB

The temple assistants wanted to show that hope in God alone overcomes any despair, fear, or worry we may face.

I have faced many times where I could not see the way. I felt there was no answer to what I was facing deep in my soul and life.

Then God showed up. He is the hope and the way out of everything. Through the Holy Spirit, we are guided to His truth. We can depend on God to keep us from getting into those same pits over and over again.

HOPE FOR YOU

Are you in such a state that you can only see despair, fear, and doubt? Have you lost hope in God and the belief that He can and wants to bring you out safely? There is hope for you, and the Lord is waiting to show it to you. Come, trust, depend, and receive the truth.

Day 332

WAIT ON THE LORD FOR YOUR HELP

He lifted me out of the pit of despair, out of the mud and the mire. He set my feet on solid ground and steadied me as I walked along.

—Ps. 40:2 NLT

David knew when he wanted an answer quickly from God, sometimes God's answer was to wait. David had come to know that normally we do not get into these situations quickly and God wants to make sure we see all the benefits of waiting before helping us out of them.

My Mother always told me I chose to do things and live life the hard way, and God would always punish me and it would never get any better. She instilled hopelessness in me because that was the way she lived her life. She cursed God instead of praising Him. I was confused for a long time.

After hearing her talk and seeing her disbelief for many years, I believed her lie that God was punishing me, and that I was never going to be good enough to enjoy the victorious life He had for me.

But God has shown me He loves me very much, and He had a plan for my life all along; even though many times I could not see it. He has shown me that waiting on Him is worth it, and that even in the wait, there is His hope over the fear, doubt, and despair.

My Mother finally let God love her too; and we were able to see God's plan at work in our lives together.

HOPE FOR YOU

Are you waiting on God for the answer to what you are facing, or are you trying to figure it out and make it work yourself? Come out of the dark into the light of God and let Him show you the wait is worth it.

Day 333

OUR VICTORY OVER
FEAR IS IN GOD

There they are, overwhelmed with dread, for God is present in the company of the righteous.

—Ps. 14:5

D avid knew the only way to face and overcome the fears and dread of this world was total belief in God alone. He knew that even though it looked as if we were fighting a losing battle, there was no doubt God was with us. And we win.

I have spent many wasted hours focusing on what I can't, don't, and will never have or be rather than what I have, what God has done for me, and what He has waiting for me. There is no doubt God is with us, in us, and for us. So there are no fears, doubts, or dreads that I ever have to allow myself to focus on again.

HOPE FOR YOU

What are you focusing on? Do you feel you are fighting a losing battle or do you see God's victory for you? Today He is ready to free you from your prison of fear.

Day 334

HE WILL KEEP YOU IN PEACE SO THAT FEAR HAS NO PLACE

You will guard him *and* keep him in perfect *and* constant peace whose mind [both its inclination and its character] is stayed on You, because he commits himself to You, leans on You, *and* hopes confidently in You.

—Isa. 26:3 AMP

Isaiah told the people what God had revealed to Him regarding the future. He wanted them to know that those who chose to believe in the Lord by committing to, leaning on, and hoping in Him will receive constant peace in their lives, no matter what will come. We can make that same choice and know the peace that overcomes any fear or doubt.

We cannot avoid what goes on around us, but we can choose God's way to handle it all. For many years I thought I had to take care of everything, and did not see that I had a choice to let God do it through me.

It is God I needed to trust and depend on, not my own ways. Once I realized the choice I had, I have never been the same. I am a more peaceful person, and I see my life through the perspective of God rather than my own.

HOPE FOR YOU

Are you living in the constant peace of God? Or do the world and people shake you to the core? God has constant peace waiting for you; come and trust Him today.

Day 335

DWELL WITH THE LORD, AND EVIL WILL FLEE

> Because you have made the Lord your refuge, and the Most High your dwelling place, There shall be no evil befall you, nor any plague or calamity come near your tent.
> —Ps. 91:9–10 AMP

This writer assures us of the hope and peace that we can have by keeping the Lord first in our lives. We will have fear to face and all that comes with it. But God will protect and send His angels to guard those who trust in Him completely.

I have seen this in action in my life. I can be the most discontented, discouraged, and fearful person when I take my life out of the hands of the Lord—when I take control of my own life. I lived that way for many years, even going to church and acting as if I was faithful to Him.

But when God showed me I was not living the victorious life He had intended for me, my life changed on the inside. Did my circumstances change so I could live the perfect life? Certainly not, but God showed me that life could be faced differently, and now I see how He protects me and leads me in His ways and not my own.

HOPE FOR YOU

Are you on a roller coaster ride of life? Are you getting weary and want to give up? God has a plan for you and He is waiting for you come and find it His way.

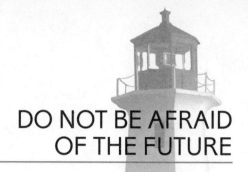

Day 336

DO NOT BE AFRAID OF THE FUTURE

> And when you hear of wars and insurrections (disturbances, disorder, and confusion), do not become alarmed *and* panic-stricken *and* terrified; for all this must take place first, but the end will not [come] immediately.
>
> —Luke 21:9 AMP

Jesus wanted us to know that our future is secure in Him. We are not to be afraid of what we hear, but we are to trust in Him to take care of us through anything.

In my lifetime I have seen much of what the Lord said would come. I have seen the wrath of war and the terror of weather and the evil they bring upon others. It seems to get even worse as the days go on.

I used to let myself get caught up in the world of trying to figure out and plan the future. Then God showed me clearly that I can refuse to enter into the belief of others that we are living in the "last days" and trying to define when the Lord will return for us, His church.

I have a simple understanding of not living in fear and letting the Lord control my days. I live everyday in the expected hope of His return for us. It could be as I write these words, and that will be just fine because He is in control of it all.

HOPE FOR YOU

Where are your thoughts and life focused today? Are they on a future of hope, joy, peace, and contentment or on the fears of everyone else? Look up, your redemption is near, and there is nothing to fear.

JESUS CAME SO WE CAN ENJOY LIFE, NOT FEAR IT

The thief comes only in order to steal and kill and destroy. I came that they may have *and* enjoy life, and have it in abundance (to the full, till it overflows).

—John 10:10 AMP

Jesus came to give us life for eternity and also a new beginning right now. He wants us to live life to the fullest and not let anyone rob us of it.

For too many years I let the thieves of this world rob me of the full life I have as a believer and follower of Jesus Christ. I let everything besides God control my thoughts and life. I gave in to every fear that came along. Then God showed me that was not His plan for me, and that I had at my fingertips the gift of life now and forever.

HOPE FOR YOU

Are you living life in the fullness of God or in the fears of this world? Today you can be free to live as Jesus intends and know the abundance He has for you.

Day 338

WHY LIVE IN FEAR OF OTHER GODS AND FORGET THE TRUE GOD?

Of whom have you been so afraid and in dread that you lied *and* were treacherous and did not [seriously] remember Me, did not even give me a thought? Have I not been silent, even for a long time, and so you do not fear Me?

—Isa. 57:11 AMP

Isaiah was letting the people of Judah know that God was not pleased with those who pretend to love and serve Him but at the same time live in fear and dread of other gods and the people who worship them. Isaiah knew that God would expose these people for who they were. He was not pleased with them.

God has not always been pleased with the way I chose to live my life. I let the world and other gods come in and wipe away the memory of His saving grace for me. Then those things became my focus, not God.

Bur God is faithful. He never left me and He knew my heart wanted to love and honor Him. He is a God of second chances or more—as many as it takes to bring us into the knowledge of putting Him first and living the life and plan He has for us.

Who would ever have thought God could take a fearful person like me and show through me that His Words are the truth? Then take me to a new level of living so that I can help others learn His truth too?

Hope for You

Are you living in dread and fear of other gods or in honor and reverence of the Lord? Are you trying to live in both worlds? Choose the real truth. God is waiting.

Day 339

OF WHOM SHALL I BE AFRAID?

The Lord is my Light and my Salvation—whom shall I fear *or* dread? The Lord is my Refuge *and* Stronghold of my life—of whom shall I be afraid?

—Ps. 27:1 AMP

D avid knew the truth of this statement from an unknown author. "Unwavering confidence in God is our antidote for fear and loneliness." David had experienced the deep, dark pit of fear that we can become prisoners of when we do not allow God to be our Light and Salvation. That lonely place when we forget that God alone is our Refuge and Stronghold.

I can remember the dark and lonely prison of fear that kept me bound so that I could not remember the God of my salvation. I forgot that He alone was the answer. I spent many years serving my sentence in that prison of doubt until ten years ago when, at the lowest point of my prison life, God showed me how to break the chains that held me and truly know He is my Refuge and Stronghold.

HOPE FOR YOU

How long is your prison sentence? Are you ready to escape with no fear of ever having to go back? Today God is waiting to show you how.

Day 340

THE DESIRE OF THE RIGHTEOUS
WILL BE GRANTED

The thing a wicked man fears shall come upon him, but the desire of the [uncompromisingly] righteous shall be granted.

—Prov. 10:24 AMP

S olomon knew the wisdom of God always involves a choice. God is not one of command and demand without loving and honoring Him first. God will not impose Himself on us. God wants us to choose to love and serve Him.

Growing up, I did not see the goodness of God. I only saw the fear I thought He had created in my family. I worked to please, serve, and love Him; but out of fear and dread rather than love and honor.

I did not see the choice God gave me. I only saw the results of others who had failed to live up to His commands and demands and had eventually given up and lived life apart from Him.

But God never gave up on me. He knew I would someday "get the message" and that it would change me forever. I no longer fear death or anything else that would rob me of the goodness of my Lord and Savior.

HOPE FOR YOU

Are you afraid of dying and of choosing to live as well? Do you see God as a commander and demander, or as a loving Father, friend, and the one who loves you so? Today choose God and let Him show you the difference.

Day 341

GOD WILL SUPPLY EVERY NEED

And my God will supply all your needs according to His riches in glory in Christ Jesus.

—Phil. 4:19 NASB

Paul was writing to his friends from his final prison cell before he was beheaded. He had faced many tests and trials in his journeys to share Christ. They were not only with the Jews, but with the Gentiles as well. He had come to know that Jesus would supply all that was needed to live—even the courage to face death.

I had heard these messages from Paul preached over and over again, but the reality and truth did not become personal to me until I faced death several times.

Death has no fear for me now, but I see that for many others the thought of it still does. Usually the ones who fear death are not content to know we will all face it at some time. They have not let God meet their needs in this life, so how can they know He will take care of them in death as well?

I have been just like many of you; nothing could satisfy me. There was not enough food and money to give me the peace and comfort I longed for. I finally found only Jesus can, and He is enough and all I ever need. Jesus paid the price so I would not have to fear death but face it knowing His love is all I need, and I will see Him and be able to thank Him in person.

HOPE FOR YOU

Have you personally met Jesus, and is He enough for you? Are you living in discontentment and nothing seems to be working for you? Join the Joy, Peace, Contentment (JPC) force today. Set the Lord first in your life, feed on His Word, and He will give you the joy, peace, and contentment you need to meet anything that comes your way—even death.

Day 342

I SHALL BE SAVED FROM MY ENEMIES

I will call upon the Lord, Who is to be praised; so shall I be saved from my enemies.

—Ps. 18:3 AMP

Are you in need of protection and a new way of life? David was, and He knew how to receive it. He called upon God in true faith, and he was saved from his enemies.

It is the same for all of us. Each of us has to come and call upon the Lord in true belief and He will save us from all our fears, the enemies that seek us, and the loss of joy in our lives.

We can search the world over, as I have done, and there is nothing besides true belief in the Lord Jesus Christ that can save us. He told us there are no other ways to the Father but through Him, and no other way to live forever in Heaven except by Him. It was a long journey for me to come to that simple truth, but when I did, it changed my life forever.

HOPE FOR YOU

Are you still seeking something else in the place of saving faith in Jesus Christ alone? I can assure you He is the only way, and today can be the day you see that for yourself.

Day 343

DO NOT WORRY ABOUT WHAT TO SPEAK OR SAY

When they bring you before the synagogues and the rulers and authorities, do not worry about how or what you are to speak in your defense, or what you are to say.

—Luke 12:11 NASB

Jesus knew His disciples would never be able to confront the religious rulers and authorities in their own strength. He sent the Holy Spirit to live inside of each believer. And by accepting that truth, the disciples would not have to worry about defending themselves to others.

It is an accepted fact that one of the biggest fears in our country is speaking in front of others. This includes sharing our faith with those who do not believe and who have the authority to damage our livelihoods and way of life.

At one time in my life I wanted to be a Country Western Gospel singer. I loved singing for anyone who would listen. But I was terrified about having to speak to anyone. I let my fear of speaking override my gift of singing for the Lord.

But God did not give up on me. He led me to a company that saw some potential in me. They provided the training and experience I needed to become a speaker and corporate manager. I had a full career of encouraging and serving others to do the same. This prepared the way for me now to share the good news of the Lord without fear of others. I will forever be grateful that God did not give up on me. And who knows? That deep down desire to sing can still become a reality!

HOPE FOR YOU

Are you afraid to speak to anyone? Today, be set free from that fear. The Holy Spirit is ready to show you how. Then you will be able to share with many the good news of Jesus Christ.

Day 344

WHY LIVE AS A CAPTIVE? GOD WANTS TO SET YOU FREE

> Yet you have forgotten the Lord, your Creator, the one who put the stars in the sky and established the earth. Will you remain in constant dread of human oppression? Will you continue to fear the anger of your enemies from morning to night?
>
> —Isa. 51:13 NLT

I saiah told the Jewish people they were not honoring the true God at this time. Instead they feared Babylon. They had reason to fear the Babylonians, who could take them captive, but they also had a loving God who wanted to save them from their fears.

We are not so different from those Jewish people centuries ago, are we? There is so much fear all around us coming from every source, that we have forgotten the one who created us and the earth. God has the power to set us free from our fears.

We are even trying to take God out of everything we hold dear because we do not want to commit and submit to the one who loves us so much. We want to be the god of our own lives and do not realize that God will never let us do so for long.

At one point in my life I thought I could handle my life without God. God knew all along that I did not have the power or authority to do so. I failed miserably. But God forgave me and showed me how to begin again to allow Him to be in total control.

HOPE FOR YOU

Are you leaving and putting God out of your life? Are you able to handle your fears? God is waiting for you to choose Him, and He is willing to forgive and forget.

Day 345

BE STRONG, YOU WHO PUT YOUR HOPE IN THE LORD

So be strong and courageous, all you who put your hope in the Lord!

—Ps. 31:24 NLT

These words, written by either David or Jeremiah, give us the message of commitment and total dependence on the Lord so that we can be strong and have the courage to face, confront, and overcome our fears—God's way.

I have not considered myself strong, nor have I had the courage to face and confront my fears. That is why I let them control me for so long.

I have finally learned that it is not my strength and courage which confront and overcome the fears of my life. Rather it is the hope that only the Lord can give and show me how to have His strength and courage in my life. Then I can face and overcome fear—His way.

HOPE FOR YOU

Are you living in the strength and courage of the Lord, or are you trying to face and confront your fears in your own strength and courage? Choose God today and live victorious.

Day 346

WHY ARE YOU WORRIED ABOUT FOOD?

Jesus knew what they were thinking, so He said, "You have so little faith! Why are you worried about having no food?"
—Matt. 16:8 NLT

Jesus was not as concerned about the disciples not having food as He was about the faith they had in Him. Even though He had provided food on many occasions, they still did not see He would take care of them. Jesus wanted to make sure they understood His principles and what it would take to become a true follower of His.

I can really understand the disciples in this situation. Even though we know Jesus can do miracles and has all the power, we still think we have to be or do something too. It is too simple to believe that it is all about Him and that we don't have to do anything except receive His gift.

I did not feel worthy enough to receive His free gift to me until I came to know that belief was just a trap of Satan. I lost precious time believing Satan's lies rather than the truth of the Lord. But God still loved me and now I am able to believe it is truly all about Him. I am blessed He chose me to love.

HOPE FOR YOU

Are you still living in only a little faith as the disciples were? Do you feel you aren't worthy of God's gift and so have not totally received it from Him? Today can be a new day for you. Believe, trust, and put all your faith in Jesus and not in yourself or others.

I WILL NOT BE TERRIFIED

> So we take comfort *and* are encouraged *and* confidently *and* boldly say, "The Lord is my Helper; I will not be seized with alarm [I will not fear or dread or be terrified]. What can man do to me?"
>
> —Heb. 13:6 AMP

The writer, possibly Paul, wrote to the second generation Christians who had lost faith and trust in the Lord. It is easy to become discontented and fail to remember that the Lord is here so that we do not have to live as non-believers do.

I was once the materialistic gal; having been raised without the love and things I saw others had in life, I thought I had to work hard to earn my place and that I deserved to be rewarded for doing so. God was in my life, but He was not my life.

It took me years to realize what I had allowed to happen, and then understand His ways and what life was really all about. It was hard to trust God alone for everything and not want to go back to my old ways.

I have learned how great it is to be a giver, saver, and spender in that order. I have God's balance in my life to overcome all the insecurities and fear that materialism creates in our lives.

HOPE FOR YOU

Do things and having the best come ahead of God being first in your life? What is the order of how you take care of the resources God gives you? His ways bring peace and security.

Day 348

THE LORD BLESSES WITH RICHES AND NO TROUBLES

The blessing of the Lord brings wealth, and He adds no trouble to it.

—Prov. 10:22

S olomon realized he was blessed to be considered the richest man who ever lived. But he also knew he had not used the wealth as God intended. God requires wealth to be used wisely. God gives us wealth so that He can teach us how to use it to honor Him.

I once did not see how the resources I received could make any difference at all in the lives of others. The need looked too overwhelming and I had obligations to my family as well. The truth was I did not want to give up my resources because I had based my security in them instead of in God. What a selfish view of life.

Clearly I did not trust and depend on God to take care of me, nor did I understand His principle of giving. But God changed my heart and helped me see it truly is "more blessed to give than receive" as stated in Acts 20:35. I am so grateful and thankful that giving is first in my life; and God has never failed financially or otherwise to take care of me.

HOPE FOR YOU

Are you a giver or a taker? Is your security found in your wealth, or in God? It is a choice. Make God's choice for your life now.

Day 349

TRUST GOD AND SEE HIS RESULTS

And let us not lose heart *and* grow weary *and* faint in acting nobly *and* doing right, for in due time *and* at the appointed season we shall reap, if we do not loosen *and* relax our courage and faint.

—Gal. 6:9 AMP

Paul knew how hard it was to keep doing the right things for God and receive no thanks nor see any results for his efforts. He challenged the Galatians to keep on doing what is right and trusting God for the results. In God's timing we will receive the blessings, if we do not give up.

I am one who focused on end results, not on the lessons learned getting there. I was a good corporate leader through and through. But blessings did not come fast enough for me.

I would give up too easily and move on to something else that I thought would get quicker results. I did this in all areas of my life. I ended up working for 40 years with little of the true blessings God had for me.

My relationships and spiritual life were not too pretty either. I didn't think I looked any different than anyone else in America. But God knew there was a different plan for me. He took me to the bottom so that I could come full circle to the top—His way. I thank Him for not giving up on me. I now make the commitment to run my race in life His way and not my own.

HOPE FOR YOU

Are results more important than God in your life? Are you sacrificing the blessings He has for you to receive them? God wants to show you His plan now.

Day 350

IS YOUR SLEEP SWEET?

When you lie down, you will not be afraid; when you lie down, your sleep will be sweet.

—Prov. 3:24

Solomon knew God wants us to trust Him with everything. And when we do, we will be at peace and be able to rest well at night. God knows the design of our bodies requires rest. He does not want anything to interfere with that process.

Do you have trouble sleeping? Do you have fearful nightmares? God has designed us to be able to rest, no matter what is going on in our lives. It is a proven fact that lack of sleep is a major problem in America.

Why don't we sleep? Don't we realize that much harm can come to our bodies when we do not rest well? I have found when I do not allow God to guide and control my life, I am not at peace. Then I have trouble sleeping.

My fears have kept me awake many times in my life. But now I have learned that I need to make sure I am at peace with God in all areas. Then I can rest well, and have the sweet sleep of life.

HOPE FOR YOU

What is it that makes you afraid of going to sleep? What prevents you from getting the proper amount and the kind of rest you need? Sleep is to be peaceful. Unless you unload your mind and renew it in the Lord and let Him control every area of it, you will not be getting the sweet rest He has for you.

DO NOT FEAR WHAT SURROUNDS YOU

I will not fear the tens of thousands drawn up against me on every side.

—Ps. 3:6

How could David keep from being afraid when all he could see were people surrounding and getting ready to kill him?

What is the major difference between us and King David, who reigned thousands of years ago? The answer is that David knew where his true help came from. He also was willing to submit, admit, and humble himself and cry out to our one true God for help.

For many years I thought I was supposed to be wise enough to work out my own problems independent of God. When my plans did not work out, God was the next option.

How messed up my concept of God and my relationship with Him was. But now I know God is ready to take care of my every need. I can rest in Him to handle it all and show me the right choices to make before I get to those fearful times.

HOPE FOR YOU

Are you living independent of God? Do you run to Him only when things are not working out? Stop and see the big picture. God is first and we are not to live without Him in control. Get your priorities and thinking focused on Him first and experience the difference.

Day 352

IS YOUR HEART FEARFUL?

> Though an army besiege me, my heart will not fear; though war break out against me, even then I will be confident.
>
> —Ps. 27:3

Are you living a life of total confidence in God? Or is it one of fear? In our world today, fear is accepted and really expected, isn't it? But God's ways and thoughts are opposite of ours. David knew that even though he was surrounded by armies and everything looked hopeless, God would take care of him.

Fear can be a dark force that controls us. It can seem like a real person. I can remember living in my fears. My heart would pound and I felt all alone. I also remember when I asked God for help. He took away the feeling of fear and gave me one of confidence in Him. Fear did not control me. He did, and that is the way I choose to live.

HOPE FOR YOU

Today are you living in the bright freedom light of God? Are you totally satisfied in Him? Or are you allowing fear to rob you of the joy, peace, and contentment God has for you? There are lots of fears we can let control us, but God says we don't have to let anything but His light and salvation be the controlling force and way of life for us. God truly is *"The Lighthouse of Hope."*

Day 353

LIFE IS MORE IMPORTANT THAN CARES, PROBLEMS, AND OURSELVES

And [Jesus] said to His disciples, therefore I tell you, do not be anxious *and* troubled [with cares] about your life, as to what you will [have to] eat; or about your body, as to what you will [have to] wear.

—Luke 12:22 AMP

Jesus spent a lot of time speaking about not being anxious or troubled. So why are we? Do we not trust and depend on Him? Life is more important than the things of this world and ourselves, but do we really believe that?

I once thought that living a life free of anxiety, worry, and fear was not possible. Why did I believe that? I did not trust and depend on Jesus with my fears and worries. Therefore, He could not help me.

When I finally reached the end of being able to handle it all alone, I realized how I had hurt God. I had let if affect not only my life, but others that were living it with me. I did not take time to spend with God in His Word so that He could show me daily the plan for my life.

HOPE FOR YOU

Are you too busy worrying and living in fear to ask God for His help? Do you believe and trust God to handle it all, and that change can come to you? Today is the day to make the choice—God or you. Which will it be?

Day 354

TRUST GOD; DON'T BE AFRAID

Surely God is my salvation; I will trust and not be afraid.

—Isa. 12:2

Are you afraid to trust even God? Are you afraid He wants to change you into someone you don't want to be? Isaiah tells us we need to realize who God is. He is our creator. He created us for Himself, not the other way around. We sinned, but even then God has a way for us to still be His.

It all takes total trust in Him. In this world it is very hard to trust. We have seen so many broken trusts, lies, and deceit taking place that it doesn't seem we can see those who are to be trusted.

I had a lot of issues with trust. My life was formed out of lies, and they just kept building. I finally came to the place where Jesus freed me from the chains of my past and showed me He is the only One I can trust forever.

HOPE FOR YOU

What or whom do you trust in today? Are you afraid or at peace? God wants to show you His way if you will only trust and obey. There is a constant reminder all around us. Pull out your wallet or purse and find coinage and bills and read these words over and over again, "In God We Trust."

This is no accident or coincidence; God can and is to be trusted.

Day 355

DO NOT BE FRIGHTENED BY THOSE WHO OPPOSE YOU

> Whatever happens, conduct yourselves in a manner worthy of the gospel of Christ. Then, whether I come and see you or only hear about you in my absence, I will know that you stand firm in one spirit, contending as one man for the faith of the gospel without being frightened in any way by those who oppose you. This is a sign to them that they will be destroyed, but that you will be saved—and that by God.
>
> —Phil. 1:27–28

This letter was written to the Philippians by Paul, as he was in prison. He wanted to encourage the believers to be in unity and stand strong in their faith of the message of Jesus Christ.

Does your life portray the gospel or are you always complaining and criticizing what is going on around you? Is it all about you or all about Christ? God wants to work mightily in each of us. But how can He if we are out of unity, first with Him, ourselves, and others in His church?

I spent too much time and effort judging and reacting to the ways of the church world instead of learning to see the plan God had for me and for others. I was not an encourager; I was a discourager. I ended up afraid and alone. But God saw my need and showed me how to begin again and become the person He had in mind all along.

HOPE FOR YOU

Are you living in unity and are you at peace with everyone? Do you criticize and cause others not to want to listen or be around you? Are you living for God or for yourself? Be honest and God will show you how to have peace and unity in your life.

Day 356

BANISH ANXIETY AND CAST OFF TROUBLES

So then, banish anxiety from your heart and cast off the
troubles of your body, for youth and vigor are meaningless.
—Eccles. 11:10

Solomon looked back at his life and knew he had not done what mattered most. In his later years, he drew close to God, but for most of his life, he lived apart from God. He is encouraging us to choose God and follow the plan God has for us. We are not to live in anxiety, fear, and the troubles created by living separately from God.

We would all choose to live some things differently if we had the ability to do so. But God, when He created each of us, knew what our choices would be and how our lives would turn out.

God placed us in families—in the skin and parts of the world where He wanted us to be. I would not have chosen the family I grew up in. But I now see there was a plan, and I am blessed to be able to say I thank God for it.

God carried me through all the anxieties, fears, and troubles created by my past. He showed me how to live in spite of the circumstances. He gave me new beginnings over and over again, even when I did not deserve them. God brought me to this place where I am content and I can help others see His plan for them as well. Why? Because God saw my heart and loved me for wanting to bring Him glory, and help others see life is truly all about Him.

HOPE FOR YOU

Where is your life at now? Are you older and looking back, or are you young and looking forward to life? In either stage, is God first and are you living His plan or your own?

Day 357

THE LORD LIFTS THE BURDENS

The Lord opens the eyes of the blind. The Lord lifts the burdens of those bent beneath their loads. The Lord loves the righteous.

—Ps. 146:8 NLT

The writers of this psalm were probably just returning from exile to Jerusalem. They were telling us that the greatest joy God receives is to be trusted and worshiped.

I have disappointed God and many others in my life. I didn't always see the reason God created me, and I didn't live my life as His righteous child. But God never left me out in the cold. He brought me to the place He had for me all along—that of total trust in Him alone.

I want to spend time and live God's way for me. He showed me part of that plan includes being an encouragement to others; so that many will see that God is the answer to all their cares and burdens. No matter how big or small our fear is; God can be trusted to handle it all.

HOPE FOR YOU

Are you one of God's righteous ones? Are you accepted, forgiven, and living as the saint of God which you are? Do you know you are a special work of art that God created? Are you trusting and worshiping God alone? He is to be trusted.

Day 358

THE PEACE OF JESUS OVERCOMES THE WORLD

I have told you all this so that you may have peace in me. Here on earth you will have many trials and sorrows. But take heart, I have overcome the world.

—John 16:33 NLT

Jesus summed up all His teachings with these words. He wanted to make sure His disciples understood how to live and go on once He was no longer with them.

Did the disciples understand right away after seeing and living with Jesus? It took them many trials and sorrows before they realized the impact of the Lord on them and the world to come.

I am so excited that I was introduced to Jesus at an early age. Through all my fears, anxieties, and the messy life I let myself be led into, He still cared enough to give me His peace and the knowledge that this is not all there is to life.

I have much to be thankful and grateful for, and I am still focused on seeing what God has in mind for me even in this season of my life. The good news is, Jesus has been with me and will be with me through all the struggles. Our victory has already been secured by Him alone.

HOPE FOR YOU

Do you know the peace of Jesus? Do you know the victory has already been won for you? Find out how to live through and overcome all the trials and sorrows of this world.

Day 359

DON'T WORRY, THE HOLY SPIRIT IS HERE

When you are brought before the synagogues, rulers, and authorities, do not worry about how you will defend yourselves or what you will say.

—Luke 12:11

Jesus taught the disciples not to worry—especially as He sent them out to preach His good news message. He knew they would face opposition just as He did. He wanted them to know that even though He would not be with them in person, He was sending the Holy Spirit to live inside of them, to give them peace and guidance no matter the situation.

What a comfort to know that we have the Holy Spirit to defend us and guide us on the way God has for us. Not much was ever said or taught to me about the Holy Spirit. I knew that once I received Jesus, He came to live inside me. That was all I knew.

Now I know that is not all there is. The Holy Spirit is such an amazing part of our God who is three in one. The Holy Spirit has a big job and often gets left out in the teaching and preaching we hear. I remembered that it was by the Holy Spirit that Mary conceived Jesus; but did you know I realized just recently that it is by the power of the Holy Spirit that Jesus was raised from the dead?

God has shown me that the Holy Spirit is a very important part of our spiritual lives, and we are not to leave Him out. I am grateful He lives inside me in the deepest part and is the one who enlightens me about the saving grace and knowledge of Jesus. I don't have to be a world renowned theologian to know Him and to share the truth of Him. He shows me I am not alone, and He will always be there to direct my journey of life.

HOPE FOR YOU

Is the Holy Spirit alive in you? Find out today the truth of His being and the reason Jesus sent Him to each of us.

Day 360

DO NOT LOSE HEART OR GROW WEARY

> Just think of Him Who endured from sinners such grievous opposition *and* bitter hostility against Himself [reckon up *and* consider it all in comparison with your trials] so that you may not grow weary *or* exhausted, losing heart *and* relaxing and fainting in your minds.
>
> —Heb. 12:3 AMP

The writer knew that the Christian life centers on hard work. He knew that fear, discouragement, and despair always have a way of creeping in and trying to destroy the meaning of Christ in our lives. The key to staying strong is to trust the Holy Spirit to help us keep our eyes on Jesus and what He has done for us. Then the battle is won, and we don't grow weary and lose heart.

I admit I have taken my eyes off Jesus many times. I have seen the darkest hours of my life come and I still went my own way. It is not a pleasant feeling and sight to see a life wasted by trying to live man's ways and not God's. God does not want that for any of us.

Jesus knows how hard it is to keep focused on the big things of life instead of letting all the little things overshadow it. God gives us so many ways to resist that lifestyle. He gives us His Word to read over and over again; He gives us others in our lives to bring Christ to us in a fresh new light.

Jesus gives us the Holy Spirit to keep us on the right path. What more do we need to see to believe that God is real and we can overcome anything that comes our way by faith in Him alone?

HOPE FOR YOU

Have you lost the "big picture"? Is God alive and well in your being? Come now and see all that Jesus has for you through His Holy Spirit alive in you.

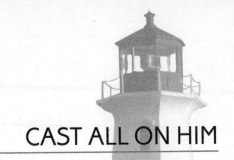

Day 361

CAST ALL ON HIM

> Casting the whole of your care [all your anxieties, all your worries, all your concerns, once and for all] on Him, for He cares for you affectionately *and* cares about you watchfully.
> —1 Pet. 5:7 AMP

Peter wrote to Christians who were being scattered and persecuted. He wanted them to know to totally depend on Jesus Christ alone, and not give up. He knew the pain and sorrow of life, and yet he knew Christ was the only way to true life.

Often my pride has gotten in the way of knowing my Lord. I was taught to be defensive to avoid added punishment. I carried lies and cover-ups for many years.

But with God, the first thing He wants from us is to become humble and to admit we need Him. This has been the hard part of my journey because I have lived in a world where admitting need showed weakness. I even lost worldly rewards for doing so.

But God has shown me His forgiveness many times. I am excited about the changes God has made in my life once I admitted my need of change. God is always at work in my life. What a blessing to know it is all about Him and not about me.

HOPE FOR YOU

Have you admitted you need a Lord and Savior? Is there anything you have not given to Him? God cares for you and wants to make a change in your life now.

Day 362

TRUST THE LORD AND BE RESCUED AND PROTECTED

The Lord says, "I will rescue those who love me. I will protect those who trust in my name. When they call on me, I will answer; I will be with them in trouble. I will rescue them and honor them."

—Ps. 91:14–15 NLT

The writers knew the God of all and that He was the one to trust totally. What a picture of love and promise for us!

I have often felt I was not worthy to be rescued and protected. I thought I had to earn the right to be loved by God when all He wanted from me was my love and honor. It has nothing to do with my feeling worthy, but rather is all about how worthy the Lord is to be glorified and honored.

It has taken me many miles and many years to see how much God loves me. He is true to His promises. God never gave up. That is why no matter what happens, nothing can shake the love of God from my life. I will praise Him all the days of my life and will be forever with Him; all because of what Jesus Christ did for me on the Cross.

HOPE FOR YOU

Do you know God loves you, worthy or not? Do you know what His love for you is based on? Today is the day to confront this truth and see how big God is.

Day 363

REMOVE ANXIETY AND TROUBLES NOW

> So then, banish anxiety from your heart and cast off the troubles of your body, for youth and vigor are meaningless.
> —Eccles. 11:10

Life in the Lord is all about choices. Solomon shows that even though people say it doesn't matter what we do when we are young, it does matter. How many times have you said, "If only I could go back and make some different choices, my life would be better?"

The good news is, God has forgiven your past choices and He sees you right now where you are. You can choose not to be anxious and to let go of troubles. Seek Him, even if you have never done so before.

It is never too late to begin again. I know that to be so true. I am now a senior citizen in age, (but not in mind and body), and I am beginning my third career. I don't have to live as if my life is over. It isn't. (And I love getting my senior citizen discount.) I don't mind sharing my age and weight. I love the life God has given to me. I love laughing, traveling, helping, and giving to others.

HOPE FOR YOU

God has a plan and purpose for all of us at each and every stage of our life. It is not time to sit and moan and groan even if life is not as we thought it would be. After all, life is not about us. It's all about God. Now let go of all the past and move to where God wants you and can use you now. "We are products of our past, but we don't have to be prisoners of them" (Joyce Meyer).

Day 364

TAKE COURAGE, THE COMING OF THE LORD IS NEAR

You, too, must be patient. And take courage, for the coming of the Lord is near.

—Jas. 5:8 NLT

James, the half brother of Jesus, was not a believer when Jesus was alive. It was only after His death that James saw the big picture and became one of the first pastors of the early church. He believed then that the Lord's time to return was near. It could happen at any time.

I haven't always been excited to hear that the Lord Jesus could return at any time for us. I kept thinking I had to clean up my life, live better, get things in order, and get ready for Him.

The truth is, we don't know when the Lord is coming back. What do I want to be involved in when He does come back? That is the important part. Do I want Him to find me living in His joy, peace, and contentment, or do I want Him to find me in my prison of fear, worry, and despair? The answer is very clear to me now. How I choose to live matters to God and He wants me to be strong, patient, and ready at any moment for His return.

HOPE FOR YOU

Are you ready for the Lord's return? What will He find you doing? Will He be honored and praised, or forgotten and cursed? There is still time to make the choice for Him.

Day 365

WE ARE NOT CRUSHED OR DEFEATED

We are hard pressed on every side, but not crushed; perplexed, but not in despair; persecuted, but not abandoned; struck down, but not destroyed.

—2 Cor. 4:8–9

Paul reminds us that even though we may think we are at the end of our rope, we are never at the end of hope. Even though our bodies are weak and we struggle with sin, God does not abandon us or destroy us.

I live in North Carolina where we breathe and live College Basketball. I love watching all the state teams, (we have 4 major ones, and of course each of us have our own favorite) and have seen many times where I felt there was no way my team could possibly pull off the win. How wrong have I been, because that is when I saw the practice, determination, unity, and coaching on display to allow them to overcome any fear or despair and win.

I have thought many times that I was at the end of the line. I did not want to—and could not—go on. But God came to me in those times and gave me the encouragement and hope to go on in spite of all that was happening around me. Just as with my favorite basketball team, there is never any time that God leaves us without His hope. He knows that our fears, anxieties, and worries will bring us closer to Him.

HOPE FOR YOU

Are you living as if it were the end of the line? Or are you excited about what the Lord still has for you to be and do? It is a choice and one that you must make. Choose Him today and see where God wants to lead you.

Day 366

BE DELIVERED AND HONOR GOD

> And call upon me in the day of trouble; I will deliver you,
> and you will honor me.
>
> —Ps. 50:15

The writer of this psalm was Asaph, one of David's chief musicians. He shows that God desires our thanks, trust, and praise.

I have made a complete circle in my life in the Lord. He gave me the courage to call on Him for help in facing and overcoming fear. He delivered me from hopelessness and gave me encouragement; so I share this journey with you.

Isn't it just like God to take this illegitimate child from a beginning that didn't appear to be worth much to anyone; through a life filled with tests and trials, just so He can receive all the praise and glory now? And He is showing me there is still more to come; how exciting!

HOPE FOR YOU

Where is your life headed? Is it bound by fear and hopelessness, or is it one of honoring, thanking, and praising God? It is a choice. Call out to God now and be changed.

EPILOGUE

I hope this journey through the pages of this book points you to the only answer and solution for facing your fears, worries, cares, problems, depression, disappointments, discouragements, and frustrations; that of knowing Jesus Christ as your personal Lord and Savior.

This book is not intended as a "self-help" devotional, but as a "God-Help" resource for your everyday life. God wants you to know how much He loves you, and how you can have a victorious and glorious life with Him in control.

Life is all about *Him* and not about you. It is forever. How you spend each and every minute of every day counts, and one day in eternity, you will see that.

So my friends, (and you are because you made it to the end of this book), do not miss a moment of what God has for you. No longer dwell, focus, or become overwhelmed by your fears. Know you can cry out and come to the one God who will forgive, forget, and give you a new beginning. Learn you can walk in the joy, peace, and contentment of the Lord and live in His freedom and hope.

I pray for your journey, and I hope to meet many of you, if not here on earth, then in eternity with our Lord in Heaven.

Living fearlessly and victoriously in Him,

Sue Falcone